SAVING FROM THE WRECK
ESSAYS ON POETRY

SAVING FROM THE WRECK
ESSAYS ON POETRY

PETER PORTER

With an introduction by John Lucas

TRENT BOOKS

Published by Trent Books, 2001

Trent Books
Department of English and Media Studies
The Nottingham Trent University
Clifton Lane
Nottingham NG11 8NS

Printed in Great Britain by Goaters, Nottingham
ISBN 1 84233 055 1

Contents

Acknowledgements

All the articles printed in this collection were originally given as lectures, radio talks or contributions to literary conferences. Many were subsequently printed in magazines or issued as off-prints. The dates, venues and circumstances of each piece are given either at the beginning or at the end of each essay. I should like to thank the conveners and organisers of these occasions for inviting me to address their audiences.

I must apologise for the unusual persistence of certain ideas about poetry which recur throughout this book. What did not obtrude while I was writing, or would not have been noticed by my various audiences, becomes almost a set of 'idées fixes' when these talks are collected between covers. I have edited my utterance to reduce repetition to a minimum, but a fondness for certain passages of poetry and for a few aphoristic insights cannot be completely erased. I hope that the reader will discover in practice that, being concerned with one subject — Poetry — each article may be seen as a variation on a single theme.

I should like to thank the Department of English and Media Studies at the Nottingham Trent University for suggesting that I gather my scattered pronouncements on poetry together, and for publishing them under their Trent Books imprint. My special thanks go to Carmen Glover, who transcribed each piece from my confused and confusing manuscripts with remarkable skill and patience. Without her discernment my views on the subject would have remained as inscrutable as cuneiform tablets. Lastly I am grateful to Professor John Lucas, who is the proper begetter of this book — not just for his Introduction, but for his generous encouragement over many years of my poetry, and for believing that an unacademic commentator might have something interesting to say about poetry.

Peter Porter

Introduction

To the unwary or inattentive, Peter Porter's by now famous pronouncement that poetry is a modest art makes him its enemy. Yet the essays included in this book reveal him to be among the wittiest, shrewdest, and most eloquent champions of the art he practises with such distinction. However, as these same essays also show him to be temperamentally opposed to certain claims that have been and continue to be made on poetry's behalf, and given that what he regards as the claimants' dangerous or vacuous immodesties prompt him to reprisals which are customarily fired by wit, it's entirely possible that beef-witted Ajaxes will continue to be wounded by Porter's refusal to march to their loud huzzas.

In a word, Porter's cast of mind is anti-Romantic. And so, although he believes that great poets are, as he says, extremely clever men and women, this doesn't lead him to conclude that poetry is truly philosophical. "In fact, looking right down the long vista of English poetry, I can't see anyone who might be called a philosopher as well as a poet." And that goes for political philosophy as well as ethics and metaphysics. No unacknowledged legislators here. Poems, as he more or less echoes Mallarmé in saying, are made with words, not ideas. Or, in his own formulation, the poet's essential need is "to follow the tread of language rather than the thread of thought." This doesn't exonerate the poet from the need to make sense, but the sense a poem makes isn't the sense that philosophy seeks. For philosophers, words are a means to an end, and any other medium enabling them to reach that end would do just as well. But for poets words are the essential medium in which they move, in which they rejoice. "Has there ever been as great a mind working with words as Shakespeare's?" Porter asks, more or less rhetorically, and throughout the following pages he comes back, time and again, to Shakespeare's pre-eminence, at one point brilliantly disposing of T.S. Eliot's preference for Dante's "la sua voluntade è nostra pace" over Lear's "As flies to wanton boys, are we to the gods;/They kill us for their sport." Porter smells "a sort of snobbery in [Eliot's] and Pound's elevation of Dante's allegiance to an organic Christendom over Shakespeare's local and proverbial loyalties. In practice, Shakespeare's plays rely on Europe's classical inheritance and on the Bible as much as *The Divine Comedy* does." Besides, one could "cite Dante's Florentine spite as being more parochial than anything in Shakespeare." Elsewhere, he suggests that the difference between Shakespeare's and Sidney's sonnets is the difference "between the gamiest Freudian case-history and Amateur night in the Petrarchan Academy. Shakespeare's poet-hero", he adds, "is the Rat-Man of the High Renaissance." Not even Randall Jarrell could have improved on that.

To say this isn't to offer such remarks as definitive. It is, however, to say that they goad the reader into attentiveness. The poets Porter likes best have a similar attentiveness. They are alert to the world about them. Hence, his indifference to, amounting to distrust of, the egotistical sublime. Wordsworth is very little mentioned in these pages, and the only poem of his which Porter discusses, "A Complaint", is found to be pervaded with "a sort of selfish grievance" and "perhaps pompous outrage." This is to put negatively what others, mustering against what they see as the high fortresses of philistinism, would trumpet as necessary ingredients of the poetic temperament. But altogether elsewhere Porter is lying in wait. "One is forced back on the important truism: a poet is a person who writes good poems. In all other matters, there is no uniformity of poetical signs. Even beautiful, haunted, poetical young men may turn out to be poets."

This remark is made in the course of the essay on George Crabbe, a poet high in Porter's own Pantheon. To understand why that should be, you have to read the essay itself, a characteristic performance, throwing off *aperçus* as it goes, offering now a lesson in the use of the couplet, next an account of how poetry can deal in the heartrending and still produce "a feast of language", later an exact account of what is wrong with Britten's depiction of Peter Grimes: "He cannot both be the brute fisherman and the lost dreamer of his song in the pub the night of the storm." Porter is nevertheless "fully conscious of Britten's greatness as a composer", and anyone who knows anything at all about Porter will be quick to understand that this isn't routine praise. Because he has such a *grasp* of musical matters he's scornful of those who vaguely gesture towards poetry's musicality. He notes that music doesn't have to be merely euphonious. The harsh and dissonant are also intrinsic to music, though that is not what commentators typically mean when they allude to poetry's musical qualities. Moreover, writers tend to reach for vague generalities about music's power in defiance of proper understanding. Porter records Stravinsky's contempt for Proust's "warbling" about the "profundity" of Beethoven's late Quartets.

In sharp contrast to these vague pieties, Porter repeatedly puts his knowledge of music to good use, not merely in "The Shape of Poetry and the Shape of Music", but — to choose almost at random — in a discussion of the organist, Charles Avison, which occurs towards the end of his essay on "Browning's Important Parleying". Here, he comments that "Browning loved music but he also envied it its power of reaching directly to human emotion, its freedom from the distorting lens of opinion and meaning." Illuminating as the entire passage from which this remark comes undoubtedly is, it's perhaps no more so than another in a later essay, "The Poet's Quarrel with Poetry", where Porter suddenly and entirely persuasively fast-forwards from Browning to John Ashbery. "The Browning of our day", he calls the American poet, and quotes from "And *Ut Pictura Poesis* Is Her Name" to make his point. Porter on more than one occasion says that he is no scholar. This may be a defensive shield put up to guard him from the darts of presumed experts, which is understandable given that the occasion for many of these essays was an Academic conference or set of lectures. But which Browning scholar could so suavely make the connection with Ashbery? Porter's criticism is invaluable because it is, to use the title of another essay, "News From the Front". Such news comes with the imprimatur, no matter how quizzically endorsed, of someone who is himself a true poet. (Hence, I will remark in passing, his cherishable put-down of Leslie Stephen's sniffy criticism that "when boy cannot be made to rhyme with employ, Crabbe is very fond of dragging in hoy." Well, why not, Porter asks. "If Stephen had tried rhyming in English, he'd have had more sympathy with Crabbe".) Still, on this Front "there is not just one enemy and one alliance — writers shoot it out in an anarchy of artistic loyalty and ambition."

From what's been said so far we can make out the shape of Porter's enemies. What of the allies? It would be unfair to list the poets discussed in detail in the following pages and say "These be thy Gods." Rochester, Pope, Crabbe and Browning are here because at different times a variety of people and institutions asked Porter to talk about them. They asked him because they knew he could be trusted to say something interesting about these poets and for that matter many others who are mentioned *en passant*. This matter of trust is important. On more occasions than I care to remember I've sat in a lecture room to hear an academic announce that due to "pressure of events" he or she hasn't after all been able to "prepare" the lecture we've come for, but that we'll no doubt be interested to hear again the lecture which they *have* brought, and which was given with great success on a previous occasion. Or maybe we'll be offered the treat of a chapter from a forthcoming book, or … . Porter may like to present himself as less than scholarly, but he's entirely professional. He's also far more-wide ranging in his interests and sympathies than most scholars I can think of. If you put the names of all the poets mentioned in this book end to end they certainly wouldn't exhaust Porter's allegiances. The most notable absence is Auden, at least in the sense that there is no essay devoted to his work. On the other hand there is scarcely an essay when he isn't either quoted or alluded to, or where his presence can't be felt. This may in part be because there is a habit of thought Porter shares with Auden, which shows itself in the seemingly casual stitching together of names and ideas in order to make what we come to recognise as not so much an argument as a judgement. Take, for example, the instance where Porter says that it is with Pope and Browning that English poetry comes on course again — "a Shakespearean course after too much epic and lyric. And Browning, while a lesser poet than Pope and a much less perfect one, has more variety, especially in the forms he chooses. It is a miracle that Pope can be so wide ranging in one poetic form — the couplet. I can think only of Domenico Scarlatti in music as an equal genius similarly self-confined to one sort of structure. But Pope doesn't take Browning's risks with human character, and has the satirist's perfection-seeking in typology, the Theophrastian roundness. Browning is cruder but wider."

This kind of acute wit (in the eighteenth-century sense) is everywhere you look in these essays, and it goes with the darting, glancing style of utterance that may owe something to the German epigrammatists Porter so admires, although it's more likely that they are kindred spirits, adapts all at pinning the truth by means of apophthegm. I seem to have known forever that Wallace Stevens is in some respects "a cross between Henry James and a serial aphorist", but in fact Porter throws the remark off towards the end of the last essay included in the present collection. In this essay, "A Place Dependent on Ourselves: Poetry & Materialism", he circles once more round a subject which continually preoccupies him: poetry's being about the real world and yet its dependence on language. For a certain kind of theorist you can't have it both ways. Language is self-reflexive. It tells us about itself and — perhaps — our many and fractured selves. It can't tell us about whatever lies beyond its cage. All utterance is locked into an inescapable subjectivity. This post-modernist fatalism is not for Porter. As he says, it isn't merely that "language was invented to convey meaning", but that "language is tribally owned and must therefore generalise." It follows that "the masterful poet is able to be recognisably particular while keeping to language's inherited orthodoxies." Poetry may be a modest art, but it is a social one. And like love, to adapt Richard Wilbur, it calls us to the things of this world. Porter might even go so far as to agree with Novalis, who, mystic though he was, nevertheless held that "poetry is the genuine absolute reality. The more it is poetic, the more it is real", although Porter would be quick to add that "the truest poetry is the most feigning."

To this humanist position, however wryly or sceptically it's affirmed – and if it weren't it wouldn't be truly humanist – can be added the claim that poetry lives "in the human spirit, and the magician-artist will liberate it wherever he feels instinctively it is to be found ... . In our permanent museum, the works of genius stay looking young. 'Ganymed' has the dew of Creation on it forever." This remark is made in the course of the seminal essay "The Shape of Poetry and the Shape of Music", which dates from 1980 and is perhaps as near as Porter ever comes to uttering a credo. The idea of culture — or should that be Western civilisation? — as a museum is much associated with the Modernism of Eliot and Pound and, with due modifications, it found its way into the thinking of F.R. Leavis and his Scrutineers. But Porter is blessedly different from them. Here is perhaps the appropriate moment to say that I first met him in 1962, just after the publication of *Penguin Modern Poets 2*, in which he appeared with Kingsley Amis and Dom Moraes. He'd been invited to Reading University by Ian Fletcher, a lecturer in the English Department, himself a fine poet, hugely knowledgeable, and a glittering conversationalist. After the reading a group of us went to a pub, where Porter lectured me — I can't recall why – on the need to beware of the Catholic Church. What impressed me was less the witty vehemence of his attack on Rome than how much he seemed to know about Church history. From Rome we passed to Wallace Stevens — a comparatively recent discovery for me. I thought I knew a good deal about Stevens, but Porter knew far more. Stevens led Porter on to other American poets, some of whom I'd barely heard of, after which he came round to English writers, brought in German poets (he'd been reading the Hamburger & Middleton *Modern German Poetry 1910-1960*), and after he'd done with that topic .... Well, I can't remember who or what came next, but by the time he'd finished even Ian seemed weeping ripe for a good word.

On me, and I suspect most of the others who formed a silent ring about him, the effect was entirely liberating. It certainly rent the veil of Leavisian solemnity which was draped over most English departments at that time and even darkened Reading. Not that Ian was a Leavisite, any more than was the great head of the department at Reading, D. J. Gordon. But the Leavisites seemed scattered everywhere, blown by a bleak, reproving wind off the fens, and the moral rigour (as they saw it, moral vanity it looked to others) of those epigoni who appointed themselves the master's true followers was as depressing as it was oppressive. If, for example, you said you thought Dickens a great novelist you were looked at as though you'd confessed to some unpardonable sin. I can remember the delight with which I came across D.J. Enright's remark, made of one particular Leavisite who was always trumpeting his moral health, that "wanting to stand for Life he usually ends up standing on it." And Geoffrey Grigson caught the spirit of Leavisianism when he said that for him the term evoked a wintry bathroom with threadbare lino. Literature had nothing to do with pleasure. Spotty young men scarcely out of short trousers were quick to assert that "there was nothing for the mature mind" in Shelley, or Browning, or Auden, ("undergraduate cleverness"), or anyone Leavis had dismissed from the Great Tradition. Only those who were "on the side of Life" could be admitted to the Canon. And very few understood about Life. If you wanted to read those who didn't — Joyce, for example — you felt you had first to wrap their books in plain brown covers. G. S. Fraser told me that on an occasion in the late 1950s, when he gave a talk at Cambridge about Burns, he and his subject were both dismissed with contempt. Fraser quoted the lines "My love is like a melody/ That's sweetly played in tune". "What's music to do with love?" a Downing student asked down his nose, and would not stay for an answer. Only Lawrence could be trusted to deal with love in a suitably mature manner.

Inevitably some Leavisites had found their way to Reading. One even came to the pub with us. From time to time I sneaked a view at him. What I saw was heartening in the extreme. As the evening wore on he gave up trying to score points off the visitor and his fixed sneer slowly gave way to a look of glum defeat. Porter was faster on his feet, he knew more, he was blessedly witty, and he seemed naturally to breathe an air of relish for literature and ideas. Whether he was aware of the effect he was having I've no idea. But, as I say, on me it was liberating and wholly beneficial.

Of course, he had and has his preferences, but usually in an uncensorious way. He also has a breadth of sympathetic understanding that sets him apart from many, perhaps most, of those who write about poetry. This gives what he has to say a kind of relaxed authority which is very different from laying down the law. For a long time, the law about eighteenth-century poetry — poetry of "The Augustan Age" it was revealingly called — was that it testified to "the gloom of the Tory satirists." These satirists were, so the scholars agreed, the upholders of Reason, Truth and Nature. In "Rhyme and Reason" Porter seems to be following this orthodoxy until he comes to discuss "The Cave of Spleen" in the fourth book of *The Rape of the Lock*. Before quoting a lengthy passage, he notes that "Pope is inspired to conjure a vision of a light-hearted Dantesque Inferno — as though Michaelangelo's Last Judgement had been repainted by Tiepolo". He then quotes nearly 40 lines (he always quotes generously, he assumes his readers will want to have the pleasure of experiencing the poetry he is praising), and continues:

> You can feel, towards the end of this passage, that Pope is going into overdrive; his fantasy has stoked up on his language until traditional devices like personification, metaphor and alliteration begin to live a life of their own. And he is frequently at this pitch throughout his best poetry. Far from being a mincing poet, a namby-pamby one (to appropriate the name he bestowed upon Ambrose Phillips) or even a classically restrained poet, he is baroque and grotesque. But the poise of the verse never slips: the more violent the vision, the more exquisitely phrased the language will be.

I don't see how this could be bettered. And of course it at once frees Pope's poetry from those iron fetters in which it had been cramped by generations of scholars for whom Augustanism meant Restraint. Similarly, I don't know of anyone who has written more illuminatingly about Browning than Porter — as for example, when tapping into his own deep familiarity with Italy, its culture and history, he here remarks that Browning "arriving in Italy in the tumescence of the Risorgimento, was able to imagine the Italy of the great days of the New Learning, which were also the less great days of the decline of the Communes into signorial despotism, as no English poet, except Shakespeare, had done. I find, reading Browning's many different approaches to his Italian subjects, a convincing small-town worldliness, a conspiratorial scribblers' ambience, a freshly-coined opinionatedness. It is the Paradise of the Word."

Porter's admiration for Browning must be at least partly linked to the belief he succinctly expresses in the last essay here, that "There are no unpoetic subjects." Rochester has therefore as good a right to be considered a poet as Dryden. His poems include "a profound view of love offered by a sceptic whose experience of fashion and pleasure has given him a taste for extremes." None of which would matter if Rochester were less than the master of words and verse forms. But Porter's comparison of Rochester's translation of a few lines from Lucretius with one by C.H. Sisson establishes Rochester's superiority as poet beyond reasonable question.

As with virtually all of the essays gathered together in this book, "Rochester: The Professional Amateur" started life as a lecture. They have been arranged in chronological order of composition, which means that Crabbe comes before Pope. I don't think this matters, and anyway the essays don't have to be read in the order in which they are printed, any more than do the essays in *Poetry and the Age* or *The Dyer's Hand*, with both of which *Saving From the Wreck* invites comparison. Like Jarrell, Porter has written widely and well on contemporary poets, and like Auden he has provided introductions to anthologies he has made of other people's poetry. There's more than enough of such work to make for another, full-length book. But the present collection has a coherence that wouldn't be helped by the inclusion of further, heterogeneous material. Much of this coherence derives from Porter's distinctive voice, to which the lecture is well suited, poised as it is between a conversational tone — you are after all speaking in the presence of others and you want them to listen — and the formality that properly belongs to public performance. In one such performance, he remarks that "In his copious and generous output, Browning satisfies the haranguer which is in each of us. We are born, we talk and we die. But chiefly we talk, and when we meet a good talker we listen." What follows is the best kind of talk.

John Lucas

For Richard Connolly

Poetry and Madness

All sensible people, and this includes artists of genius, are afraid of madness and would hope to live their lives untouched by it. What Lear said in horrified recognition of his future applies to everyone "Let me not be mad". But, having said this, it is only proper to continue by adding that madness or some derangement of the rational intelligence by the obsessional imagination is one of the most common, and indeed, the most fruitful of the spurs to creativity in all the arts. But the paradox must be stressed — great works of art are like dreams, they have volition of their own, but little responsibility to their creators or their audiences. The author stays sane, but the characters explore areas of the mind which would be intolerable in life. This is what lies behind the Greek plays, behind the Christian Mass and behind the great tragedies of the Jacobean age and the novels of Dostoyevsky. Catharsis may be more praised than experienced, but it is the justification for harrowing experiences such as sitting through *Antigone* or *Othello*. What we have to be on our guard against is the soliciting of unreason, the willingness to bargain for great artistic powers with our health and our sanity.

Exceptional men of genius have brought this off, but at a tremendous personal cost. Rimbaud, for instance, seems to me the greatest of all French poets, and no one can read through *Les Illuminations* without wondering at its extraordinary prescience about the future of the world. Almost every twentieth-century phenomenon, from pollution and ecological disaster to the tribal enthusiasm of the love generation, is in Rimbaud's poem. But, despite his policy of conscious derangement of the senses, he could not stand the pace. He wrote no more poetry after the age of nineteen. And, curiously, he was a failure at his chosen worldly career of Abyssinian trader and gun dealer.

They order these things better in fiction. In Thomas Mann's novel *Doktor Faustus*, the composer Adrian Leverkuhn updates the traditional bargain with the devil in the light of nineteenth century morbid psychology. Looking at the great composers whose creativity went hand in hand with their neurasthenic natures, Mann makes Leverkuhn deliberately acquire syphilis so that the derangement of his body and mind will yield dividends in the creation of music. Behind this very voulu idea are the real stories of Beethoven, Schubert, Schumann, Donizetti, Wolf and a score of writers as well. Ours is an acutely self-conscious age — as Auden warns, there is nothing more deluding than the belief in a natural style:

> For given Man, by birth, by education,
> Imago Dei who forgot his station,
> The self-made creature who himself unmakes,
> The only creature ever made who fakes,
> With no more nature in his loving smile
> Than in his theories of a natural style.

This creature, Man, can obviously petition for suffering, hoping to gain artistic rewards. As they say in India, "very mad, very holy". We have seen all too many examples of poets in our century unable to control the daemons they have conjured up. It has become, in fact, a spurious way of living — most particularly in the United States. Americans reward their poets lavishly but they expect them to pay the highest price. Confessional verse, so-called, has claimed an authenticity not just from its excellence as poetry but because of the real blood its poets have poured upon the page. Suicide has become the endorsement not merely of genius but of seriousness. The roll call of names is ominously full — from Hart Crane to Sylvia Plath, Anne Sexton and John Berryman. But what I want to celebrate in this essay is the sort of creative derangement of sensibility which is unsought but also unavoidable. I am not referring either to the supreme artists of genius, whose works are as frightening as apocalypses but whose natures seem to have been sealed off from their imaginations — Sophocles, Shakespeare, Wagner, for instance. And as I said earlier, I don't mean the self-soliciting poets, cuddling up to their extremism and hectoring the public.

It seems to me that an important line may be drawn between the dreaming imagination and the confessing imagination. A parallel may be found in psychoanalysis. An analyst is trained to sort among a patient's conscious memories. This is a long process and even with the technique of free association remains problematic. Analysts also examine dreams, but seem to have much less success with them. In all Freud's *The Interpretation of Dreams*, there is little which seems to me to touch on the real experience of dreaming. To dream is to live while you are asleep — it is not to receive coded messages from your unconscious. For me, Freud's truly beautiful book about the nature of the world is *Civilization and Its Discontents*. This classical study explains how mankind has had to pay the price for its civilization in neurosis. Far from deploring civilization, Freud believes that the price is well worth paying. But, though we stay alive and invent great art and ingenious pastimes, we also become sick and wish to die. All the analyst can do is try to mollify that sickness. When an artist is helplessly forced to follow his dreaming self, however much he wants to stay true to his rational and waking self, then we get works of near-madness, which nonetheless are recognizable as artifacts of the real world. In some poets (and I will be dealing predominantly with poetry and only touching on painting and music), this division in themselves ushers in nothing worse than chronic melancholy or depression. In others, it goes as far as madness.

The madman, of course, has always been treated by poets and playwrights, and presumably also by primitive societies, as an oracle. When Shakespeare and Webster ran into plot difficulties they frequently resorted to a mad scene, and there is no reason to presume that this was just because their hardened audiences liked to laugh at deranged people. The much more likely reason is that the mad are licensed to speak of what the sane must always suppress. The jester or fool could always excuse himself by calling himself mad. In *King Lear*, there is a plethora of mad truth-tellers, of which the Fool is the closest to sanity. Indeed, *Lear* is a play almost entirely about madness — whether of dotage, disappointment, ambition, baffled lust or shock. Edgar adopts the role of Mad Tom as an excellent disguise to get near a court devoted to hearing the truth in unpalatable forms from sententious lunatics.

The mad scene in a poetical drama is the closest literature can show to the structure and organization of ordinary sane dreaming. Dreams are inevitable in their unfolding but not logical — they are seamless but full of non-sequiturs. And like the monologues of madmen, they observe no taboos of subject matter. It is interesting to look at the development of opera, which had its heyday two centuries later than the poetic drama. While Ophelia could only hint at a total lyricism in her madness, Donizetti's Lucia could sing her delusion in a completely artificial but utterly convincing way. It seems to me that poetry is always aspiring to the condition of music (the much discredited but misunderstood observation of Walter Pater), and that the technique of the dream is one way to achieve this. The difficulty lies in the ordering of a dream by the rational intelligence — one simply can't cut corners and hope to achieve the right result.

Poetry has always been forced to stick to the brute facts of life, however unmusical they may be. Attempts to write pure poetry almost always fail, at least in English. Mallarmé may bring it off, but Swinburne cannot. And this is where the poet suffering from delusions of the mind can succeed: he can make the insoluble brute facts of the world more lyrical by finding associations for them which the rational intelligence cannot reach. But, as I said previously and as I shall continue to stress, he has to do this innocently. He has to be genuinely deluded and this means usually that he doesn't know that he is saying anything out of the ordinary. In fact, when I come to the illustrations from poetry in the second part of this talk, I shall be drawing on the eighteenth century mainly. No century has such a reputation for calm and sanity. The psychologically disturbed poets of the eighteenth century earned no support from their fellow men for their derangement. It made them either pariahs, fit for persecution, or secret melancholics deeply ashamed of their deviation from reason. Yet the roll call of their names is impressive. Christopher Smart, William Collins and William Cowper were all certifiably mad; Jonathan Swift, Alexander Pope, Samuel Johnson, Matthew Greene and William Blake were either morbidly depressed or ecstatically bemused, and Thomas Gray, Charles Churchill and George Crabbe kept a hold on their reason by self-discipline only. There is no better illustration of the state of mind we call manic-depressive than the diaries of James Boswell.

In all these men, the spirit of poetry was fighting for liberation from the prosaic world of everyday life in the Age of Reason. But each and every one was devoted to reason, and believed he was fulfilling its obligations. Or, when he knew he wasn't, he felt guilty for not doing so. Since their time, there have been many poets caught in the same nets, none of them wishing to be deviant from the norm but all unable to help themselves. Coleridge, Clare and Tennyson in England; Gerard de Nerval and Baudelaire in France; Hölderlin, Mörike and Trakl in Germany; Leopardi in Italy — the list includes some of the most distinguished names in the history of European literature. Their heirs today would seem to be poets like the Americans Galway Kinnell (author of *The Book of Nightmares*) and James Wright, rather than the suicidal confessionals, though Sylvia Plath has much in common with the more gentle tradition I have sketched in, as does the Piedmontese poet, Cesare Pavese. On the whole, it is those who stay away from psychoanalysts who are likely to produce the best visionary poetry. The sort of verse which R. D. Laing conjured up in his book *Knots* is a dire warning of the strangled cries put out by the unconscious when it tries to solicit inspiration.

To work at all, art has to be at the service of one or other of the great myths which have dogged mankind from prehistory onwards. When we come to examples of the poetry of Christopher Smart we shall see how all his visionary material is offered up to the Christian God in a sort of super-serviceable litany which excludes nothing from its list. The only great repository of myth outside Christianity available to Europeans is the storehouse of classicism celebrated in the art of Greece and Rome. Looking at painting, we see how the artists mixed their classical pantheon of gods with the Christian. One such artist, who is deeply poetical in his pictures, is worth examining in a little more depth here, the fifteenth-century Florentine painter, Piero di Cosimo. He has always been a favourite with literary men, on account of the very explicit iconography of his pictures. But he suits me as well, since we know from Vasari that he was sufficiently eccentric to be dubbed "mad".

Piero came late in the procession of Florentine masters beginning with Masaccio who made the fifteenth century the great age of European Renaissance painting. But he is just before Mannerism, so that his madness is in his subjects not their treatment, and he has none of that spurious glow which fills the pictures of men like Pontormo and Rosso Fiorentino. His famous pictures, "The Battle between the Centaurs and Lapiths", "The Discovery of Honey", "The Invention of Fire", "Perseus delivering Andromeda" and the "Hunting Scenes" in the Metropolitan Museum of Art in New York are violent, nightmare pictures which nevertheless differ absolutely from the Northern apocalyptic style of Hieronymous Bosch, Piero's almost exact contemporary. Bosch is a redemptive painter — his horrors are to warn and to lead to a new transfigured world. Piero di Cosimo takes us back to the deep past of mankind: it was out of the woods which Piero drew that Man, helped by the fire of the gods, first came. Piero shows civilization's origins and warns against our neglecting the sources of our modern world in Nature, and in Nature's amazing mutations.

Piero is the most poetical of painters in that he produces the greatest lyrical effusion with the least distortion of reality. Even his sea monsters, like the one Perseus has bailed up to release Andromeda, are scaly and real enough to feature at a fish market. As man, the supreme creature, departs too far from the Nature which made him, Piero warns, then the monsters of evolutionary possibility come back into view. His message is still alive today, in a world raped almost to death. W. H. Auden summed up Piero's personality in his poem, "Woods", the second in the series of *Bucolics* he wrote in the 1950s:

Sylvan meant savage in those primal woods
Piero di Cosimo so loved to draw,
Where nudes, bears, lions, sows with women's heads,
Mounted and murdered and ate each other raw,
Nor thought the lightning-kindled bush to tame
But, flabbergasted, fled the useful flame.

Man, the lightning-tamer, must still look back at the primal woods he came from. Telling such a message in Florence of the High Renaissance required an obsessional and cunning nature, and Piero developed such a character through eccentricity to the point of madness. The classical world, as understood by Florentine Humanism — the teachings of Marsilio Ficino and Pico della Mirandola, say — was optimistic and ecumenical. Piero doesn't fit into the Neoplatonic mould so brilliantly outlined in Edgar Wind's *Pagan Mysteries of the Renaissance*. He is an Edenist, not a Utopian. Like the poet Smart, his work is a hymn to the Garden of Eden and an illustration of aboriginal calamity. Such a nature was bound to be at odds with his society, and so we find Vasari describing him as "living the life of a wild beast rather than a man". "He never allowed his room to be swept and ate only when he was hungry; nor would he have his garden watered or his fruit trees pruned; but let the vines grow wild. From stains of filth thrown against the wall, he would conjure strange scenes, combats of horses, curious cities, and the most extraordinary landscapes." Vasari also describes Piero's tour-de-force, "A Triumph of Death for the Florentine Carnival":

> The triumphal car was draped in black cloth, with skeletons and crosses on it. It was drawn by coal-black buffaloes. Within the car stood a colossal figure of Death, scythe in hand, while around him were covered tombs which opened when the procession halted. At the sound of a wailing summons, moaned through trumpets, the figures of the dead raised themselves half out of their tombs and seated their skeleton forms thereon while they sang the words, Woe, lamentation and penitence.

Piero's corpses were fresh from the mortuary and bore the old Florentine legend

As you are, so once were we,
As we are, so shall you be!

Vasari continues:

> Piero studied nature with a zeal that made him oblivious of
> time or labour. No effort was too severe, he endured any
> hardship willingly for the mere love of study. He allowed
> himself, for instance, no other food but hard-boiled eggs,
> and these he cooked only when he had a fire to boil his
> glues and varnishes. Nor did he cook them six or eight at
> a time, but by fifties. He kept them in a basket and ate them
> when he felt hungry. This mode of existence suited him
> perfectly; any other seemed to him the merest slavery.

Fifteenth-century Florence was a surprisingly liberal city, tolerating a
high degree of eccentricity in its artists, but by the eighteenth century the
march of reason had pushed the dreaming nature of poets and painters
underground. Between the Renaissance and the Age of Enlightenment
gaped the fosse of religious bigotry, the Reformation and the Counter-
Reformation. Now, the only deliverance for Europe came from overseas
— the Age of Reason was also the Age of Colonial Expansion, the
beginning of world capitalism. Into this ethic of success, the poets had to
fit somehow. We know, from hindsight, that the method they finally
adopted was Romanticism, a rejection of the world they lived in. But
before the birth of Romanticism there lived some of the greatest poets in
English literature, and all, to a greater or lesser degree, show themselves
at odds with their unpoetic world. This may seem a controversial statement
to make about men like Pope and Dryden, yet it seems to me that a close
reading of their poetry shows a disaffection with the prosaic and an attempt
to establish some sort of *paradis artificiel*, if only to impose an order on
the material of their world. Satire, after all, is really a version of pastoral.
It is a way of making the hateful manageable. Not all poets adopted the
satirical mode, though it is predominantly the means employed by Dryden,
Pope and Swift.

In an earlier generation, Rochester had prefigured Rimbaud in a form
of demonism — Rochester's finest poems are like the calm at the centre
of a severe neurasthenic storm. But Rochester died young and was never
mad though violently self-destructive. The purest case of a man's vision
prevailing over the spirit of his times is that of Christopher Smart. Smart's
dates are 1722 to 1771, the very centre of the Augustan calm. That calm
was in the social order: overseas England was fighting France in the Seven
Years' War and other conflicts which were to lead to her becoming the

world's leading colonial power, a fact which Smart watched with great interest and which offered him several prophetic insights. He began as a purely conventional poet, born the son of a steward to a wealthy family in Kent, and sent by them, after a good classical education, to Cambridge University where he became a brilliant scholar. His early life was as full of promise as it was conventional in style. But there had been oddities among the successes — he was removed from Kent to Durham, to Staindrop Manor, a scene of banishment he never forgot, and this exile became an important theme in his masterpiece *Jubilate Agno*, or *Rejoice in the Lamb*, the extraordinary poem he composed during his time in Bedlam and other madhouses. Baffled love was another traumatic misfortune.

At the university, he was in a very exposed position despite his scholastic brilliance. He had no income but his Fellowship of Pembroke College, and he lacked the smooth and ingratiating skill of his Cambridge contemporary, Thomas Gray. And he drank too much. Despite winning the Seatonian Prize several times, it became obvious while Smart was in his early twenties that he could not remain at the university. He was too bizarre and intemperate. And he rendered praise and devotion to the Christian God far in excess of the decorous level favoured by his rationalist contemporaries. Yet, in fairness to the university authorities, it should be stressed that they tried very hard to keep him in his Fellowship. There was a drive in Smart himself to enter the real world, to try himself in a harder arena. He must have known instinctively that great poets are not well placed in academic communities, so he went down to London where he became a hard-working hack in Grub Street, writing almost any sort of thing which the booksellers wanted. One of his most constant resorts was to provide libretti for composers of the day, and all his life he remained fond of music and well informed of its technicalities.

Under a host of pseudonymns, the best known of which was Mrs Midnight, he turned out verses and sketches galore. He also drank heavily and made a marriage to the daughter of a London bookseller to whom he became increasingly indebted. From *Jubilate Agno*, we know that Smart felt that he had been betrayed by his wife and her family: he also recalled a childhood love for Anne Vane, his father's employer's daughter and placed far above any aspiration of his. His mind was the perfect storehouse for the dreaming intelligence: he was erudite, passionate, bewildered, and he felt himself betrayed. Religious mania grew with addiction to alcohol, and in 1757, while only thirty-five, he suffered his first confinement in a mental hospital. In 1759, he was admitted again, this time to Bedlam itself, and he remained there or in some other institution until the beginning of 1763. It was during this later confinement that he composed *Jubilate Agno*. It is usual to quote from Smart's Miltonic pastoral *The Hop Garden* or one of his effusions on the Supreme Being to show the sort of poet he was when he wrote conventionally. But I'd prefer to disinter some lines from a genre he often practised, where his achievement, though modest, is altogether less portentous and solemn — I mean his many Fables. These are not as adept as John Gay's but they are very nicely turned, as in the following, entitled "The Bag-Wig and the Tobacco-Pipe".

> A Bag-wig of a jauntee air,
> Trick'd up with all a barber's care,
> Loaded with powder and perfume,
> Hung in a spendthrift's dressing-room:
> Close by its side, by chance convey'd,
> A black Tobacco-pipe was laid;
> And with its vapours far and near,
> Outstunk the essence of Monsieur;
> At which its rage, the thing of hair,
> Thus, bristling up, began declare.
> "Bak'd dirt! that with intrusion rude
> Breaks in upon my solitude,
> And whose offensive breath defiles
> The air for forty thousand miles —
> Avaunt — pollution's in thy touch
> O barb'rous English! horrid Dutch!
> I cannot bear it — Here, Sue, Nan,
> Go call the maid to call the man,
> And bid him come without delay,
> To take this odious pipe away.
> Hideous! sure some one smoak'd thee, Friend,
> Reversely, at his t'other end.
> Oh! what mix'd odours! what a throng
> Of salt and sour, of stale and strong!
> A most unnatural combination,
> Enough to mar all perspiration —
> Monstrous! again — 'twou'd vex a saint:
> Susan, the drops — or else I faint!"
> The pipe (for 'twas a pipe of soul)
> Raising himself upon his bole,

In smoke, like oracle of old,
Did thus his sentiments unfold.
    "Why, what's the matter, Goodman Swagger,
Thou flaunting French, fantastic bragger?
Whose whole fine speech is (with a pox)
Ridiculous and heterodox.
'Twas better for the English nation
Before such scoundrels came in fashion,
When none sought hair in realms unknown,
But every blockhead bore his own.
Know, puppy, I'm an English pipe,
Deem'd worthy of each Briton's gripe,
Who, with my cloud-compelling aid,
Help our plantations and our trade,
And am, when sober and when mellow,
An upright, downright, honest fellow.
Tho' fools, like you, may think me rough,
And scorn me, 'cause I am in buff,
Yet your contempt I glad receive,
'Tis all the fame that you can give:
None finery or fopp'ry prize,
But they who've something to disguise;
For simple nature hates abuse,
And plainness is the dress of Use."

There's nothing much in this or in any other of Smart's early poems to prepare us for the shock of *Jubilate Agno*. The poem is still generally considered the work of a madman. It is precisely this "madness" which makes our century esteem it — we have learned to appreciate the pleasures of disorder through modernism in the arts and in psychology. The same "madness" would have made the eighteenth century refuse to call it poetry at all if it had known the work. For such a poem to be written in the Age of Reason almost requires madness to explain it. And Smart was held to be insane by his contemporaries. He insisted on embarrassing his acquaintances by urging them to join him in public prayer. Dr Johnson, a tortured personality himself, was much kinder in his judgment of Smart. According to Boswell, he said:

    "Madness frequently discovers itself merely by unnecessary
    deviation from the usual modes of the world. My poor friend

Smart showed the disturbance of his mind by falling on his knees and saying his prayers in the street, or in any other unusual place. Now although, rationally speaking, it is greater madness not to pray at all, than to pray as Smart did, I am afraid there are so many who do not pray, that their understanding is not called in question."

Note Johnson's surprising use of the words "rationally speaking". He and Smart were in an Augustan minority. Johnson also declared "I did not think he ought to be shut up. His infirmities were not noxious to society. He insisted on people praying with him and I'd as lief pray with Kit Smart as anyone else. Another charge was that he did not love clean linen, and I have no passion for it." Once more the great Doctor's idiosyncrasies are revealed and seem curiously parallel to Smart's. In fact, Smart was thought well of by men like Johnson, Burney, Garrick and Goldsmith. They must have admired his scholarship, since it was prodigious.

However, *Jubilate Agno* is unlike any poem in the English language, though it shows the strong influence of the rhapsodic prose-poetry of the Bible, especially the Psalms. It has lines of a poetical beauty which can only be matched in the Bible itself. Smart wrote it in emulation of Hebrew poetry. It was intended to be spoken aloud with an antiphonal effect, rather like the responses in church. The whole manuscript (and less than half has survived) is divided into long lines beginning either with the word "let" or the word "for". Smart's American editor, W. H. Bond, first alerted us to the fact that originally there must have been one "for" verse to answer each "let" verse. The "let" verses are mostly Biblical in subject matter and constitute a litany of praise of God by the animal kingdom, whose names are coupled with characters from the Old Testament. The "for" verses are more personal and often refer to Smart's own circumstances, particularly to his misfortunes. Fortunately for posterity, Smart's paranoia took the form of manic elevation of spirits and his unhappy life is transmuted in his poetry to love of God. In almost every respect, his gift was to praise. Some of his lines are incredibly moving and of a startling originality. The poem declines in quality as it goes on, but fortunately we have a complete set of antiphonal "let" and "for" verses from early on, when Smart's imagination was at its freshest. The poem opens with a remarkable flourish — immediately Smart's clarion language establishes itself, and we quickly learn to appreciate his highly concrete diction. The next few lines are a selection from the first section of the manuscript, of which only the "let" verses survive:

Rejoice in God, O ye Tongues, give the glory to the
Lord and the Lamb
Nations and Languages and every Creature, in which is
the breath of Life.
Let man and beast appear before Him and magnify his
name together....
Let Nimrod, the mighty hunter, bind a Leopard to the
altar, and consecrate his spear to the Lord....
Let Balaam appear with an Ass, and bless the Lord his
people and his creatures for a reward eternal....
Let Merari praise the wisdom and power of God with
the Coney, who scoopeth the rock, and archeth the
sand.
Let Jehoiada bless God with an Hare, whose mazes are
determined for the health of the body and to parry
the adversary....
Let Obed-Edom with a Dormouse praise the name of
the Lord God his Guest for increase of his store
and for peace.

Let David bless with the Bear — The beginning of
victory to the Lord — to the Lord the perfection
of excellence — Hallelujah from the heart of God,
and from the hand of the artist inimitable, and
from the echo of the heavenly harp, in sweetness
magnifical and mighty....
Let Bakbakkar bless with the Salamander, which
feedeth upon ashes as bread, and whose joy is at
the mouth of the furnace....
Let Huldah bless with the Silkworm — the ornaments
of the Proud are from the bowels of their Betters....
Let Anaiah bless with the Dragon-Fly, who sails over
the pond by the wood-side and feedeth on the
cressies.
Let Mattithiah bless with the Bat, who inhabiteth the
desolations of pride and flieth amongst the tombs....

It is plain enough that Smart has no very keen interest in these obscure
names from the Bible, though it was a better known book in his day than

it is in ours. His point, rather, is to take off from each name into an ecstatic order of praise of God. God in multiplicity is his inspiration. In the second and most majestic of the poem's fragments, we are close to heart of Smart's imagination. The matching of verse and response is not always close. Smart appears to have cared as much for contrast as complement and sometimes he neglects to make sure that pairs have anything in common. Nor are the lines necessarily related to each other in sequence. Therefore, I've chosen as illustrations those pairs of lines I think are the best from the 250-odd in this section.

Let Achsah rejoice with the Pigeon who is an antidote
    to malignity and will carry a letter/
For I bless God for the Postmaster general and all
    conveyancers of letters under his care, especially
    Allen and Shelvock.
Let Tohu rejoice with the Grouse — the Lord further
    the cultivating of heaths and the peopling of deserts/
For my grounds in New Canaan shall infinitely
    compensate for the flats and maynes of Staindrop
    Moor.
Let Hillel rejoice with Ammodytes, whose colour is
    deceitful and he plots against the Pilgrim's feet/
For the praise of God can give to a mute fish the
    notes of a nightingale.
Let Eli rejoice with Leucon — he is an honest fellow,
    which is a rarity/
For I have seen the White Raven and Thomas Hall of
    Willingham and am myself a greater curiosity than
    both....
Let Hushim rejoice with the King's Fisher, who is of
    royal beauty, tho' plebeian in size/
For in my nature I quested for beauty, but God, God
    hath sent me to sea for pearls.
Let Bedan rejoice with Ossifrage — the bird of prey
    and the man of prayer/
For nature is more various than observation tho'
    observers be innumerable....
Let Bukki rejoice with the Buzzard, who is clever, with
    the reputation of a silly fellow/
For silly Fellow! Silly Fellow! is against me and

belongeth neither to me nor to my family.
Let Joram rejoice with the Water Rail, who takes his
    delight in the river/
For I pray God bless the CAM — Mr HIGGS and Mr
    & Mrs WASHBOURNE as the drops of the dew....
Let Shephatiah rejoice with the little Owl, which is the
    winged Cat/
For I am possessed of a cat, surpassing in beauty, from
    whom I take occasion to bless Almighty God....
Let Zelophehad rejoice with Ascalabotes who casteth
    not his coat till a new one is prepared for him/
For the Sun's at work to make me a garment and the
    Moon is at work for my wife....
Let Andrew rejoice with the Whale, who is arrayd in
    beauteous blue and is a combination of bulk and
    activity/
For they work upon me with their harping-irons, which
    is a barbarous instrument, because I am more
    unguarded than others....
Let Philip rejoice with Boca, which is a fish that can
    speak/
For the ENGLISH TONGUE shall be the language of
    the WEST....
Let Urbane rejoice with Glanis, who is a crafty fish
    who bites away the bait and saves himself/
For the TRUMPET of God is a blessed intelligence
    and so are all the instruments in Heaven.
Let Stachys rejoice with Glauciscus, who is good for
    Women's milk/
For GOD the Father Almighty plays upon the HARP
    of stupendous magnitude and melody.
Let Aristobulus rejoice with Glycymerides who is pure
    and sweet/
For at that time malignity ceases and the devils
    themselves are at peace.
Let Herodian rejoice with Holothuria which are prickly
    fishes/
For this time is perceptible to man by a remarkable
    stillness and serenity of soul.

Smart selected his creatures not only from natural histories of his time but also from Pliny. This accounts for some of the legendary creatures he mentions. But these obscure Latin and Greek names and the even more obscure polysyllabic names from the Bible are used more for their sound than for any religious or mystical connotation. Smart observes what has been called the first principle of poetry: that it lives in the names of each particular creature in the world. So his huge hymn of praise can take in not only the richly named personages of the Bible and the creatures of Pliny but the soldiers, scholars, musicians, literati and men of affairs of his own time as well. He was mentally deranged only in the sense that he connected all the multifarious activities of the world and put them on equal terms in the mind of God. It is sane to keep them apart and assign them differing values.

Only one other complete set of "let" and "for" exchanges survives, though there are several hundred more lines extant. Smart shows himself well versed in botany and in music and a keen follower of England's progress in the wars overseas. He was a fanatical patriot, as is shown in the line forecasting that the English Tongue shall be the language of the west — a most prescient conception. Some of his flower lines are of great beauty.

> For the doubling of flowers is the improvement of the
> gardener's talent....
> For there is no Height in which there are not flowers....
> For the flower glorifies God and the root parries the
> adversary.
> For the flowers have their angels even the words of
> God's Creation....
> For there is a language of flowers....
> For flowers are peculiarly the poetry of Christ....
> For the right names of flowers are yet in Heaven. God
> make gardeners better nomenclators.
> For flowers can see, and Pope's carnations knew him.
> For the Poorman's nosegay is an introduction to a
> Prince.

He finds rhymes for all the musical instruments, and he expatiates upon the letters of the alphabet. He is always excited by lists and ordered series and by chemical and physical laws. Wherever there is pattern, Smart discerns the hand of God. But his spirits withered in confinement, though by the standards prevailing even today his asylum was a reasonable place, affording

him a bit of garden to dig in and shelter for his cat. It is doubtful that
Smart ever intended publishing *Jubilate Agno*. It was not finally brought
out until 1939. When he began it, it had both form and purpose. Later,
it degenerated into little more than a device for recording the sluggish
passage of time in his cell — he took to adding a line a day to it. But
the aforementioned cat, his beloved Jeoffry was immortalized in one of
the otherwise more barren sections in the middle of the poem. The Jeoffry
lines are the only ones that most people know. Smart is never cloying in
his praise of his cat: he always sees him as a further emblem of God. He
shows himself capable of very Blakean sympathies, as in the line "For the
Cherub Cat is a form of the Angel Tiger".

> For he is of the Lord's poor and so indeed is he called
>   by benevolence perpetually — poor Jeoffry! poor
>   Jeoffry! the rat has bit thy throat.
> For I bless the name of the Lord Jesus that Jeoffry is
>   better....
> For his tongue is exceeding pure so that it has in
>   purity what it wants in musick....
> For he can spraggle upon waggle at the word of
>   command....
> For God has blessed him in the variety of his
>   movements....
> For he can tread to all the measures upon the musick.

After his release from the asylum in 1763 Smart apparently added nothing
to *Jubilate Agno*. He did however quarry it for his famous poem, *A Song
to David*. Some authorities have suggested that it was a sort of prose
paraphrase of the metrical Song, since other prose preparations for poems
have been preserved in Smart's hand. Certainly, the feeling of *A Song to
David* is strikingly like that of *Jubilate Agno*. Yet, beautiful and original as
it is, I find its slightly metronomic versification moves me less than the
admittedly baffling and uneven *Jubilate Agno*. Smart was never incarcerated
in an asylum after 1763, but the last years of his life, living apart from
his family, were unhappy ones. They were enormously productive, however:
he completed translations of Horace, metrical versions of the Psalms and
hymns and songs for the church, notably a fine series for children.

A few of his hymns for the church year approach the level of genius
of *Jubilate Agno*, especially these much-admired stanzas from his Nativity
Hymn:

Nature's decorations glisten
　　Far above their usual trim;
Birds on box and laurels listen,
　　As so near the cherubs hymn.

Boreas no longer winters
　　On the desolated coast;
Oaks no more are riv'n in splinters
　　By the whirlwind and his host.

Spinks and ousels sing sublimely,
　　"We too have a Saviour born",
Whiter blossoms burst untimely
　　On the blest Mosaic thorn.

God all-bounteous, all-creative,
　　Whom no ills from good dissuade,
Is incarnate, and a native
　　Of the very world he made.

The last stanza contains one of the most beautiful acclimatizations of the mystery of the incarnation ever put into poetry. Smart was always able at his best to rise from the concrete to the sublime in a single gesture and this is the only way poetical afflatus can be achieved if it isn't to be corrupt or fulsome. *A Song to David*, too, ends with a superb coda of adoration, so that the last phrase, which Smart prints in capitals, is fully earned — an ecstasy of everything natural, the more remarkable for having been long and painfully filtered through the imagination of a madman:

LXXXIV

Glorious the sun in mid career;
Glorious th' assembled fires appear;
　　Glorious the comet's train:
Glorious the trumpet and alarm;
Glorious th' almighty stretched-out arm;
　　Glorious th' enraptur'd main:

LXXXV

Glorious the northern lights a-stream;
Glorious the song, when God's the theme;

Glorious the thunder's roar:
Glorious hosannah from the den;
Glorious the catholic amen;
Glorious the martyr's gore:

LXXXVI

Glorious, — more glorious, is the crown
Of him that brought salvation down,
    By meekness, called thy Son:
Thou at stupendous truth believ'd; -
And now the matchless deed's atchiev'd,
    DETERMINED, DARED, and DONE.

There is a special irony in considering Smart alongside his contemporary William Cowper. The preservation of the manuscript of Smart's *Jubilate Agno* was due to friends of Cowper's into whose possession it passed and who regarded Smart as an exemplary case of poetic mania. They preserved it because of its relevance to Cowper's own condition, though they thought it useless as poetry. Reading it beside Cowper's most celebrated poem "The Castaway", perhaps our literature's most effective extended metaphor for the abandonment of the mind to insanity, one can only conclude that in religion and poetry, as in so much else, mania is a happier state than despair. Cowper, like Clare after him, was a depressive, though Clare did have some manic periods, as when he wrote a new version of *Don Juan* in his Northamptonshire asylum, believing himself to be Lord Byron. But the truth of Clare's desperation comes in his lyric, "I am", a grim statement of the power of disappointment to rob a man of his God-given dignity and vitality. Clare left us two lines in an album which set the key for any study of the effect of despair on the creative imagination:

Language has not the power to speak what love indites.
The soul lies buried in the ink that writes.

Cowper was a man of gentle and obliging character, who nevertheless believed he was outcast from God, a persistent Sinner whose only hope of avoiding damnation was divine redemption. His habitual self-accusation probably sprang from experiences in early childhood and at a horrifying school he attended as a boy. He could not transcend it or relieve it and in 1763 he went into an asylum the very year Smart emerged from one. There he was converted to evangelical Calvinism, which only confirmed him in his sense of predestination. Afterwards, he lived in retirement in the country (being a man of some property, unlike Smart).

The worst effect of Cowper's neurosis was that the less he had to reproach himself with, the more he believed himself guilty. In a poem not published in his lifetime and dating from an early attack of madness, he wrote:

> Hatred and vengeance, my external portion,
> Scarce can endure delay of execution,
> Wait, with impatient readiness,
>> To seize my Soul in a moment.

In this poem, he speaks of himself as "damned below Judas" and ends with a description of his mental state, "fed with judgment, in fleshy tomb, buried above ground". Towards the end of his life even Christianity and the promise of redemption could not raise his mind above the storms of delirium and self-reproach. It was in this period that he wrote "The Castaway". It is a classic statement of despair, a metaphor of the soul abandoned by God, doomed to be lost forever. But Cowper was a true son of the eighteenth century. There is no violence or derangement of language in the poem, nor any of Smart's manic divergence from classical reticence. Cowper is content to describe one event at sea and then seal off his metaphor at the end.

The story is very simple. Cowper had read how, when the British ship The Centurion, commanded by Anson, was rounding Cape Horn, one of the sailors fell from the rigging into the sea. The crew were unable to help him but had to watch his struggles in the sea until he disappeared from sight. When last seen, he was swimming strongly and this left them with the terrible impression that it may have taken some time for the sea to overwhelm him. Cowper saw in this event his own struggles against insanity and despair. If he were the castaway and the ship his faith, then he was inevitably lost. Cowper keeps his metaphor clear of its implications; except at the start and again at the end, he works only on the scene of the sailor's struggle in the sea. His poem has none of the overt psychology of a modern work with a similar theme, William Golding's *Pincher Martin*. Cowper's concentration on the horror of the castaway's fate is a simpler and better way to bring home his own despair. One feels, at the end of the poem, that he has earned the right to make this frightening identification.

Obscurest night involv'd the sky,
   Th' Atlantic billows roar'd,
When such a destin'd wretch as I
   Wash'd headlong from on board,
Of friends, of hope, of all bereft,
His floating home forever left.

No braver chief could Albion boast
   Than he with whom he went,
Nor ever ship left Albion's coast,
   With warmer wishes sent.
He lov'd them both, but both in vain,
Nor him behold, nor her again.

Not long beneath the whelming brine,
   Expert to swim he lay;
Nor soon he felt his strength decline,
   Or courage die away;
But wag'd with death a lasting strife,
Supported by despair of life.

He shouted: for his friends had failed
   To check the vessel's course.
But so the furious blast prevail'd
   That, pitiless perforce
They left their outcast mate behind,
And scudded still before the wind.

Some succour yet they could afford;
   And, such as storms allow,
The cask, the coop, the floated cord,
   Delay'd not to bestow.
But he they knew nor ship nor shore,
Whate'er they gave, should visit more.

Nor, cruel as it seem'd, could he
   Their haste himself condemn,
Aware that flight in such a sea
   Alone could rescue them;
Yet better felt it still to die
Deserted, and his friends so nigh.

He long survives, who lives an hour
　　In ocean, self-upheld;
And so long he, with unspent pow'r,
　　His destiny repell'd;
And ever, as the minutes flew,
Entreated help, or cried "Adieu!"

At length, his transient respite past,
　　His comrades, who before
Had heard his voice in every blast
　　Could catch the sound no more;
For then, by toil subdu'd, he drank
The stifling wave, and then he sank.

No poet wept him; but the page
　　Of narrative sincere,
That tells his name, his worth, his age,
　　Is wet with Anson's tear:
And tears by bards or heroes shed
Alike immortalise the dead.

I therefore purpose not, or dream
　　Descanting on his fate,
To give the melancholy theme
　　A more enduring date;
But misery still delights to trace
Its semblance in another's case.

No voice divine the storm allay'd,
　　No light propitious shone;
When snatch'd from all effectual aid
　　We perished, each alone;
But I beneath a rougher sea,
And whelm'd in deeper gulfs than he.

The detail which gives the poem such life is Cowper's. The account from Anson's ship makes no mention of the cask, the coop or the rope thrown to the castaway. Like Defoe in *Robinson Crusoe*, Cowper invents from what was almost a newspaper cutting. In his earlier poem, "Alexander Selkirk", he had, like Defoe's Crusoe, found God even in abandonment. But "The

Castaway" is Cowper's final statement on the position of the soul in extremity. Outwardly, Cowper's life was more fortunate than Smart's. Inwardly, it was more dreadful.

I am aware that I have done little more than touch on a subject of enormous complexity, and also that my examples may seem to many people wildly personal and eccentric. A very different programme could be assembled from writings by contemporary authors afflicted by paranoia or manic depression. Other and more dreadful metaphors — the Nazi extermination camps, for instance, or the hydrogen bomb — might seem to hang a pall over our own poetic imaginations. But I'd like to end on a note different from either Smart's crazy elevation or Cowper's depressed decorum.

It is taken from another mad poet, the German Friedrich Hölderlin, a gentle personality whose last forty years of life were spent in the house of a Swabian carpenter and his wife. Hölderlin, a great Hellenist, saw life as redemptive but not apocalyptic. One day, late in his madness, when asked if he ever wrote poems any more, he produced a pencil and wrote these lines on a piece of carpenter's wood. They remain the perfect hope of both the sane and the deranged when facing the long recensions of human fate:

> The lines of life are various. They diverge and cease
> Like footpaths and the mountains' utmost ends,
> What here we are, elsewhere a god amends
> With harmonies, eternal recompense and peace.

1975: ABC Radio, Sydney

CHAPTER II

Saving from the Wreck

This essay is an edited and expanded version of a talk given in 1977 at the Humanities Research Centre of the Australian National University in Canberra. The theme that year at some of the Centre's conferences was Translation, and my paper was only one of many presented. Later in 1985 it was edited further and printed in an issue of the magazine Scripsi, *published in the University of Melbourne. I should like to thank the Centre's then Director, Professor Ian Donaldson for inviting me to address the conference, and* Scripsi's *editors, Peter Craven and Michael Heyward, for accepting the talk for publication. It has been slightly edited again for inclusion in this book.*

When I think of how much has been written on the subject of literary translation, I am made aware immediately of my own inadequacy in the face of so much expertise. My only qualifications are that I have translated Martial and some fifty squibs from the Greek Anthology. I once slaved over reproducing as close an approximation as I could to some elaborately versed poems in that most inflected language, Hungarian, which I cannot read at all, and I have written libretti and song cycle texts for composers. But I have decided to be fool enough to rush in on the topic because I have been steadily producing poetry in my own language for almost forty years, and I believe that the practical difficulties of writing any poetry at all should offer some insight into the ancillary task of producing a translation of somebody else's poetry. After all whatever the problems of understanding a work of art in another language, you have still to fashion a worthwhile poem in your own tongue as the one true end of your efforts.

In the first days of the production of literal cribs of the classics, the learned men who put Latin poets into elegiacs or attempted stychomythia in English were forced to write badly — what they were doing was so unnatural. Good scholars often make bad translators, since they feel no pressing need to render vividly into their own language what they understand and love already. Or, perhaps I should say that this was what happened when the translators were scholars first and poets afterwards, which means at any time from the beginning of the Nineteenth Century onwards. Before that, the better the translator or scholar was at the language in question (and it could be a modern European language as well as a classical one — Harrington rendering Ariosto and Urquhart elaborating Rabelais, just as much as versions of the Greek and Latin classics), the more relish he showed for putting it into his own tongue and the more audacious and natural he could be in his reworking.

Today, alas, the opposite is generally true. The reason for this seems to be the much wider spread of higher education and the decline of the teaching of the classics. The result has been a vast market of people only half able to appreciate what their mentors wish to introduce them to. In order to acquaint millions of readers with Virgil or Leopardi or Hölderlin, the translator must stay humble and serve the original by never straying from its literal meaning. The result isn't necessarily a travesty, yet how often must the student who has already appreciated Shakespeare and Donne in their pristine strength have wondered sadly what all the fuss is about as he picks his way through a prose crib of Horace or even Victor Hugo. Can Pushkin be as bad as he seems in English translation, verse or prose? I defy anyone to read 'The Bronze Horseman' in an English version with any pleasure. The dilemma can be better put by reversing the usual lament: if only our poets were better scholars, rather than our scholars better poets. (I speak of course with full-toned mea culpa, being no scholar myself.) In an ideal world, we would get to know the great works of literature in the languages they were written in. Pope and Dryden knew Greek and Latin extremely well and being great poets they made successful poems of their translations of Homer and Virgil.

I suspect it was Romanticism which killed the classics as a natural training for English poets, though the presence of such a polymath as Shelley in the ranks of the Romantic poets makes me hesitate to ascribe the decline solely to that. And there in the background stands Shakespeare, with his small Latin and less Greek, and his plays and poems stuffed with tags from antiquity and the pedantry of the High Renaissance. He made no direct translations, but his talent for producing metamorphoses was greater than Ovid's.

> Ye elves of hills, brooks, standing lakes, and groves;
> And ye that on the sands with printless foot

Do chase the ebbing Neptune, and do fly him
When he comes back; you demi-puppets that
By moonshine do the green sour ringlets make,
Whereof the ewe not bites; and you whose pastime
Is to make midnight mushrooms, that rejoice
To hear the solemn curfew; by whose aid —
Weak masters though ye be — I have bedimm'd
The noontide sun, call'd forth the mutinous winds,
And 'twixt the green sea and the azur'd vault
Set roaring war: to the dread rattling thunder
Have I given fire, and rifted Jove's stout oak
With his own bolt; the strong-bas'd promontory
Have I made shake, and by the spurs pluck'd up
The pine and cedar: graves at my command
Have wak'd their sleepers, op'd and let 'em forth
By my so potent Art. But this rough magic
I here abjure; and, when I have requir'd
Some heavenly music, — which even now I do, —
To work mine end upon their senses, that
This airy charm is for, I'll break my staff,
Bury it certain fathoms in the earth,
And deeper than did ever plummet sound
I'll drown my book.

The clue to the bad effect of unpoetic literal translation lies in the one word, reverence. Scholars are frequently frightened of each other and scornful of the public. I am not arguing against accuracy. My ideal translation would be as accurate as the difference between languages allows, but it would be alive and it would be a real poem. Reading a foreign poet with your finger along the line and your eye dropping down to the silt of the literal crib at the bottom of the page or going cross-eyed looking over facing pages is no way to get to know any writer. Short of a miracle which offers us all the gift of tongues, the best hope for translation is for the literary and academic industries to harness the talents of working poets and set them to the task of finding out just what will and what won't go from one language into another. There are quite a few masterpieces which have still to receive even one decent English version. My watchword would be the line by Hölderlin from his poem *Sokrates und Alcibiades* (the translation is Michael Hamburger's with one word changed): 'Wer das Tiefste gedacht, liebt das Lebendigste' — 'He who has considered the deepest truths, loves what is most alive'. Thus, in translation, as in any other department of literature, eloquence is the key. And it must be a living eloquence.

Though perhaps it would be far-fetched to claim any of that eloquence for today's poets, nevertheless a fondness for reworking poems into other languages, or at least a willingness to attempt translation on a considerable scale, is characteristic of practising poets all over the world. It is by no means an equal traffic — three quarters of the translation is putting less imperially successful languages into English. Here I should add quickly that I am talking of poetry and other forms of high art — the traffic is out of English and into the world's dozens of languages for films, popular novels, text books and economic documents. But if one thinks of Robert Lowell's *Imitations*, of W. H. Auden's versions of Dag Hammersjold's *Markings*, and poems by Ekelof, Voznesensky, Brecht, of Edwin Morgan's collected translations from European poets including the considerable feat of rendering Mayakovsky into broad Lallans, of Ted Hughes's Pilsinksy, of Christopher Middleton's and Michael Hamburger's excellent anthology of Twentieth Century German Poetry, of all the collections of European poets published in America and by Penguin books — one is inclined to say that this is an age of translation.

Of course, I have mentioned by name only a very few of the more successful enterprises known to me — the scale on which translation of poetry is undertaken today might give even the most convinced idealist vertigo. Conferences, festivals and institutions devote all their time and resources to the task of making the world's heritage of great poetry available in various vernaculars. Later on, when I come to some of my quixotically chosen categories of translation I shall express my serious reservations about the success of many of these undertakings, but I welcome the activity wholeheartedly.

What I should like to do is to suggest a few of the practical difficulties facing the man of goodwill, who has some experience as a poet, setting out to be a translator. The first thing for him to beware of is goodwill itself. It seems to me that the true message of Pentecost was not that everyone understood all the languages of the world, but that in receiving God's message each was given an illumination of the eloquence of his own language. Therefore, in facing a poem (and this would apply to any text of lapidary excellence) which the translator knows or feels to be remarkable, he must decide whether there is any parallel form in his own language which he can put it into. Often there will be, if the language is German going into English, for instance — or French, Italian and even Russian, perhaps. But the Latin and Greek classics are more problematic and I have no notion of what the chances are with Asian or African languages. One important observation about the classics should be made here — there is such a tradition of versions of them in every European vernacular that we tend to forget the very real difference between Greek and Roman poetry, on the one hand, and later European verse on the other. Pope's Homer is very accurate literally, but it would be hard to find a verse form farther from Homer's than the English heroic couplet. Accuracy of meaning alone will not produce the effect and atmosphere of the original. A student reading the Penguin Homer might understand better the epic force of the poem than he would if he read Pope's version. But he would miss much of the poetry. From Pope he would get another and different order of poetry — and this is what I mean by saving from the wreck.

> When fierce the Hero o'er the threshold strode;
> Stript of his rags, he blaz'd out like a God.
> Full in their face the lifted bow he bore,
> And quiver'd deaths, a formidable store;
> Before his feet the rattling show'r he threw,
> And thus terrific, to the Suitor crew.
>
> One vent'rous game this hand has won to-day,
> Another, Princes! yet remains to play;
> Another mark our arrow must attain.
> *Phoebus* assist! nor be the labour vain.
>
> Swift as the word the parting arrow sings,
> And bears thy fate, *Antinous*, on its wings:
> Wretch that he was, of unprophetic soul!
> High in his hands he rear'd the golden bowl;
> Ev'n then to drain it lengthen'd out his breath;
> Chang'd to the deep, the bitter draught of death:
> For Fate who fear'd amidst a feastful band?
> And Fate to numbers by a single hand.
> Full thro' his throat *Ulysses*' weapon past,
> And pierc'd the neck. He falls, and breathes his last.
> The tumbling goblet the wide flow o'erflows,
> A stream of gore burst spouting from his nose;
> Grim in convulsive agonies he sprawls:
> Before him spurn'd, the loaded table falls,
> And spreads the pavement with a mingled flood
> Of floating meats, and wine, and human blood.

That was Pope. Now for the prose of The Penguin Homer.

> Shedding his rags, the indomitable Odysseus leapt onto the great threshold with his bow and his full quiver, and poured out the winged arrows at his feet.
>
> 'That match is played and won!' he shouted to the Suitors. 'Now for another target! No man has hit it yet; but with Apollo's help I'll try.' And with that he levelled a deadly shaft straight at Antinous.
>
> Antinous had just reached for his golden cup to take a draught of wine, and the rich, two-handled beaker was balanced in his hands. No thought of bloodshed had entered his head. For who could guess, there in that festive company, that one man however powerful he might be, would bring calamity and death to him against such odds? Yet Odysseus shot his bolt and struck him in the throat. The point passed clean through the soft flesh of his neck. Dropping the cup as he was hit, he lurched over to one side. His life-blood gushed from his nostrils in a turbid jet. His foot lashed out and kicked the table from him; the food was scattered on the ground, and his bread and meat were smeared with gore.

With the various items he rescued from the hulk of his ship, Robinson Crusoe made a new life for himself on the island. I would go so far as to suggest that almost every attempt to reproduce a Latin or Greek classic in English must be a wreck, if the aim of the navigating translator is to find a closely parallel form for his version. The Bible may well be the greatest example of poetry as metamorphosis in existence. We print the ecstatic Hebrew poetry of the Old Testament as prose, and the wonderfully rich language which the committee who produced the Authorised Version of 1611 wrote in has gone on to influence every subsequent generation of English poets all the way to Dylan Thomas and, in our own decade, Peter Redgrove and Galway Kinnell. There is even a form of this sea-change which could be described as 'creative misunderstanding'. Out of a false reading of the original an artist of powerful imagination invents a new order of sensibility in his own language. The power of the Bible is so great that the many metamorphoses of its texts, though framing in turn the characters of whole nations, may still be excused the charge of being true misunderstandings.

But what of Baudelaire's enthusiasm for Edgar Allan Poe — what is insipid, monotonous and contrived in English becomes a new order of feeling in French. The French have always had a good line in misunderstanding American literature — Sartre on Dos Passos and all the nouvelle vague films makers in our own time. For sheer skill at getting things wrong, they can be matched only by Bertolt Brecht. I know that Brecht was really interested in an America of the Mind, but I can hardly sit through such pieces of Teutonic Americana as *Mahagonny, Happy End* and *Arturo Ui*. There is even something in the latter called the Organisation of Cauliflower Wholesalers, or at least the translation puts it that way. Yet, where the misunderstanding is innocent and due to enthusiasm for a fresh insight into life and literature, getting things wrong doesn't matter so much. The great keenness felt by English and American poets in the Thirties and Forties for the poetry of Rilke was almost wholly a good thing. It liberated the imagination of the Anglo-Saxon writers in a way which might have astonished its xenophobic creator. Those Chatto and Windus editions of Rilke and Cavafy stood on the shelves of a whole generation of poets. We have seen these half-understood enthusiasms run riot in recent years. In the Sixties American poets became obsessed with first Zen and then Spanish American literature. The one produced Gary Snyder among the bears, and the other a school of poets, headed by Robert Bly and James Wright and christened by A. Alvarez 'Minnesotan Peruvian'. Vallejo and Neruda have a lot to answer for. But the principle is not entirely dishonoured: an enthusiasm for translating very different kinds of culture to one's own may liberate creativity in an opposed tradition.

And we don't have to misunderstand our models — there is a mystery in the differences of languages which may inspire a completely new school of thought. After all, what was the Renaissance but the birth of modern Europe through the sedulous imitation of the past. Ezra Pound's injunction to 'make it new' would have surprised a Florentine Humanist as much as it would have disgusted him. When Romanticism ends, it becomes Classicism, but Classicism imitated sometimes turns out to be Romantic.

By coming back continually to the challenge offered the translator by the forms of poetry, I may be understressing the importance of theme or content or even of atmosphere, but I should be happy if in setting out to translate a poem I knew I could find some form in my own language which was manageable and which could be judged a pretty fair equivalent of the one in which the original was written. Sometimes the way ahead is straightforward (though the execution may be onerous). For instance, anyone translating Ariosto who didn't use ottava rima would be shirking the job. But to do it, relentlessly, stanza after stanza, as well as Harrington did in the 1590s, and without unnecessary elaboration, requires genius as well as application. I am glad to see that the new Penguin *Orlando Furioso* is in the original stanza form, though I doubt that its modernisings are as enjoyable as the wonderfully dry precision of Harrington. Take for example the famous description of the moon, from Canto 34. Astolfo has flown on the Hippogriff to the moon to recover Orlando's lost wits, since all the things which men lose on earth may be found on the moon. Ariosto suggests that they are hardly worth the looking for. Both Harrington and Barbara Reynolds, the Penguin translator, do it well, but Harrington has a drypoint feeling which suits Ariosto's combination of scepticism and romanticism. Here are stanzas 73, 74 and 78 from Harrington followed by the same stanzas by Reynolds (hers are numbered 74, 75 and 79):

> A storehouse strange, that what on earth is lost
> By fault, by time, by fortune, there is found,
> And like a merchandise is there engrost
> In stranger sort than I can well expound,
> Nor speak I sole of wealth or things of cost
> In which blind fortune's power doth most abound,
> But ev'n of things quite out of fortune's power
> Which wilfully we waste each day and hour.

> The precious time that fools mispend in play,
> The vain attempts that never take effect,
> The vows that sinners make and never pay,
> The counsels wise that careless men neglect,
> The fond desires that lead us oft astray,
> The praises that with pride the heart infect.
> And all we lose with folly and mispending
> May there be found unto this place ascending.

> He saw great Cities seated in fair places
> That overthrown quite topsy turvy stood;
> He asked and learned the cause of their defaces
> Was treason that doth never turn to good.
> He saw foul serpents with fair women's faces,
> Of coiners and of thieves the cursed brood.
> He saw fine glasses all in pieces broken
> Of service lost in court, a woeful token.

Spelling is partially modernised to make the comparison less jarring, but the punctuation, including possessives, is Harrington's original.

> Not only wealth and kingdoms, which the wheel
> Of fortune whirls at random among men,
> But what she has no power to give or steal,
> Such as the following, I also mean:
> Tatters of fame are there, on which a meal
> Is made (the tooth of Time is sharp and keen);
> Prayers to God and penitential vows
> Which sinners make with humbled knees and brows,
>
> The tears of lovers and their endless sighs,
> The moments lost in empty games of chance,
> Vain projects none could ever realize,
> The fruitless idleness of ignorance,
> And unfulfilled desire — which occupies
> More room than all the rest and more expanse:
> In short, whatever has been lost on earth
> Is found upon the moon, for what it's worth.
>
> Ruins of cities and of fortresses
> Lay scattered all about, with precious stores,
> Plots ill-contrived, broken alliances,
> Feuds and vendettas and abortive wars,
> Serpents whose faces had the semblances
> Of thieves and coiners and seductive whores.
> Phials lay broken — he saw many sorts —
> The futile service of ungrateful courts.

The final couplet of Reynolds's stanza 75 is better than Harrington's, but elsewhere she fills in with redundancies for rhymes and is softer, more received and more consciously poetic. Harrington's plainness is his strength.

For Dante, terza rima is essential — but, oh, how hard it is to make terza rima work in English. Even Byron, in his fragment from *The Inferno*, of the love of Francesca and Paolo, makes the poetry read lamely:

> Ed ella a me: 'Nessun maggior dolore,
> che ricordarsi del tempo felice
> nella miseria: e ciò sa il tuo dottore.

Ma se a conoscer la prima radice
del nostro amor tu hai cotanto affetto,
farò come colui che piange e dice.

Noi leggevamo un giorno per diletto
di Lancillotto, come amor lo strinse;
soli eravamo e senza alcun sospetto.

Per piu fiate gli occhi ci sospinse
quella lettura, e scolorocci il viso;
ma solo un punto fu quel che ci vinse.

Quando leggemmo il disiato riso
esser baciato da cotanto amante,
questi, che mai da me non fia diviso,

La bocca mi baciò tutto tremante:
galeotto fu il libro, e chi lo scrisse;
quel giorno più non vi leggemmo avante.

Mentre che l'uno spirto questo disse,
l'altro piangeva si, che di pietade
io venni men cosi com' io morisse;

e caddi, come corpo morto cade.

Then she to me; 'The greatest of all woes
        Is to remind us of our happy days
        In misery, and that thy teacher knows.

But if to learn our passion's first root preys
        Upon thy spirit with such sympathy,
        I will do even as he who weeps and says.

We read one day for pastime, seated nigh,
        Of Lancelot, how love enchain'd him too,
        We were alone, quite unsuspiciously.

But oft our eyes met, and our cheeks in hue
All o'er discolour'd by that reading were;
But one point only wholly us o'erthrew:

When we read the long-sigh'd-for smile of her,
To be thus kiss'd by such devoted lover,
He who from me can be divided ne'er

Kiss'd my mouth, trembling in the act all over:
Accursed was the book and he who wrote!
That day no further leaf we did uncover.

While thus one spirit told us of their lot,
The other wept, so that with pity's thralls,
I swoon'd, as if by death I had been smote

And fell down even as a dead body falls.

And I stress Byron because he learned from the Italians how to write good serio-comic verse in English. His excerpt of translation from Pulci's *Morgante* is really a dry-run for *Don Juan*, just as much as *Beppo* is and *The Vision of Judgment*.

But, however hard it may be to make a poem work in a parallel form, it will probably be harder still if one decides to find a different form for convenience sake, or because one is excited by the content of a poem more than by its shape and significance. Do you translate only the words — the syntax and story of a poem — or should you look into its known or supposed effect in its own language and try to interpret that in your own version, or at least allow it to structure the new poem in your own language? Sometimes I find myself willing to be very unorthodox in these matters. Throwing purity to the winds, I have been tempted to employ a method which I call, for my own ease of identification, 'lifting the footnotes up into the text'. This must be done with tact, but can, in some cases, if one establishes a loose-fitting form of verse, create the necessary background to the translator's own ease of conviction. When I came to translate Martial I despaired of matching his concision and power with any one kind of verse. Therefore, I elected to find *sui generis* some way of fitting-out each epigram in turn. I was entirely inconsistent — sometimes rhyming, sometimes using the freest of free verse, often applying devices at a whim (there is even one poem which is a concealed sonnet). I tried faithfully to bring out the point Martial was making even if this led to greater explicitness than he found necessary.

My worst inconsistency was the use of anachronism. I kept most of the Roman proper names and many of the Roman places, but freely set beside them such modern terms and references as served to explain something *quickly* to the modern reader. I was tempted to do what Dudley Fitts does in his versions of Martial — to substitute modern names and instances for Latin personages and places. He discovers some ingenious equivalents but I feel that the resulting poems have the wrong tone. My mixed method may be indefensible in theory, but it seems to me that it works in practice. The footnotes can appear in their most encapsulated form if they are used in the body of the poem. To take one very short example, a Martial Epigram, Book 3 No. 35. It is the merest squib in praise of the verisimilitude of the carvings on the Parthenon by Phidias. To find some way of describing their life-like appearance became a commonplace of the Greek epigram writers, and the tradition was pretty well worn out by the time it reached Martial. He managed to find a new gloss for it, however, and it was up to me to find a still newer gloss for his. If I quote my very brief poem (and I excuse its vulgarity on the grounds that it takes no more words than the Latin, which is some sort of feat given the different specific gravities of the two languages), you should be able to imagine the Latin for yourselves.

> Instant Fish
> by Phidias!
> Add water
> and they swim.

I did the same sort of thing in much more serious contexts, and I think more engagingly upon occasion. But before leaving my own involvement with Martial, I'd like to quote some lines I took for my book of translations from the introduction written by Mr Burnaby of the Middle Temple to his version of the *Satyricon*. He writes: 'If I have alter'd or added to the Author, it was either to render those Customs of the Romans that were analogous to ours, by what was more familiar to us, or to prevent a Note by enlarging on others where I found 'em.' The one review of my lifetime which I cherish most was of my Martial book in an American classical journal. It acknowledged all the freedoms and vulgarities and chastened me for a few howlers, but it went on to say that the old poet seemed alive in his new English clothes. It even pointed out that I had missed an important double obscenity in a passage where I had been content to let the quite-repulsive-enough notion stand. What pleased me was this — I am a much less robust person than Martial was, but I had been taken over a little by his spirit. This is a very agreeable sensation for a poet to feel in his loneliness. What Martial feels, of course, can only be imagined.

I appreciate that everything I have said depends on the idea that poetry is a special unparaphrasable order of words and that texts which are only information-carriers are not subject to the same difficulties of translation. Novels and plays are in a mid-way category. Someone once told me that a good translation of Dostoyevsky would reveal that he wrote with a supreme lack of stylistic distinction in Russian. Since Dostoyevsky is my favourite novelist, I resented the remark, yet it may be true, as I know no Russian. The grandeur of Dostoyevsky may lie in his emotional and intellectual material. And this survives in, rather than gains, by translation. Also, the novelist works at great length and wastage is part of his realism, even sometimes of his distinction. There are a few poets whose essence resides in their cast of mind, irrespective of the words it is clothed in. The best example would be Cavafy, a poet who translates very well indeed.

My last observation on the possibilities and impossibilities of translation, before I come to my improvised categories of literary renderings into English, is to do with the autonomy of sound. Rather than deal with poetry as such, I'd prefer to consider the subsidiary subject of translation of musical texts, especially of operas. Speaking personally, I cannot abide foreign opera in English, though I know that to perform it in the original frequently reduces a dramatic experience to a mere concert performance. Even if one knows Italian (say) or German tolerably well, secco recitatives and the like are often reduced to what one critic called the Glyndebourne gabble. The language of Italian opera is a highly conventional one, and the poor English translator is forced to find equivalents for the highly useable but almost meaningless diction of the hack librettists. What is one to do with all the 'dolce contentos' and 'fiero tormentos', the 'testas' and 'tempestas', with 'forestieri', 'traditore', 'naufragio', etc. of even such good libretti as Da Ponte's? To say nothing of the copious rhymes in opera seria as well as opera buffa, and the constant feminine endings. This very conventionality of the libretti for Mozart's operas makes me prefer them on the stage in their original language. Most translations become desperately vulgar or unnecessarily underlined. Who could bear to hear 'Reich mir die Hand, mein Leben/ Kommt in mein Schloss mit mir' for 'La ci darem la mano/ La mi dirai di si'. I cannot even recall the standard English translation. And if 'Now your days of philandering are over' is quite nice in English and haunted our childhoods in versions by Peter Dawson and others, it hasn't quite got the style or the overtones of 'Non piu andrai farfallone amoroso'. And as for Wagner — most of *Tristan* and *Die Meistersinger* are written in close-rhymed short lines. Admittedly, Wagner's German gives most of his fellow-countrymen with the smallest feeling for poetry acute nausea, but English translations simply kill one's suspension of disbelief on the spot. Even Andrew Porter's recent Anglicising of *The Ring* for the English National Opera doesn't seem to me much more than the merest plank washed ashore from the wreck. I think we should all learn German if we are to understand Wagner.

In many circumstances, and especially when the sound of words is reinforced by the sound of music, then sound itself is everything. This element of sound is what lies behind the extreme difficulty of bringing a poem out of one tongue and re-constructing it in another. I don't know what the linguists say on this point, but I am sure that 'To be or not to be' and 'Sein, oder nicht sein' represent two different orders of feeling, although their literal meanings are the same. Of course, one must not give up — 'say not the struggle naught availeth' — but every translator must remind himself as he sits down at his desk that it is not only societies and historical periods which change, it is meanings and their associations once they move out of one language into another. Somewhere or other his translation must acknowledge the unswervable groundbass of its original. Sometimes sound will seem almost all there is. Which may be why modern poets like to quote so much from foreign poetry in their works. In the original version of 'Letter to Lord Byron', Auden reeled off some passages in three European languages and summed up in the concluding lines of the stanza:

> ... what this may mean
> I do not know, but rather like the sound
> Of foreign languages, like Ezra Pound.

Liking the sound of foreign languages is almost as important as knowing what they mean, and should underlie the intending translator's joy in the work he has chosen to make a version of. Then, in his turn, he should ensure that his new poem enjoys just as great an autonomy of sound in his own tongue as well as its checkable quotient of meaning.

By literary translation we mean the changing of a work of art from a foreign language into our own. If the original text is not a work of art, then the problem of translating it is merely one of accuracy and economy.

But a literary text is a made object in the same way that a painting or piece of sculpture is, and therefore has to be remade whenever it is translated. The ways of doing this are legion and I have drawn up a few categories of them, less for any serious purpose than for amusement's sake. Nevertheless, within these pigeonholes, many of the chief kinds of literary translation can find a resting-place. Not that all of them pretend to be works of art: all however claim to have understood the original as a work of art and to offer some form of English equivalent, whether for study or as a fully-worked autonomous piece of writing.

Category One I have named the *Uncompromising Scholarly*. There is plenty of it about. The best place to look is in the Loeb Classical Library series, where the Greek and Latin originals are frequently faced by English cribs of unbelievable woodenness. When one first encounters some of these versions (and they are not all bad — the Martial cribs by W.C.A. Ker, for instance, are quite good), one concludes that they are attempts to follow the conventions and word order of the original, and this accounts for the tortured English. But it is rarely as simple as that. One begins to appreciate that these learned men thought they were writing lyric, epic or dramatic poetry and that they became more poetical the further they departed from the usage of their day. Behind much of their dramatic translation lies the spectre of Jacobean blank verse, no matter what classic devices are in the foreground. Or, in lyric poetry, the ghosts of Tennyson and Swinburne can be seen. Personally, I think Gilbert Murray's translations of Greek drama are preferable to many modern and much drabber efforts, but the specially enriched Swinburnian music of the choruses is hard to take and must be impossible to perform. But other and lesser men than Murray have made an extraordinary meal of the Greek plays. To take just one example close to me at the moment. Euripides' *Helen* is in the Loeb series in a version by A.S. Way, a fine scholar. Here are the opening lines of the play in his version.

> These be the Nile's fair-flowing virgin-streams,
> Who, fed with white snow melting, not with rain
> From heaven, waters Egypt's lowland fields.
> Lord of this land was Proteus, while he lived,
> Dweller in Pharos' isle, and Egypt's king,
> Who of the Maids sea-haunting wedded one,
> Psamathe, widowed wife of Aeacus:
> And to this house she brought forth children twain,
> A son, Theoclymenus, — for that honouring

> The Gods his father lived, — a noble daughter,
> Named Eido, 'mother's pride', while yet a babe;
> But since she grew to bloom of spousal-tide,
> Theonoe they called her, for she knew
> Heaven's will for things that are and things to be,
> Inheriting from her grandsire Nereus this.

Now this isn't too bad and is nothing like as stilted as the translation becomes later in the play. It is not Way's fault that 'Mother's Pride' is now a well-known brand of English sliced bread, yet he ought to have avoided that pre-packaged phrase. Indeed, it is such already-wrapped phrases, which bedevil translation from the Greek, because the Greeks liked them in their own tongue: in ours however they are either ludicrous or supererogatory. The fault in this passage seems to lie less in its diction, worn and poetical as that is, than in its unspeakableness as dramatic poetry. Here the English pentameter doesn't sound like anything Greek, but just like another academic exercise in sub-Shakespearean. Half-timbered verse, in fact. I'd like to quote the same passage in a version I was once working on. Mine is not fine poetry: the speech is after all only recitative and Helen has to get through a pile of information for the audience right at the start. Nor is mine quite as accurate as Way's. And I am well aware that poetic fashions change and that I may be just profiting by a modern fondness for poetry in the vernacular. But I believe mine to be speakable on the stage, and that in discarding the pentameter I have avoided all hauntings of Jacobean. I have used syllabic verse throughout — eleven and nine syllables in such recitatives as this one. Elsewhere versions of nines, sevens and fives — any odd number, in fact, to escape the iambic beat, or at least its dominance.

> You are in Egypt, whose ever-fertile Nile
>   nourishing the delta fields is fed
> by high snows melting, not by rain. The last king
>   of all this land was Proteus, who
> governed from his island-palace, Pharos. His
>   wife was one of the sea-nymphs, Psamathe,
> Aeacus' widow, and she bore Proteus
>   two children: a son Theoclymenus
> and a daughter Eido. Her mother lavished
>   love on Eido as a child, and when
> she grew to womanhood her name was changed to

    one more fitting to her special gift,
  divine foreknowledge; called Theonoe, she,
    like Nereus her grandfather, sees
  beyond this world to the purposes of the gods.

Now any comparison of these two versions would raise issues which could
occupy days of discussion. I've got the information down, but where is
the Greek decorum, the constant reference-making — where too the music,
the metrical ingenuity? My answer must be that they're still on the ship
with Euripides and she's fast on the rocks. My translation has been built
on the shore from bits of the Greek original. But I do assert that it's a
proper English structure and is habitable, if not very comfortable.

  Sometimes the UnEnglish English of these old scholars amounts to a
sort of genius — as in Housman's immortal parody of a typical speech
from a Greek play:

CHORUS: O suitably-attired-in-leather-boots
             Head of a traveller, wherefore seeking whom
             Whence by what way how purposed art thou come
             To this well-nightingaled vicinity?
             My object in inquiring is to know.
             But if you happen to be deaf and dumb
             And do not understand a word I say,
             Then wave your hand, to signify as much.
ALC: I journeyed hither a Boeotian road.
CHORUS: Sailing on horseback, or with feet for oars?
ALC: Plying with speed my partnership of legs.
CHORUS: Beneath a shining or a rainy Zeus?
ALC: Mud's sister, not himself, adorns my shoes.
CHORUS: To learn your name would not displease me much.
ALC: Not all that men desire do they obtain.
CHORUS: Might I then hear at what your presence shoots?
ALC: A shepherd's questioned mouth informed me that —
CHORUS: What? for I know not yet what you will say.
ALC: Nor will you ever, if you interrupt.
CHORUS: Proceed, and I will hold my speechless tongue.
ALC: This house was Enphyla's, no one's else.
CHORUS: Nor did he shame his throat with shameful lies.

ALC:	May I then enter, passing through the door?
CHORUS:	Go chase into the house a lucky foot.
	And, O my son, be, on the one hand, good,
	And do not, on the other hand, be bad;
	For that is very much the safest plan.
ALC:	I go into the house with heels and speed.

And more recently, there have been some deliberate experiments in capturing the force and oddity of original classical poetry in English translation. Gavin Ewart, one of the most resourceful of living English poets, has translated Horace insisting on the same word order as the Latin but still keeping a measure of English sense and syntax. The result is wonderful to behold if weird to listen to. Here is Ewart's version of Horace's Ode, Book 2, No. 20.

Not with worn nor weak shall I be carried
wing biform through liquid air
      poet, nor on earth shall I stay
      longer, and the envy greater than

of the city I shall quit, not I of poor
blood parents, not I whom you call,
      dearest Maecenas, shall die
      nor by Stygian shall be bound wave.

now now settle on legs rough
skin, and white I am changed into bird
      above, and are born light
      on fingers and shoulders feathers.

now than Daedalean more famed Icarus
I shall be seen of groaning on shores Bosphorous
      and of Syrtes Gaetulan singing
      a bird on Hyperborean fields.

me Cochian and who hides fear
of Marsa's cohort Dacian and furthest,
      will know Geloni, by me taught
      will learn Iberian and of Rhone the drinker.

far be with pointless threnodies
and grief unseemly and complainings;
    restrain outcry and of the grave
    put aside the empty honours.

But Ewart is enjoying himself at the expense of the Latin. More bewildering is Louis Zukofsky's aim in translating Catullus of finding English words which are homophones — or nearly so — while still being approximate translations of the Latin. The outcome is pretty dreadful but suggests a good game to be played in churches on the Grand Tour. Monumental inscriptions can be highly amusing transcribed ad hoc in the Zukofskian manner. I give a simple example- 'Si monumentum requiris, circumspice' becomes a Scots explainer's version of Ezra Pound — 'See mon you meant 'em to wreck queries. Sir, come speak ye!' The difference between Ewart's and Zukofsky's Latin renderings is in their intention: Ewart is mocking generations of crib-preparers and teachers in Public Schools. He is out to demonstrate to the wishful-thinking British that it is not so easy a matter to 'think Roman', and that the British Imperium should not identify smugly with the Roman. Zukofsky is trying to match up English and Latin, but also to startle us into accepting Catullus as a precursor of Modernism. Zukofsky's has all the seriousness of the German American tradition.

Altenus, remember *kind intimacies*? false? They elated us,
I am not to commiserate, rue a dull kiss — and to be cool?
I'm — my prodigal, I am not to doubt failure or perfidy?
Men's false acts, human impieties, leave the Gods cool in the sky?
Why do you neglect them, desert me to misery and malice;
ah, you! what end do men face, whom have they then, what faith to
    feed them?
Care to do as you bid, animus trod there by iniquity,
inducing me to love more and more as tho all love were for me.
And now you take them all back, yourself and your words and their
    acts as
winds that irritate, carry a thick nebulous air — you've seen it.
Say you have blotted us out, yet the Gods remember, and Faith
    does —
why, they post to you this moment making you repent that fact too.

My second category I call the *Aesthetic Scholarly* and it's really just to cover Gilbert Murray and his followers. It incorporates a fine principle, that a lover of original poetry in one language will want to put it into equally convincing garb of his own time. It is distinguished from category one by a recognition that English won't accommodate classical forms and that distortions of word order ought at least to be according to modern practice, and not ancient. But it suffers from inappropriateness often enough.

Now comes the third of the categories — the *Recreative Scholarly*. While appreciating how much these headings overlap, I can claim some significant (if approximate) differences among them. I believe this recreative mode to be the repository of the great versions of the classics in English. Some are in forms quite unlike the original, as with Pope's Homer (quoted earlier) and Dryden's Virgil. The material has not been tampered with, but the verse form and, even more importantly, the tone are very different. These two great English men of letters have tamed three great epics. It matters less in Virgil's case, because Dryden is arguably one propagandist translating another, but Pope's sensibility and Homer's are miles apart. I haven't time to question the role of rhyme in English and will content myself with saying that the most serious English poetry tends to eschew rhyme. Rhyme and its supporting syntax are the basis of the couplet, so Pope, the greatest craftsman in the history of English literature, simply turns Homer into somebody else in his version. So did the Hellenistic world of course in its thousand and one glosses and pedantries. What started heroically soon became a groundbass for commentators.

The other sort of recreation I have in mind is the adaptation of a foreign masterpiece into the same form in our language. This is seldom done by poets of the absolute first rank but usually by master craftsmen who are also scholars. Thus, there is a difference between Harrington translating *Orlando Furioso* into English ottava rima and Spenser writing *The Faerie Queene* in an allied English stanza, albeit with an alexandrine at the end. Such a translation is always truthful to intent and meaning and also as loyal as possible to the original form, but will inevitably be modified by the need to produce real art in the translator's language. Italian is not only more mellifluous than English and far easier to rhyme in, but paradoxically it is dryer and lighter as well. *The Faerie Queene* is a much more baroque work than Harrington's *Orlando*, which is why it is harder to read, if more rewarding to study. There is a case for putting some prose translations into this category — Florio's Montaigne, for instance. I'm not sure where to place the standard versions of the great European novels in English. Mostly, in one of my later categories, the *literal*, I think, but a few may belong here: Burton's *Arabian Nights* does.

Category Four is the *Exuberant Scholarly or Over the Top!* This follows on from the recreative and merges into a later one, *Imitation*. Whatever is there in the original is twice as much there in the translation. The English language, having enormous resources of vocabulary and synonyms, and being bendable in all directions, encourages elaborations of the original which sometimes amount to new conceptions. To succeed in this category, the translator should be a polymath or even a sort of word-dazzled pedant. Sir Thomas Urquhart's Rabelais is a locus classicus of this genre:

> Hem, hem, gud-day, sirs, gud-day. Et vobis, my masters. It were but reason that you should restore to us our bells; for we have great need of them. Hem, hem, aihfuhash. We have often-times heretofore refused good money for them of those of London in Cahors, yea and those of Bourdeaux in Brie, who would have bought them for the substantific quality of the elementary complection, which is intronificated in the terrestreity of their quidditative nature, to extraneize the blasting mists, and whirlwinds upon our vines, indeed not ours, but these round about us. For if we lose the *piot* and liquor of the grape, we lose all, both sense and law. If you restore them unto us at my request, I shall gain by it six basketfulls of sausages, and a fine pair of breeches, which will do my legs a great deal of good, or else they will not keep their promise to me. Ho by gob, *Domine*, a pair of breeches is good, *et vir sapiens non abhorrebit eam*. Ha, ha, a pair of breeches is not so easily got; I have experience of it myself. Consider, *Domine*, I have been these eighteen days in matagrabolising this brave speech . . . a town without bells is like a blind man without a staff, an ass without a crupper, and a cow without cymbals. Therefore be assured, until you have restored them unto us, we will never leave crying after you, like a blind man that hath lost his staff, braying like an ass without a crupper, and making a noise like a cow without cymbals. A certain Latinisator, dwelling near the hospital, said since, producing the authority of one Taponnus — I lie, it was one Pontanus the secular poet — who wished those bells had been made of feathers, and the clapper of a foxtail, to the end that they might have begot a chronicle in the bowels of his brain, when he was about the composing of his carminiformal lines. But *Nac petetin petetae, tic, torche lorgne*, or *Rot kipipur kipipot put pantse malf*, he was declared an heretic. We make them as of wax. And no more said the deponent. *Valete et plaudite. Calepinus recensui.*

Recently, the English humorist and critic, Richard Boston, compared several passages of Rabelais with Urquhart's translation and showed how great were Urquhart's additions and how splendidly excessive his imaginative embroideries of the original. Scott Moncrieff's Proust might possibly be considered in this category, if one feels that Jamesian English is even more serpentine than labyrinthine French. Here, too, some of Ezra Pound's fantasies and variations belong. Certainly much of his Confucian anthology, *Cathay* and possibly *Homage to Sextus Propertius*, though the latter is more properly an imitation. I think the most beautiful example of this sort of exuberance is to be found in music, and since musical metamorphosis is easier to follow than literary, I offer it here as a guide to the kind of elaboration I have in mind. I am thinking particularly of Stravinsky's re-working of Pergolesi's slender tunes in his ballet *Pulcinella*. The word pastiche should be forgotten from the start. *Pulcinella* is not only a supremely beautiful and witty score, and a veritable handbook of original orchestration, but it sums up two centuries' development of musical style. At this stage in our culture, we westerners live in a permanent museum, and it is to clear-minded lovers of the past like Stravinsky that we owe our ability to go on making real art in our own lifetimes. I regret only that I can think of no poet, novelist or dramatist so culturally and historically Protean in his inventiveness as Stravinsky — not even Auden or Thomas Mann or Nabokov or Joyce.

I have nothing very interesting to say about the category I call *Literal*, except that it is by far the biggest. To get a modern English novel into German or Russian is hard enough, so the notion of literalness is not one to be taken for granted. I once read a long letter sent to my friend the Irish novelist, William Trevor, by his German translator, detailing all the points of difficulty in the version of Trevor's novel *The Old Boys* he was preparing for a German publisher. The trouble began with the title, which doesn't seem an oxymoron in English but is impossibly so in German. And I would never have thought the word 'snapdragon' presented much difficulty until I read this highly educated German's tentative guess that it might be some sort of flower. It is perhaps a chastening thought that the greatness of Tolstoy, Dostoyevsky, Ibsen, Strindberg and even Cervantes has to come to most of us through filters of such complexity and sensitivity as were demonstrated in this German translator's letter. Many people tell me that the standard translations of Thomas Mann by Helen Lowe Porter do less than justice to the beauty of the original. My German isn't good enough to enable me to judge. Even with novels and philosophical works, one feels that something must be lost, though not as much as with poetry.

I like to think that philosophers might call on poets for translations of their aphorisms. Empson's line from his poem *Aubade*, 'What is conceivable can happen too' is a beautiful rendering of Wittgenstein's 'Was denkbar ist, ist auch möglich'. My favourite aphorist, Lichtenberg, goes beautifully into English. Yet it was Lichtenberg who defined a camel as a horse translated into Dutch. That very valuable series, the Penguin European Poets, prints helpful literal cribs and gives most space to the original in its own language. The Rimbaud by Oliver Bernard and the Hölderlin by Michael Hamburger are conscientious literal translations.

My penultimate category, *Imitation*, is one much used by contemporary poets. Robert Lowell, as I said earlier, calls his book of worked exercises from European poetry, *Imitations*. The same applies to his version of Racine's *Phedre* and to Richard Wilbur's and Tony Harrison's acting texts of Molière — the latter are more remarkable for being rendered in rhyming couplets. But Harrison went on to blot his copybook badly when he translated Aeschylus for the National Theatre in London. Their production of the *Oresteia* was remarkable for the use of masks and the menacing groupings of the chorus. Harrison Birtwistle's score was hardly ever quiet and turned the plays into an operatic experience. Fortunately it often drowned both the individual characters' lines and the chorus's chanting, which was a mercy since Harrison chose to render the Greek into early English alliterative verse. The following passage is wholly characteristic. Clytemnestra is speaking.

> Look at him, Shaggermemnon, shameless, shaft-happy,
> ogler and grinder of Troy's golden girlhood.
> Look at her, spearprize, prophetess, princess,
> whore of his wartent, his bash back on shipboard.
>
> They've got their deserts the two of them now.
> There he lies. She's sung her swansong and lies
> as she should do stretched out alongside him,
> his 'dear's' death a side-dish to the banquet of his.

Worse than the portmanteau words and the vulgarisms is the ill-chosen dactylic rhythm, which becomes maddening at the end of a long night in the theatre. Yet I suppose that as a genre Imitation is no more than an impatient wing of the Recreative Scholarly. It is this sort of translation that Vladimir Nabokov rails so much against. The basic rule seems to be that the translator finds in a finished work of art the bones of one of his own. He is struck by a form of pre-echo. He is somewhat like an archaeologist or a paleontologist. Some of his new constructs deserve to be called, as the old *National Geographic* magazine put it, 'our artist's impression' and may be no closer to the original than the Hanging Gardens of Babylon were to the prints of our childhood. An Imitation should stop short well before the point at which it becomes a variation on someone else's theme. There are some splendid Rimbaud enlargements by Peter Redgrove and similar workings of Rimbaud, Laforgue and Corbière by Martin Bell and Douglas Dunn, which are too deviant from their sources to be claimed as Imitations. Bell's rendition of Rimbaud's *Democracy* catches the spirit of the original much better than most literal cribs do.

> The colours on parade, dipping past the filthy bricks of this garrison town. Boots, newly issued, stutter on the cobbles; but we can keep step.

> We'll be posted overseas, to the big Base Depots. White buildings in long straight lines, like the Big City itself, but with everything laid on, just for us. It'll be the biggest best-run brothel in the world. If the students riot it'll be us reservists who're called out.

> East of Suez or thereabouts — where the cold beer is grateful to the clay that gurgles it up and the temper rises nicely after meals. We'll make the black bastards work: leader-writers will talk about the Commonwealth.

> Anywhere to get away from home. Glad to be back in the army, we'll use our loaves alright. We can't pass exams but we get our feet under the table. Everyone else can get fucked. Progress we call it.

> by-the-right-quick-MARCH.

Much of the modern output of imitations is from Romantic European poetry, but there were similar things in the past. It is very interesting to compare William Wycherley's play *The Plain Dealer* with Molière's *Le Misanthrope*. The English play is based on the French but it is very unlike it. Wycherley is sombre, baroque, extravagant and complicated. Molière is classical, restrained and a model of expository clarity. Also, Molière writes in verse and Wycherley in prose. If I prefer Wycherley, that is only because I know English better than French and like the doggedness of English character more than the thin reasoning of the French. Dr. Johnson's two poems *London* and *The Vanity of Human Wishes* are surely Imitations of Juvenal, by my definition. In a like manner, Juvenal and the Roman satirists and elegists were imitating the Greeks. But I have to admit that at its most characteristic Imitation is really a form of creative writing rather than a department of translation proper.

Which brings me to the last of my categories — the last and most shameful — the *Ecumenical Slovenly*. Its heart is in the right place but its brains are underdeveloped. I assign all sort of enterprises 'devoutly to be wished' to this category — anthologies by many hands from obscure languages which none of the translators reads, magazines from the Iowa translation centre giving surveys of the latest poetry from any part of the globe, books dutifully undertaken by grateful American poets repaying kindnesses done them in Europe. There is a dangerous notion lying behind this category. I heard it put by Ted Hughes, who, though a fine poet, talks agreeable nonsense in public. If only the poets of the world could get together, he argued, they could help repair the damage done by the politicians. Personally, I think they'd almost be capable of starting a third world war.

The Rotterdam Poetry Festival has morning sessions each day when as many of the assembled poets as can be corralled into a luxury suite settle down to the task of translating the work of a master of one of the world's more obscure languages into their own tongues. When I was there, in 1976, the language was Yiddish and the poet the sixty year old Israeli, Abraham Sutzkever. English was the medium of communication though I was the only person present whose native tongue it was. We dutifully rendered a poem or two poems a day into our own languages. They were collected at the end and published. I gave up very quickly. Mr Sutzkever's first poem was in a tight ballad metre, with end-rhymes which reminded me of Kipling, so I set out to put my poem into the same metre in English and to rhyme it. I didn't find the task too hard, but my colleagues were horrified. They thought I had degraded a serious work of art. Their own versions, all of them in free verse, sounded sonorous enough (in the languages I understood, because there were Turkish, Polish and Hebrew versions as well). But they seemed to me to have changed an unassertive ballad into a piece of the modernistic oracular. Too much goodwill was at fault, I believe.

I think we simply have to admit that much of what passes for translation today is just organised dissemination of misinformation. I find it hard enough to know whether the regular issues of the London-based *Modern Poetry in Translation* magazine are a fair indication of what is going on in the major European languages. And I cannot begin to be sure of anything when the verse comes from Scandinavia or the Middle East or South America or Asia. I must admit that there is a lot of poetry I shall never get to know. What I have seen of a lot of it in translation doesn't make me want to follow it up. There are, after all, according to that big St James Press reference book, more than 1000 poets writing in English alone at the present moment. How many people reading this essay have read even fifty of them in any depth? When I set out to write the British Council's pamphlet on British Poetry since 1960 (I didn't finish the task: it depressed me too much and my colleague Anthony Thwaite took it over) I listed 150 poets working in the UK whose work was known fairly intimately to me. I could only muster about fifty names among foreign poets I'd read in translation.

I suppose we must remember that, rich as our own language is, three quarters of the world's great literature will have to come to us in translation, unless we can learn to read fluently in other tongues. And I take heart from the fact that there are great rewards to be had from works in translation — insights and aspects of life which change our very way of looking at the world. I may have misunderstood him, but I owe much of my now habitual feeling of the tribal currents in human society to reading Rimbaud's *Les Illuminations*. I read them in French but I always liked to check on the English gloss. So with Thomas Mann, with German lieder, with Laclos's *Les Liaisons Dangereuses*, with Grimmelshausen and with Ibsen — just to name a random selection of European writers and their works which are dear to me and which I read in English, with cross-checkings into their own languages (except Norwegian, of course). In their cases I feel that somehow the ship escaped wrecking, though that may be my own illusion. But, wrecked or not, we need these argosies from other languages. And I am sure that we shall go on trying to bring them safely to land.

1977: Canberra. HRC Conference on Translation

CHAPTER III

The Shape of Poetry
and the Shape of Music

I am honoured to be addressing you tonight, since my auspices are so
distinguished. They derive from the fame of your much-loved poet and
musician, James McAuley, in whose memory these lectures have been set
up, and also from the eminence of the man who gave the first McAuley
Memorial Lecture, Alec Hope, whose own place in the Republic of Letters
is an assured one.

James McAuley was a true musician, and I am only a collaborator with
composers. But McAuley was firstly a poet and so am I, and I have dared
to bring together the two practices of music and poetry in my address.
The talk which follows is about a number of different aspects of the
relations between the two arts. Inevitably, it will be music which dominates
the argument. But I shall be using words, whether I talk about literature
or music. Before you conclude that I traffic only in truisms, I suggest that
you consider that it is very difficult to say anything really useful about
one art in the medium of another. Or, more honestly, only words can
serve as purposeful means of communication. In London, Hans Keller has
been trying to establish that the truly significant way to comment on music
is in music. I have heard several of his structural analyses, where he
composes musical commentaries on existing masterpieces. You hear the
opening bars of the composition and then comes music by Keller which
amounts to discourse upon or examination of the previously announced
section of the 'finished' work of the composer. So it goes on until the
end of the movement: the composer's score, then Keller's commentary.

It does not work well. I remember Keller's analysis of the first movement
of Mozart's Piano Concerto in C Major, K503. All I got from Keller's
own music was the expected confirmation that Mozart knew what he was
doing when he chose the notes and just the notes he did. You can use
words to talk about other words, and words to talk about music, but, *pace*

Hans Keller, you cannot describe music in terms of music. Or words, in terms of music, of course. This is not to say that a great deal which happens in musical composition does not derive from pre-existing works — music talking shop about music, as it were. Both literature and music have done this since the first setting up of a canon. The model for art remains that of metamorphosis: imaginations, great events, are all transformation scenes. It is no surprise to learn that Shakespeare's favourite poet was Ovid. Today, especially, artists have become ever more self-conscious creators of variations on themes. This may reflect the richness of mind of the creator, as with Eliot in poetry, Thomas Mann in the novel and Stravinsky in music, or it may be mere chic, as much that gets played at contemporary music festivals reveals: gobbets of Mahler, phrases from Schubert, tincture of the Beatles and Hard Rock manifest themselves and disappear in a welter of music-theatre events. Good or bad, our use of the past is one of the best ways of getting to know us.

Art *abo ovo* is almost impossible, yet the permanent museum is a place which insists on our knowing the ground plan and behaving therein with decorum. When even Pound's injunction 'to make it new' has been itself thoroughly historicized, we would do well to let the true creator, the imagination, guide us through the haunted world we live in. With all this in mind, I ask you to remember the limitations of my means tonight — my own intelligence, of course, but also my having to use words about music instead of the sounds themselves. There is a vast quantity of music not connected in any overt way with literature, and I shall even refer to some of this on occasions, but the equally extensive territory of music linked to words will be my chief area of reference. I shall not wittingly do what a distinguished son of Tasmania, Mr Peter Conrad, did in his book on the literary origins of romantic opera, which is to turn music into substitute literature. I shall respect its autonomy. And before I leave this part of my exordium, I must affirm my dislike of the habit of literary men to be enthusiastic only about opera. This is a vulgarism which I am surprised to discover in the writings of W. H. Auden, perhaps the most distinguished collaborator with musicians this century or at least since Hugo von Hofmannsthal. Early in his career, Auden could refer to his fondness for lieder. In *Letter to Lord Byron*, in 1936, he wrote,

> I like Wolf's Goethe-Lieder very much,
> But doubt if Ganymed's appeal will touch
> That marvellous cry with its ascending phrases
> Capitalism in its later stages.

This was at a time when he wrote that he was 'not bad at reading the slower movements', and when, in *Letters from Iceland*, he tells how he enjoyed sight-reading the March of the Priests from *The Magic Flute* on a harmonium in an Iceland cottage. But after meeting Chester Kallman, it was opera all the way for Auden. Since this led to the creation of *The Rake's Progress* and, a little further down my list of enthusiasms, to his Henze operas, *Elegy for Young Lovers* and *The Bassarids*, I should not complain. But I find many of Auden's *obiter dicta* on the relationship between words and music arbitrary, and his later libretti filled with fustian, with pastiche of the pastoral and even with doggerel. His translations of the Mozart operas are neither good versification nor good for singing. He has given us so much, we should take only the good from him and excuse him his more peculiar injunctions. Opera, which I too recognize as perhaps the greatest of all the arts, can represent an escapist and trivializing taste. It is not the be-all and end-all of literary-musical collaboration. So I shall concern myself with songs, hymns, cantatas, and even purely instrumental music as well as operas. I hope too to retain some of the Old Adam of poetry in what I say.

Although each of the major arts has resemblances to its sister arts, each is autonomous and differs from the others quite clearly. Music and literature are both bound by time, which the plastic arts are not. They must be encountered and understood sequentially. One thing follows another, and gains significance by what has preceded it and what will follow it. On the other hand, you take in a picture or a piece of sculpture at one moment. If you remain for an hour in front of the one, or walk round the other a dozen times, you are only deepening your vision, you are not extending it beyond the boundaries of your first encounter with it. Appreciating a picture or a piece of sculpture is a cumulative process: reading a poem or listening to a musical composition is a sequence of encounters. The material of the plastic arts is presented all at once: the material of poetry and music is offered in a continuous stream and may combine the sense of journeying with the phenomenon of a natural force — a Heraclitean flux, like a river or a stream of particles. Music and literature could not work without memory, while there is a real sense in which you might say that a painting has no need of memory. Certainly a photograph insists on being always in the present, and allows nothing to perpend.

However, music has links with pictorial art which it does not share with literature. Literature has no intrinsic reality: it is wholly an art of symbols. Because we are so familiar with words, we think they are more real and everyday than are notes of music or colours on canvas. Yet they are symbols we have learned and they have no existence outside the meanings they convey.

Playing about with words as pure sound will not change this. Onomatopoeia works only when the mimetic noises are fixed firmly in their sphere of operation by overt meaning. A picture, though it may reflect reality, exists as an object in its own right. This is even more true of music, an abstract system of sounds which is totally real at the same time. The fact that we associate these sounds with emotions and parts of the concrete world does not detract from music's self-sufficiency. Most analyses of the language of music are forced to take their examples from settings of words. Since we know from the words what the mood of a composition is, we can work out a language or even a syntax (usually a matter of rising or falling major or minor intervals) to cover musical expressiveness. But remove the words and the situation becomes much less clear. In his pioneering volume, *The Language of Music*, Deryck Cooke is able to amass a convincing set of examples of composers' using particular intervals and harmonic relationships to establish moods. From Josquin to Britten, the chief human passions have been represented by the same musical formulae — the intervals, not the notes, are the same of course. Yet this so-called language is no language at all in the ideas-conveying sense of the word, as we use it in a fully verbal art. Music serves dramatic and lyrical states of mind with peerless expressiveness, and works beautifully in harness with words, but it does not borrow from literature any system of references. If we call Schubert the most poetic of composers and Tennyson the most musical of poets, we do not suggest that either would have excelled in or even aspired to the other's art. Unfortunately, exchange between the two arts tends to be all of one order. When words are set to music they become the property of the sounds and surrender their independent life. Schubert immortalized hundreds of minor poems in his songs (as well as some major ones), but Tennyson was tone-deaf. The current of concern tends to run one way — from poetry to music.

By what process then does the literary work become the musical work? The composer does not, in my view, just set the words to notes and especially does not, as the literary men of the Florentine Camerata seemed to believe, add to the eloquence of poetry by rhetorical emphasis. Instead, he uses the words to make a tone- or sound-poem in its own right. Thus great musicians are able to write inspired music to doggerel, provided that that doggerel serves a great idea. The arias with which Picander, Marianne von Ziegler and Salomo Franck supplied Bach for his cantatas are set with the same devotion as passages from the Bible. Some commentators (Auden was one) even believe that the best music requires the worst poetry, or perhaps the most conventional poetry. The thinking here is not as perverse as it may seem. Purely literary value can be too intense and local to be improved by musical setting. Musical elaboration or melismata find themselves anticipated and therefore rendered superfluous by literary development.

The process of setting words to music would seem to go something like this. Firstly, some underlying idea or Platonic outline in the whole verbal structure engages the composer. It might show itself in a phrase or trick of language, but it is more likely to be the message of the piece and thus found in a novel or play as readily as in a poem or fragment of prose. The composer makes his setting serve the living idea he has received, and in general is not governed by the poet's handling of the words. Those syllables which make up the words are just the consonants and vowels he needs to launch his music. Sometimes he may illuminate part of the verbal structure when it happens to coincide with compositional necessity. This happens whether the poet is Shakespeare, Goethe or a sentimentalist like Friedrich Rückert. Once the words have taken possession of his imagination, he orders them about like a sergeant major. Technical competence and economy are useful in the writer but literary merit, outside the ability to inspire the composer, is not important. Always, as I have stressed before, the notion in the poem must be a great one, though its greatness need be apparent only to the composer, not to any observer or commentator. Arnold Schönberg has given us an account of his reactions to Schubert's songs which demonstrates exactly this point, though from the opposite direction. It is worth quoting here as I want to use Schubert as my first major example of the interaction of words and music in the production of complex art. And because I know from James McAuley's poems and from other sources that the German *lied* was high among his loves. Schönberg wrote:

> In several of Schubert's songs, well-known to me, I was ashamed to discover that I had absolutely no idea what was going on in the poems on which they were based. But when I read the poems it became clear to me that I had gained absolutely nothing for the understanding of the songs thereby, since the poems did not make it necessary for me to change my conception of the musical interpretation in the slightest degree. On the contrary, it appeared that, without knowing the poem, I had grasped the content, the real content, far more profoundly than if I had clung to the surface of the mere thoughts expressed in words. For me, even more decisive than this experience was the fact that, inspired by the sound of the first words of the text, I had composed

many of my own songs straight through to the end without troubling myself in the slightest about the continuation of the poetic events.

Now, I shall twist Schönberg a little here and say that when he writes of 'the sound of the first words' he means the mysterious over-all impact of the poem — what I call, in fact, its idea or notion. That is where poets score over prose writers in setting musicians' imaginations to work. Not just in tailoring language to comely shapes, to lines and stanzas and metrical contrivances, but in preparing essences of feeling which the composer sees in a flash are waiting to liberate music in him. If anyone following my argument concludes that I am now contradicting myself — having previously asserted that literary merit is not important to a composer — I can only claim that the excellence which poetry has which acts as inspiration to composers *is not necessarily literary excellence*, but a sort of pre-echo of the musical form, something unaccountable, directly from the Platonic Cold Store.

I shall now take two Schubert songs as examples of what I mean. One is well known, his setting of Goethe's early poem 'Ganymed'. The other is a piece of doggerel by Johann Seidl, 'Das Zugenglöcklein', a strophic song from the very end of Schubert's life.

My taste for Goethe's poetry is underdeveloped, to say the least, but I can see the elements of greatness in this piece of Germanic Hellenizing. Schubert makes of it a strikingly poetic creation, where the neo-classicism of Goethe's poem is reborn as an utterly unaffected adventure in God-making. From the legend of the beautiful youth translated to heaven to be cupbearer to the gods, the abstract-minded Goethe chose to emphasise the emotion of union with the infinite. Schubert accepts this as his centre of concern also, but he travels much more eventfully. Ganymede's translation into spirit will be no triumph if he is not fully human from the start. He carols about the Spring and he is equipped with nightingales, but Schubert's way of moving through the element of thought is superbly poetic. The nightingale's trills are conventions, pianistically speaking, but to have denied them expression would have been priggish and Schubert is never a prig. Schubert journeys back to a freshness of vision for which the word 'myth' is an over-studious label. The Greek story is re-made in our time. Great art is always a renaissance. Schubert's musical language is purely Viennese, just as Shakespeare's language is Jacobean English, but the spirit of myth is recreated by each of them when they confront the past because for them the past is an eternal present.

Some critics, Alec Robertson especially, have described the sequences which lead up to the final climax of 'Ganymed' as commonplace, but they do not strike me that way. It is Goethe's poem which rushes forward in spurts: 'Mir! Mir!/ In euerm Schosse/ Aufw' arts!/ Umfangend umfangen ...' The great cry 'Alliebender Vater' closes the case for both poet and composer. Schubert has found the poetry of Goethe's vision, and we appreciate suddenly that this poetry is not in words but in a great notion. Today many critics repeat the shibboleth that poetry is made of words, not of ideas, thinking it safer to echo Mallarmé and William Carlos Williams. But poetry lives not in words nor in notes, but in the human spirit, and the magician-artist will liberate it wherever he feels instinctively it is to be found. Thus, concentrating on style is a terrible distraction. In our permanent museum, the works of genius stay looking young. 'Ganymed' has the dew of Creation on it forever.

What then of 'Das Zugenglöcklein', which is even-tempered doggerel which would have no appreciable merit if Schubert had not seen a vision behind it? Well, it belongs to that beloved vein of Schubert's, the wanderer or pilgrim song which inspired so many instances of the *andante con moto* steady procession through a landscape of plenitude or despair. The welcoming bell draws the wanderer home, in subtle variants of the strophic melody. The same bell will one day be a passing bell, but is not yet. Each time the melody returns it is not quite as it was before, and there are the usual Schubert modulations on the way. The bell sounds on an E flat beautifully and variously placed within the texture of the piano accompaniment. Here is the gemütlich equivalent of such sombre songs as 'Der Wegweiser' and 'Das Wirtshaus' from *Die Winterreise*.

It may seem that I am offering a depressing message to poets and lovers of poetry, telling them that great music is made happily enough from mediocre verse. Indeed, I am, but I am also moving on to a more encouraging, and even liberating idea. This is that both poetry and music act as an illumination of the real. The greatest poets have the least need of the arcane: they can make the most shining of structures out of everyday material. What we see is transfigured, but it keeps the lineaments of its ordinariness. Thus the process of inventing a poem and the process of composing music are similarly concerned with thematic transformation. When George Herbert turns cottage brooms and kitchen tables into great religious poetry, he is doing the same thing that Beethoven does with the notes of the common scale. Poets can learn from composers how to be more poetical, and that is a lesson needed desperately today. The battles between fixed and open forms, between tradition and modernism, between the shock of recognition and the challenge of the new are, finally, unreal engagements. Each true poet has the hard task of quickening the dust of the real, and his only resources are statement, contrast, development and counterpoint — the same as those used by musicians. Prose can afford to argue, to be discursive and compendious. It is like the sounds of Nature: it has not been selected and winnowed for its immaculate shape. Poetry is a selection of words from the whole store available, as music is of natural noises. Thus the two arts are doing the same thing, but they often help each other only as isolated acts of kindness.

Words may centre a composer's vision and a poet may learn to structure his poem from the thematic process natural to music. The plastic arts play their paradigmatic part, too, as Rilke, one of the supreme masters of metamorphosis, recognized. His poem 'To Music' suggests a number of changes which imagination imposes on literal truth.

> Music: breathing of statues. Perhaps:
> stillness of pictures. You speech, where speeches end.
> You time,
> vertically poised on the courses of vanishing hearts.
> Feelings for what? Oh, you transformation
> of feelings into ... audible landscape!
> You stranger: Music. Space that's outgrown us,
> heartspace. Innermost ours,
> that, passing our limits, outsurges —
> holiest parting:
> where what is within surrounds us
> as practised horizon, as other
> side of the air,
> > pure,
> > gigantic,
> > no longer lived in.

Or, as Robert Browning, a poet who not only loved music but understood its workings and its wonders, makes the Abbé Vogler, a composer musing in the organ loft, discern:

> Or else the wonderful Dead who have passed through the body
>   and gone,
> But were back once more to breathe in an old world worth their
>   new:
> What never had been, was now; what was, as it shall be anon;
> And what is — shall I say, matched both? for I was made perfect
>   too.

Abbé Vogler appreciates the Platonic scheme of this perfection. Music and poetry bring us a vision of something that cannot be wholly achieved here on earth. 'On the earth the broken arcs; in the heaven, a perfect round.' It is those broken arcs which poet and composer have to work with. There is no point in pretending that they are not broken, that man's reach does not exceed his grasp. Poetry to be transcendental must recognize its limits. I am out of sympathy with those overreachers who say that poetry (and music too) must contain everything, that it must be as large as the multifarious world it lives in. This creed of gigantism ends up having to pretend that cosmic significances lie in what are merely compendious instances. I mean poetry of the colossal and inclusive sort — Charles Olson's *Maximus Poems*, even Pound's *Cantos*, and in music Olivier Messiaen's *Turangalila Symphony*, to say nothing of the ululating ecstasies that Karl Heinz Stockhausen finds in the air around him. If one wants to see the garlands which hang from Heaven, one listens to the prelude which Bach wrote round the chorale 'Schmücke dich, o liebe Seele', one of the eighteen Leipzig chorales. Attempts to storm Heaven fall to the ground. The least poetical place that ever existed was the Tower of Babel.

I have said that poetry and music are both created by the means of thematic transformation. I want further to discuss some of the special headings under which poetic shape can be perceived, but before doing so I shall touch in some shades of the happier topic of poetry and music in close professional relationship. The troubadours, the minnesingers and the itinerant monks who wrote the medieval English carols and the *Carmina Burana* were poet-musicians. The name of Guillaume de Machaut is found in both histories of music and histories of literature. With the Renaissance, however, specialization sets in. Poetry is honoured but music enters its time of autonomy. The authors of the words of Josquin des Pres's chansons are mostly unknown — he may have written some of them himself. In England, at least, the High Renaissance brought poetry and music together in close relationship. Shakespeare's plays are peppered with songs and, though he did not compose his own settings, he wrote his dramatic poetry with music in mind. There is a sense in which some of his greatest works resemble musical dreams, equivalents of the late Romantic tone poem. *Hamlet, A Midsummer Night's Dream and The Tempest* are unfolded in the usual five acts and many scenes, but are more expressively fantasias on themes.

We know that Shakespeare held that music was an expression of the central harmony of existence. Scholars refer to this as a Neo-Platonist commonplace, but in performance we feel a much more original energy at work. Lorenzo and Jessica on their bank, sung to by the choiring heavens, are surely telling us that, in the mind of this supreme poet who saw the unswervably evil nature of so much of the world, there was a place for a divinely-promulgated beauty: grubby souls were touched by the serenity of invented sounds. Shakespeare worked towards such absolutism: he seems to have been the supreme example of those persons whom Auden described in his poem, 'In Praise of Limestone' — those 'whose greatest comfort is music,/ Which can be made anywhere, is invisible,/ And does not smell.' Music as a practical aid in Shakespeare's plays, and as a maker of symbolic platforms for his thought, could provide a lifetime's study. One example will have to suffice. If one takes the famous line in *Antony and Cleopatra* where a soldier remarks to a companion, just before Antony's last and disastrous battle, ''Tis the god Hercules whom Antony loved, now leaves him', it hardly matters which sounds the incidental music makes. The laconic stage direction remarks: 'hautboys beneath'. The occasion comes out of Plutarch, and perhaps music beneath the stage was often used for manifestations of spiritual change, yet the moment is profoundly Shakespearean: the gods speak to us ambiguously — often in oracles, and for their deepest impartings, they use music, the supreme oracle. In *The Tempest*, Caliban, the monster, hears the island's noises as consoling music, but to Ariel they are only mischievous messages.

Milton's father was a composer and contributed a madrigal to *The Triumphs of Oriana*. Alas, we do not know who wrote the words of many of the madrigals and lute songs which so bedecked the Jacobean age. Any poet who could claim the composition of 'Fine knacks for ladies' or 'Thule, the period of cosmography' should be happy to do so. I hope Dowland and Weelkes wrote them themselves, and that Orlando Gibbons, who had such good taste in poetry, is the author of the words as well as of the music of 'The Silver Swan'. One man shone in both capacities — the two-handed genius, Thomas Campion, who was also a doctor and contriver of masques. He championed classical metres in English poetry, always a brave thing if not an impossible one to do. His poetry is of the highest possible quality. So is his music; though I find it rhythmically a little turgid beside Dowland's, Morley's and his friend Rosseter's. Campion's songs are usually melancholy, with a tendency towards hymn-tune phrasing. But once heard, songs like 'Never weatherbeaten sail' and 'The cypress curtain of the night' are not lightly forgotten.

Purcell and Bach seem to have been largely indifferent to poetic quality as such, though Purcell collaborated with Dryden, and if we look at the libretto of *Dido and Aenea* with an unbiased mind, we will see that Nahum Tate's text is a masterpiece of compression and clarity. If 'Thus on the fatal bank of Nile/ Weeps the deceitful crocodile' is less than moving verse, 'Great minds against themselves conspire' and 'When I am laid in earth' are true examples of dramatic poetry.

Bach had the Bible to fall back on, plus the Lutheran inheritance of hymns and prayers. There is good reason to suppose that the texts of a number of Bach's church cantatas were compiled by the composer himself, drawing heavily on the Bible and on the pietistic poets of his church. The two-hundred-odd cantatas which have come down to us are priceless storehouses of poetry and music working towards the sublime. Fitted as they had to be into the Sundays of the church year with their prescribed epistles, gospels and hymns, they encompass the whole Christian mystery in the most poetical outlay. As I stated previously, inspired words are set alongside those of hacks like Picander, but the over-all relationship of words and music is nothing less than a new version of Creation. The imagery of Bach's music encompasses raging dragons, the flowing waters of the Jordan and the exile-echoing waters of Babylon, the Sages of Sheba on their camels, the dove descending, the trumpet in Zion, the alder trees of Leipzig waving above the dolours of a funeral, the Watchman's horn, the Bridegroom's coming — the list is endless.

Consider two of the lesser-known cantatas — Number 187, 'Es wartet Alles auf Dich', and 71, 'Gott ist mein König'. The first is a meditation on Matthew's account of the Sermon on the Mount, mixed with the Psalmist's injunction that all things wait upon God for their sustenance. In the alto aria with obbligato oboe, 'Gott ersorget', Bach paints the waving fields of grain which divine beneficence has placed before man. The oboe weaves one of the most extended melismas that even Bach composed. Bach sermonizes on God's care for his world. This is the poetry of truth, a Shakespearean extension of the real. 'Gott ist mein König', was written early in Bach's career and is the only cantata to be published in his lifetime. Since Bach may well have chosen the words himself, I like to imagine him settling on an obscure text from Psalm 74, verse 19, which makes up the most inspired number in the score, a chorus accompanied by recorders and a full orchestra of everything except percussion. One does not have to practise the fashionable art of hermeneutics to believe that all artists love mystery, that a richness of harvest will follow upon a divine lead into obscurity. This chorus uses just one sentence, 'Du wollest dem Feinde nicht geben die Seele deiner Turteltauben' — 'Thou wilt not deliver up the soul of thy turtledove to the enemy.' This prayer for the delivery of the soul, addressed as a turtledove, becomes a recorder decorated barcarolle of the most lulling sort. Bach, like Schubert, moves in and out of the crowded imagery of a poet's world. Without words, his faith, so strenuously insisted on in his absolute music, would have lacked its most human dimension.

Mozart and the composers of the nineteenth century show a different approach to the marrying of words and music. Mozart was lucky to find in Lorenzo da Ponte a supreme librettist, but one who was so skilful a craftsman he left the provision of the poetry in their dramas to Mozart. In turn, *Don Giovanni* and *The Magic Flute* spawned a thousand poems and dramas, as the new literary romanticism discovered that in music it possessed the perfect demonic spur to creation. Shelley wrote his lyric 'I arise from dreams of thee' to fit the A major duet from Act I of *La Clemenza di Tito*. He had heard Mozart's operas with Leigh Hunt, but I doubt that he had much of an ear for music. His, though, was a pattern which thousands of poets and writers followed in the nineteenth and twentieth centuries.

Byron, Kierkegaard, Shaw and many others followed Mozart into Don Juan's world. Music was not only, as Shaw wrote, 'the brandy of the damned', but it had become by this time the only resource of artists addicted to the high style. Auden asserted that only opera could now approach an heroic dimension possible to poetry in Shakespeare's time. Thomas Mann retold the Faust story in musical terms — the composer Adrian Leverkuhn sells his soul to the Devil to become the new innovatory genius. Gretchen has disappeared: Schönberg's twelve-note system is his total lure. Even Rimbaud's visionary poems, looking into the tribal future of the advancing industrial democracies, see time as being punctuated by music. Poems now want to be pieces of music, and so escape from the burden of meaning, especially if they are written by Mallarmé.

The whole question of opera is too big a topic to be more than sketched in here. Berlioz and Wagner wrote their own libretti. The first had good taste and the second did not, but Wagner is much the more successful artist. Wagner was wholeheartedly the tone-poet, even though we learn that he used to give readings of his operatic texts to swooning circles of admirers. It was the words and not the music of *Tannhauser* which mad King Ludwig of Bavaria loved. Yet, what strange texts they are! The short rhyming lines of *The Mastersingers* are even harder to listen to without wincing than the invented saga style of *The Ring*. Blessed are those who hear the German of Wagner's operas only as sound.

Verdi and Puccini took enormous trouble to get their libretti right, but poetry was the smallest of their considerations. They went for theatrical effectiveness every time, and in this respect Puccini was a much better judge of the book of an opera than Verdi. It was Verdi's way to present his librettists with very full prose paraphrases of the action and dialogue of his operas and ask them just to versify his words. Piave, generally dismissed as a hack, fulfilled this task better to my mind than the more literary Boito. The libretti of *Macbeth* and *La Traviata* are both masterly adaptations. And I am pleased to think that Verdi's genius has conferred proverbial familiarity on the modest Piave's well-tailored phrases. 'Caro Nome', 'Dite all giovane', 'Di Provenza il mar il suol', 'addio del passato' and the rest are more than signals to us to sit up: they illuminate the ordinary with a poetry which lies beyond verbal poetry. In the entombment scene in *Aida*, Verdi preferred his own draft to his librettist Ghislanzoni's version, and the words are the most moving in the opera, clichés though they be if separated from the drama and its musical clothing. 'O terra addio, addio, valle di piante' — 'Earth, farewell, farewell this vale of tears.'

Verdi demanded effectiveness and *brevità* from his librettists, but he did not have Puccini's perfectionism of dramatic form. Commentators praise *La Forza del Destino* for its Moussorgskian scale and epic humanity, but was there ever a more sprawling ill-judged dramatic sequence in a great opera? Puccini, though incapable of Verdi's nobility and humanity, would never have settled for such a piece of ineffective theatre. Reading his letters to his literary collaborators, one wonders time and again at Puccini's patience and natural instinct. His endless sorting out of motives and characters together with the right scenic words amounts to a strange perfectionism. Strange, because Puccini is still thought of in serious musical circles as a blood-and thunder *verismo* composer, with an intolerably sentimental taste into the bargain. Yet *La Bohème* is a work of Mozartian classicism at least in its shaping and formal invention. Puccini and his librettists, Giacosa and Illica, went to enormous trouble getting the libretto perfect, and its final shape must be judged by the very highest standards, especially if the process of selection, condensation and elaboration be seen against the loquacity of Murger's original novel. *Madama Butterfly* also shows Puccini as an artist possessing a deep-lying poetic spirit — seizing pathos from the corny theme of Long's and Belasco's boulevard play.

Puccini could be tasteless: he is, I think, in *Tosca*, despite its effectiveness, and wholly so in his horse opera, *La Fanciulla del West*. But the Dante masquerade *Gianni Schicchi* is another superbly original boiling-down of material to reinforce dramatic effectiveness. If he was taken by the immediacy of Belasco's showmanship, he had more sense than to respond to the *fin-de-siècle* posturings of D'Annunzio. The master of morbid fustian wooed Puccini continually to work with him. Mosco Carner, in his study of the composer, has unearthed a spiteful little verse where the disappointed poet refers to Puccini's habit of murdering ducks while hunting on Lake Massaciuccoli, that swampy mud-bath at the foot of the Apuan Alps where Puccini's villa stood. D'Annunzio wrote

> Ecco il lago Massaciuccoli,
> tanto ricco di cacciagione,
> quanto misero d'ispirazione.

which may be rendered: 'Behold Lake Massaciuccoli: such riches of waterfowl, such poverty of inspiration'. If D'Annunzio wasn't what Puccini wanted, the composer nevertheless needed a poet before he could write at all. His greatest though unfinished masterpiece, *Turandot*, comes from a play by Carlo Gozzi worked up into a libretto by Renato Simoni, a scholar and orientalist, and Giuseppe Adami, a man of letters. In 1920, when *Turandot* was in the planning stage, Puccini wrote to Adami:

> If I touch the piano my hands get covered with dust. My desk is piled up with letters — there isn't a trace of music. Music? Useless if I have no libretto. I have the great weakness of being able to write only when my puppet executioners are moving on the scene ... If only I could be a purely symphonic writer! I should then at least cheat time ... and my public. But that was not for *me*. I was born so many years ago ... and Almighty God touched me with his little finger and said: write for the theatre — mind, only for the theatre.

I do not know of a more moving statement of a composer's admission of his dependence on the literary priming of his pump. Admirable as the works of Adami and Giacosa were (and I can testify to Giacosa's quality, having encountered some of his original plays), these men were not the finest of poets in their own right.

The collaboration of Richard Strauss and Hugo von Hofmannsthal offers a fascinating example of two men of genius using and being used by each other. Their operas propose a peculiar distribution of the effectiveness of genius. Hofmannsthal, who had begun his career as a precocious semi-hermetic poet, ended it attempting transcendental novels and dramas. He had wide learning and natural good taste. Strauss, however, was the better man of the theatre and much the more wholehearted creator. Hofmannsthal's collaboration with Strauss shows in strikingly clear terms that if one cannot orchestrate one's own plays as Shakespeare did — the supreme dramatic poetry being a sort of autonomous music — then the next best thing is to offer one's vision to a composer of genius who, if he is sympathetic enough, will be aroused to bring to fruition the original poetical vision. *Der Rosenkavalier* and *Arabella* are perhaps operas in which the poet rose to match the composer's vision. *Die Frau ohne Schatten*, however, is an opera where the genius of Strauss goes against its native grain and attains a special incandescence in the process.

The story is impossibly complex and symbolic, but it embodies Hofmannsthal's favourite theme of the supernatural power of the ordinary, of the holiness residing in marriage and fecundity. Strauss was stretched to match the idealism, but Hofmannsthal could never have made his insight effectively poetic in words alone. The end of Act I, when Barak the dyer returns to his hut where his sluttish wife is asleep and hears the voices of the watchmen exhorting the city husbands and wives to love each other, since by such love a bridge is built between the living and the dead, is of a profundity which Strauss rarely attained. It is as if the Muses put two relative deficiencies — Strauss and Hofmannsthal — in each other's way the better to encompass sublimity. It is for such moments that words and music come together. At other times they speak with the tongues of their otherness, but here they succeed in that business which Corvo delineated out of *The Symposium*, 'The Desire and Pursuit of the Whole is Called Love'. Without going too far into the disputed territory of fashionable non-connection, nevertheless one can say that great works of art may require a strong element of unsympathy, even of misunderstanding. In his old age, Strauss worked to rather boring librettos by Joseph Gregor, an Austrian archivist, but here too he happened upon moments where words and music lay in wait for each other. He seems to have warmed up specially for the ends of his first acts, since at that point in *Die Liebe der Danae* he produces a supreme moment, reminiscent of the exact point in *Die Frau ohne Schatten*. Jupiter arrives in Danae's kingdom, on shipboard, disguised as Midas. Out of their two hardly-idealistic expectations Strauss makes another of those transfiguring annunciations of which he is so expert a compounder. What could be more poetical than that worldliness and fleshly expectation should be irradiated by the divine? Once more we feel that poetry is not an art of words or an art of music but a state of illumination which may need both as its contrivers.

Auden with Stravinsky, Benjamin Britten with Auden and a variety of other writers, Brecht in full flight — these must keep for another time. There is, however, one great nineteenth-century area which fits into this section of my exposition. I have touched on it already in talking about

Schubert. I mean those songs where the texts are not written specially for music, but which are seized upon by composers as ideal vehicles for their imaginations. By this time it was too late for Campion-like poet-composers, though Robert Schumann, with his fine literary style and natural sympathy with Romantic expression, is almost the type. Instead, one finds a newly-paramount literary upsurge given a more certain immortality by its being adopted by a group of contemporary musicians. It is hard for someone whose native tongue is not German to know how good the poets of the late eighteenth and early nineteenth century are. I must come out in the open and confess that if I appreciate Heine and Goethe and Schiller, it is because I first heard them in the notes which Schubert, Brahms, Schumann and Wolf chose for them. Eduard Mörike owes a great debt to Wolf's inspired settings of his poems. Mörike is a gentle soul whose mixture of domestic and transcendent images makes him one of the most attractive personalities in any country's poetry and almost unique in German. Yet I doubt that I could have seen into poems such as 'Auf ein altes Bild', 'Um Mitternacht' or 'Gesang Weylas' without Wolf to guide me. I find it very strange that the purest spirit of all in German poetry, Friedrich Hölderlin, remains in general unilluminated by his musical confederates. Brahms set him, but something elusive, some self-sufficiency in his verse, seems to have diverted composers from his work — at least until recently when Britten found inspiration in six of Hölderlin's shorter poems, the fragments of his Opus 61. A living tissue unfolds in Hölderlin's poems, such as 'Der Rhein', in a 'heavenly length' which is as poetic as Schubert's great C Major Symphony is symphonic.

The epitome of this quest can be found in the single stanza which Schubert took from a long poem of Schiller's entitled *Die Götter Griechnlands*. 'Schöne Welt, wo bist du?' asks Schiller of the golden past of Greece and the first morning of the world. Schubert allots it a yearning phrase in A minor. And answers it immediately in the major: 'Kehre wieder, holdes Bluthenalter der Natur' — 'Come back, fair burgeoning time of Nature'. He quotes this again in the third movement of the A Minor Quartet, a bitter-sweet summing-up of Vienna and the Hellenistic past. Louis MacNeice wrote in his *Autumn Journal* about ancient Greece, that 'it was all so very different and all so long ago'. Schubert shows that we can only bring the past to life when we live in the present — a Jacobean present, a Viennese present, a modern British or Australian present. The Muses were fathered by the pure spirit of creation, Zeus himself, upon Mnemosyne, goddess of memory. Through their mother they thus mediate between the living and the dead.

It will not have escaped your attention that my examples have been taken from German and Italian composers and that so much of the poetry I have referred to is in those languages. This is because I think the supreme artistic achievements in music were made by German and Italian composers. By the same token, I think the greatest art in the English-speaking world is poetry. The shapes of poetry are in the deepest sense analogous to those of music, and I must speak, however cursorily, about some of those shapes and about English-language poets' attempts to attain what Walter Pater said all art tends towards — 'the condition of music'. I like to divide poetry into three states which I call, simply enough, Deep Form, Middle Form and Light Form. In the first I locate all those structures which not only require elaborate rule-following by the poet but which depend in great part for their effectiveness on the reader's or hearer's awareness of the rules and on the extent of their satisfaction. In this category come sonnets, fixed stanzas including *ottava rima, terza rima*, rhyme royal, quatrains and the rest — odes, villanelles, some sorts of alliterative saga-styles and poems with refrains. Antiphonal and musically imitative forms belong here too. Into Middle Form I put those ways of writing poetry which have proved perhaps the most fertile of all in English. The demands of rules are less severe here and work more as a discipline on the poet than as devices of recognition and satisfaction for his audience. Such are blank verse, heroic couplets and tetrametric couplets. Perhaps Projective Verse and structures such as Pound's *Cantos* belong also. As do those forms I call gamesplaying with more than one constant. Pope and Shakespeare are the masters of this enormously fruitful domain. Syntax is as important as any directly mnemonic or musical device, as a few pages of Pope's *Moral Essays* or Shakespeare's late plays will show. Light Form is perceived as poetry by being thought of as such by its sensibility, by the place where you encounter it and by its tone. Technical features are less important. Here I place syllabics, free verse, gamesplaying with only one constant (such as the requirement that every line must end with the definite article or that each line must contain words of only a set number of syllables, etc.), some antiphons and responses and imitations of the rhapsodic poetry of the Bible, all prose poetry and anything which seems to acquire memorability *sui generis*. Truth to experience and the inherited shaping of language may be all the form such poetry needs, just as story-telling or a fine eavesdropper's ear may be all that is required for a novel. Badly achieved poetry usually has form wrongly used or form in excess of need.

Strangely enough, nobody asks where form comes from. Why is poetry from the early ages of the world so complex? Today our idea of complexity is complexity of reference or meaning — classical complexity is of shape. Was it to aid recognition and memorability that difficult metres and rules were contrived? I lose my way in the standard explanations. Plato's notion of each work's aspiring to an ideal template is not much help. If we have not seen a form, what chance have we of recognizing the work which reproduces it? It would seem that in some way shape satisfies us whether it is mimetic or arbitrary: it touches some subliminal valve we have in us designed to appreciate it. I heard a scientist once declare, 'A bee is a device invented by a gene to make more genes like itself.' Shape in poetry is that which brings about a satisfaction which leads to the production of more poetry. It is easy to forget, however, that experience makes a shape in memory also. Therefore subject matter must be said to have at least a secondary shape, by virtue of its selection from experience and its 'fictional' concentration on some aspect of a whole continuum of experience. What is poetry, therefore, but 'the supreme fiction' as Wallace Stevens put it?

Back with my three categories, we notice that the English genius is, as ever, to develop the middle way. Why are English poets less devoted formalists than most Continental ones? Perhaps this is due to our language, which in its turn reflects the temperament of the people, making them indifferent to classicizing. There is no serious or comedic drama in English written in rhymed verse throughout. In French or German there is little drama before the nineteenth century which is *not* rhymed. Our tongue is poor in rhymes, but it is more than that — our sense of seriousness is upset by what we think of as the tinkling and trivializing effect of rhyme on the stage. In those tropes of Middle Form, in the medium-length social poem or in plays in a mixture of blank verse and lyric prose, we find the greatest achievements of the poetic mind in our language. Here are the designs and devices which may be said to reflect the processes of musical composition. I consider Pope to be the most musical poet in English, though he may not have cared for a note of formal music. His lines, 'Those that do to church repair/ Not for the doctrine but the music there', would suggest that he was suspicious of music. But music teaches us to relate words by their adjacency or their sympathy and not merely by overt meaning. It further reminds us that syntax is the most important element in poetry, the poetical equivalent of harmonic construction. I have chosen an example from Pope's 'Epistle to Burlington' as the first of a short anthology of quotations to end this talk. There has been all too little poetry spoken so far this evening. I have chosen deliberately a not very well known piece so that I shall not be guilty of resorting to special pleading. Pope is rebuking the false taste for magnificence in some noblemen's gardens. The passage is mellifluous enough — what makes it musical to my ears is its economy and the perfect balance of the meaning with the sound.

> At Timon's Villa let us pass a day,
> Where all cry out, 'What sums are thrown away!'
> So proud, so grand, of that stupendous air,
> Soft and Agreeable come never there.
> Greatness, with Timon, dwells in such a draught
> As brings all Brobdingnag before your thought.
> To compass this, his building is a Town,
> His pond an Ocean, his parterre a Down:
> Who but must laugh, the Master when he sees,
> A puny insect, shiv'ring at a breeze![1]

That seems to me as directly musical as 'Break, break, break' or 'Tears, idle tears'. Indeed its progress is most like the forward-moving impulse of a movement by Mozart or Haydn.

Now I am coming forward two centuries to Wallace Stevens, the most musical of poets in the sense that his works tend towards the condition of music. The passage I shall read is the pavane-like ending of his long poem, *Esthetique du Mal*. Art, says Stevens, is the greatest enhancement of the real. We do not make poems or pieces of music to escape from reality, but to know it better. Part 15 of *Esthetique du Mal*:

> The greatest poverty is not to live
> In a physical world, to feel that one's desire
> Is too difficult to tell from despair. Perhaps,
> After death, the non-physical people, in paradise,
> Itself non-physical, may, by chance, observe
> The green corn gleaming and experience
> The minor of what we feel. The adventurer
> In humanity has not conceived of a race
> Completely physical in a physical world.
> The green corn gleams and the metaphysicals
> Lie sprawling in majors of the August heat,
> The rotund emotions, paradise unknown.
>
> This is the thesis scrivened in delight.
> The reverberating psalm, the right chorale.

One might have thought of sight, but who could think
Of what it sees, for all the ill it sees?
Speech found the ear, for all the evil sound,
But the dark italics it could not propound
And out of what one sees and hears and out
Of what one feels, who could have thought to make
So many selves, so many sensuous worlds.
As if the air, the mid-day air, was swarming
With the metaphysical changes that occur.
Merely in living as and where we live.

Finally, a prayer to invoke the Patron Saint of Music herself Saint Cecilia, hymned and honoured from earliest times to the present, and not just on her own day, November 22nd. From Dryden, Purcell and Handel to W.H. Auden and Benjamin Britten, himself born on Saint Cecilia's Day, as was also Wilhelm Friedemann Bach, first son of Johann Sebastian, a musical child taught the keyboard by his father on such pieces of pedagogy as the *Trio Sonatas*, the *Two- and Three-Part Inventions* and the *First Book of the Forty-Eight Preludes and Fugues*. In Eden we were all listeners, but what we heard were the unimprovable sounds of Nature. Since the expulsion, we have made much more beautiful and complex sounds for ourselves. And called them poetry and music. Great men worked hard to invent them for us, and it behooves us to be grateful and to go on reading, listening and applauding while human time continues. Auden left us this advice in his 'Anthem for Saint Cecilia's Day':

In a garden shady this holy lady
With reverent cadence and subtle psalm,
Like a black swan as death came on
Poured forth her song in perfect calm:
And by ocean's margin this innocent virgin
Constructed an organ to enlarge her prayer,
And notes tremendous from her great engine
Thundered out on the Roman air.

Blonde Aphrodite rose up excited,
Moved to delight by the melody,
White as an orchid she rode quite naked
In an oyster shell on top of the sea;
At sounds so entrancing the angels dancing

Came out of their trance into time again,
And around the wicked in Hell's abysses
The huge flame flickered and eased their pain.

Blessèd Cecilia, appear in visions
To all musicians, appear and inspire:
Translated Daughter, come down and startle
Composing mortals with immortal fire.

1980: Hobart. James MacAuley Memorial Lecture. Printed in Quadrant, *1980.*

Note
1. The full passage is quoted on page 114.

CHAPTER IV

Rochester: The Professional Amateur

Rochester's reputation as a poet is hedged by confusions, presumption and downright prejudices. It is not possible to write about his poetry with that detachment which, in any other poet as eminent and as long dead, would be automatic. Of the two main reactions, uneasiness with his sexual content has proved less debilitating than modern huffiness at his being one of the nobility. Perhaps this attitude is not so modern, since it lies behind Pope's dismissive remark that Rochester was "a holiday poet". Yet Rochester is not only the most accomplished English poet between Milton and Pope, but prefigures, in his own heroic couplets, that tone of deep-cutting urbanity which is Pope's mark of style, and which becomes the most effective instrument of invention in English poetry after the Caroline high noon.

There are important things Rochester could do which were alien to Pope (writing lyrics which are so much more than song-texts for instance), and even more important ones which Pope was master of and which lay outside Rochester's ability. The point is not that Rochester is Pope's equal or Dryden's superior, but that he passed on the baton to Pope and thereby to the rest of English Poetry. It never went through Dryden's hands. Many of one's own prejudices must be declared, if not cleared away, before the verse itself can be decently assessed. Rochester's male chauvinism (countered by his willingness to invest women with the highest independence as swashbucklers), his diabolism, his clubbableness, his aristocratic disdain for publishing, his insistence on drinking and telling, his death-bed conversion — all these are qualities which make him an uneasy figure for literary men to handle. We clerkly persons have never been much at ease with the Restoration writers, especially the Court wits. This distance was already apparent to Pope, no leveller but a man of the affluent middle class who did not care for self-destruction and diabolism. But Rochester, like all the best writers, shows us the restless human spirit moving in a universe where morality only becomes itself after it has been tested by experience. He and his friends were much more than cynical show-offs. They were the sons and heirs of long-exiled cavaliers, men and women distrustful of even their own legitimation. Behind their masks of fashion, their charades to relieve boredom and their sexual predatoriness, was a Hobbesian anxiety about the state itself. What would hold up, what would keep anarchy at bay? Certainly their privileges meant much to them, but they had few illusions about them. What came back with King Charles was anxiety as well as idleness and horseplay. We should consider the hangover Cromwell's Protectorate must have given the following generation. Under him serious music flourished, the state enjoyed deep peace and there was little sequestration of property or interference with the opponents of the Commonwealth. There can never have been so liberal a dictator as Cromwell, and the expansion of England, to become both an imperial power and a moral force in the world, was begun by him.

Many of King Charles's courtiers saw this well enough, though they would have wished some other source of it. The Restoration led to a diminution of England's seriousness and effectiveness. There was nothing to do but act up. Rochester demonstrates, in the brief passage of time between his teenage poems welcoming the King's return and the sombre late masterpieces, a whole spectrum of disillusion with his friend, the King, and with the whole of what we would now call the English Establishment. The motives behind his most scurrilous satires and lampoons were certainly not all disinterested or moral ones, but there is an undoubted element of frustrated patriotism among them. Rochester was always a man to go too far, and there is an impossibilist, idealist side to his scorn:

> All monarchs I hate, and the thrones they sit on,
> From the hector of France to the cully of Britain.

With this frustrated patriotism goes Rochester's classicism. He translated a number of Latin passages which suggest his philosophical viewpoint, that of the disciplined pagans, such as Lucretius and Seneca. The way the Roman poets wove their theology into a realistic picture of life as men must endure it appealed to Rochester — at least, if we go by what he chose to render from their works into English. His version of lines 44 to 49 of *De Rerum Natura* may be no more than a brief exercise, though the fragment could simply be all that survives (together with a more tentative version of the opening of the poem) of a larger undertaking. But even in isolation, these lines form a beautifully apt statement, as fine as anything ever put into epigram form:

> The gods, by right of nature, must possess
> An everlasting age of perfect peace;
> Far off removed from us and our affairs;
> Neither approached by dangers, or by cares;
> Rich in themselves, to whom we cannot add;
> Not pleased by good deeds, nor provoked by bad.

It is doubtful that Rochester could have kept this up, but I am tempted to show how precise and poetical his mind was by contrasting his version with that of the same passage by an admired poet of our own day, C.H. Sisson:

> Divine nature cannot be other than nature
> Subsisting for endless time in an unspoilt peace
> Far away from ourselves and the things that touch us;
> For deprived of pain, and also deprived of danger,
> Able to do what it wants, it does not need us.
> Nor understands our deserts, and it cannot be angry.

Rochester's direct involvement with the classics is tiny beside the translations of them made by Dryden, or Pope's use of them as perennial touchstones, exemplified in *An Essay on Criticism*. But his frame of mind recalls one Latin poet particularly, Martial. It has usually been understood, if not acknowledged, that poetical skill is not the same thing as "poetical temperament". Neither Martial nor Rochester had such a temperament. They were realists first, exaggerators afterwards, and transcendentalists almost never. Later on in this essay I shall liken Rochester's work to that of modern American writers, to Wallace Stevens and John Ashbery. But I don't mean to suggest that he had any trace of the Emersonian sublime in him. He became almost an analyst of language because of his impassioned detachment, yet his temperament was classical. Martial looked at Domitian's and Trajan's Rome in very much the way Rochester regarded Charles's England: appalled by fools more than he was upset by knaves. Classicism means keeping technique in the foreground. It suggests that hatred of humbug is a better guiding principle than righteous indignation. Rochester and Martial join hands across the centuries in being castigated as the dirtiest poets in the Pantheon. They should not mind the opprobrium, if they can also claim credit as the greatest realists.

There is ample evidence in Rochester's work of a pleasing gentlemanly lightness and detachment. There is also, as everyone knows, some coarseness of sensibility; but nowhere will one find carelessness. Amateur, in the old and correct sense, Rochester was, since he did not challenge the convention of the time which kept gentlemen from publishing. But he was not amateur at versification, and his freedom from the restraints of the market, together with his restless imagination, led him to become an innovator, the chief mark of his innovation being a lightness in the use of the couplet which was his direct gift to Pope. His dozens of squibs and lampoons also show a rhythmic and syntactical freedom which is quite unlike carelessness. Even the broader pieces in ballad rhythm aim for epigrammatic memorability rather than the anacreontic longwindedness produced by the more knock-about Restoration versifiers.

> To some cellar in Sodom Your Grace must retire
> Where porters with black-pots sit round a coal-fire;
> There open your case, and Your Grace cannot fail
> Of a dozen of pricks for a dozen of ale.

When one considers pieces like this, a whole armoury of light-verse lampoons with their air of improvisation, one is at the heart of the suspicion with which literary critics have tended to look at Rochester. Many famous (and professional) poets wrote similar pieces, if less well; but their scatological works are customarily set apart from their main output, and are seen as deliberate relief from high-mindedness. Rochester's case is different: his main compositions and even his more deliberately decorous writings are likely to break into scatology at any moment. It is this gentlemanly looseness which criticism has been uncomfortable with. Rochester's unwillingness to separate large formal designs from the improvisings of a rhymers' club has done his reputation harm.

The case is even stronger if his songs and lyrics are considered. In their splendid ease of utterance, in their perfect judgement of what is transferable to verse from the lineaments of music, and in their memorability, they are the finest lyrics between Shakespeare and W.H. Auden. They are essentially etchings in lyricism, townee vignettes, if set against the wash-and-watercolour of the great English lyrical tradition — Keats and Tennyson, for instance. Yet while these song pieces can be exquisitely limned and as far as possible from all raucous effects, they can also be libidinous and anti-Romantic. Generations of commentators have relished the lyric called "Love and Life", especially its first stanza:

All my past life is mine no more;
        The flying hours are gone,
Like transitory dreams given o'er
Whose images are kept in store
        By memory alone.

But it is no more perfect or delicate in tone than "A Song of a Young Lady to Her Ancient Lover", "The Mistress", "To a Lady in a Letter" and "On Mrs Willis". I might seem to be stretching things in claiming delicacy for these last two sets of quatrains, but I find the noun just when the almost lacy precision of Rochester's writing is examined:

Whom that I may describe throughout,
        Assist me, bawdy powers;
I'll write upon a double clout,
        And dip my pen in flowers.

Here, as so often, Rochester is realistic and original, and his amused recognition of the disrupting effect of the uneuphemistic language of the upper class on the make-believe of poetry contributes largely to his modernity. It is, after all, something to be the only writer with a claim to classical standing in English literature who directly refers to menstruation. And to this taste for realism he adds imaginative conceits which raise some of his pornographic poems to the level of fantasy. It is not certain whether Rochester wrote *Sodom*, but there is reason for thinking it was composed by a group of wits including him. In one scene there is a splendid example of tenderness dressing up as obscenity for its own protection, which, if it is his, expands one's appreciation of his use of pornography in poetry. The scene where Prince Prickett and Princess Swivea enact a kind of sexual catechism is very funny and at the same time sweet. Here is some part of that elusive arcadian sexuality we have heard about from populist libertarians. When the Princess shows him her cunt, she explains:

It is the workhouse of the world's great trade;
On this soft anvil all mankind was made.

I cannot imagine a more reflective and gentle description. Even the jokey realism of their encounter is without any desire to hurt:

Prickett: I'm in. I vow it is as soft as wool.
Swivea: Then thrust and move it up and down, you fool.

But pornography is morally equivocal, to say the least. *A Ramble in St James's Park* is excellent poetry by any standards, but it doesn't hesitate to "do the dirt on sex" (in D. H. Lawrence's priggish phrase). Style intervenes, of course, as it does more tastefully in the gamier songs. The whole poem is more comic exaggeration than disgust. It is Rochester's way to impose ruthlessness on ranting, so that verbal baroque becomes well-pictured grotesquerie:

> But cowards shall forget to rant,
> Schoolboys to frig, old whores to paint;
> The Jesuits' fraternity
> Shall leave the use of buggery;
> Crab-louse, inspired with grace divine,
> From earthly clod to heaven shall climb;
> Physicians shall believe in Jesus,
> And disobedience cease to please us,
> Ere I desist with all my power
> To plague this woman and undo her.

With such imaginative conceits, Rochester inflates his black comedy to high artifice. Pope carried this way of writing to its apogee in *The Rape of the Lock*, ('Maids turned bottles cry aloud for corks'), and in some of his Horace Imitations (themselves owing much to Rochester's *An Allusion to Horace*). He might have found the crab-louse's progress apt, but his good taste would have precluded his using it. Nor would he have been happy with the casual reference to religion which follows. Even more Popean is the fantastical pastoral sketch of the Park which occurs early in the poem:

> There, by a most incestuous birth,
> Strange woods spring from the teeming earth;
> For they relate how heretofore,
> When ancient Pict began to whore,
> Deluded of his assignation
> (Jilting, it seems, was then in fashion),
> Poor pensive lover, in this place
> Would frig upon his mother's face;
> When rows of mandrakes tall did rise

> Whose lewd tops fucked the very skies.
> Each imitative branch doth twine
> In some loved fold of Aretine,
> And nightly now beneath their shade
> Are buggeries, rapes, and incests made.

Put into pentameter, this could be a fantasia on Piero di Cosimo carried out by a less cautious Alexander Pope.

Signior Dildo exhibits the same exaggeration, but this time ventures into the ballad-form and the anacreontic. It is hard to know whether libertine raillery such as Rochester's is merely male chauvinism, or whether it has a serious undertone. Rochester may be scolding what Vieth calls "the promiscuous noblewomen of the Restoration Court" because their flagrant affairs could lead to instability of privilege and the state. If that notion seems pitched too high, it might be more reasonable to suggest that *Signior Dildo* at least among his lampoons is unflinching in locating sexual lust as the prime effrontery offered by aristocratic women:

> The Countess of Falmouth, of whom people tell
> Her footmen wear shirts of a guinea an ell,
> Might save the expense if she did but know
> How lusty a swinger is Signior Dildo.

Rochester's development as a poet was steadily towards greater exuberance. His earliest poems, such as "A Dialogue between Strephon and Daphne", already assault the pastoral eclogue with the shock tactics of irony and surprise endings, but they stick pretty closely to the mode they mock at. A few years further on, though a long way to advance in so short a life, we find him in "The Mistress" perfecting a genre of realistic love poem which is truthful, ambiguous and yet passionate. There are slight echoes of the Strephon and Daphne exchange in this poem, but its tone is quite different. Cleverness and cynicism have fled, and so have mechanical contrivances. Irony, an awareness of mixed feelings, has taken their place. The poem abounds in received phrases and examples from poetic stock, but they are never used without being specially placed in an ever-expanding field of irony. I think it worthwhile to quote the poem entire. It is quite long by the standards of Rochester's lyrics, but no stanza is dispensable if it is to be fully understood. The antepenultimate stanza, for instance, one of the finest declensions in his entire corpus, must come exactly where it does in the argument.

An age in her embraces passed
    Would seem a winter's day,
Where life and light with envious haste
    Are torn and snatched away.

But oh, how slowly minutes roll
    When absent from her eyes,
That feed my love, which is my soul:
    It languishes and dies.

For then no more a soul, but shade,
    It mournfully does move
And haunts my breast, by absence made
    The living tomb of love.

You wiser men, despise me not
    Whose lovesick fancy raves
On shades of souls, and heaven know what:
    Short ages live in graves.

Whene'er those wounding eyes, so full
    Of sweetness, you did see,
Had you not been profoundly dull,
    You had gone mad like me.

Nor censure us, you who perceive
    My best beloved and me
Sigh and lament, complain and grieve:
    You think we disagree.

Alas! 'tis sacred jealousy,
    Love raised to an extreme:
The only proof 'twixt her and me
    We love, and do not dream.

Fantastic fancies fondly move
    And in frail joys believe,
Taking false pleasure for true love;
    But pain can ne'er deceive.

> Kind jealous doubts, tormenting fears,
> And anxious cares, when past,
> Prove our hearts' treasure fixed and dear,
> And make us blest at last.

In the "Dialogue between Strephon and Daphne", the end is a cynical shock, the girl explaining, with a touch of O. Henry, that she has been unfaithful all along while her more sententious lover was working himself up to his disclosure of intent. It reads like an exercise. "The Mistress" is well stocked with paradox, it begins seriously and spaciously, in a near Petrarchan manner, but the irony is planted from the start: these quatrains, as has often been pointed out, sound almost ecclesiastic, Isaac Watts *avant la lettre*. Rochester keeps up the Neo-Platonic tone, but he mixes proverbial drinkers' wisdom along with it. It is a song, after all, and you can feel a presence such as Campion's behind it — solemnity and levity enjoying the same stately metre. The fourth stanza is very Campion-like — "Short ages live in graves". Cynicism is shown as the proper path to truth. There are no shocks, no *trompe l'oeil*, and there is nothing indecent. Instead, we have a profound view of love offered by a sceptic whose experience of fashion and pleasure has given him a taste for extremes.

In this sense Rochester is a forerunner of Baudelaire and Rimbaud. His "dérèglement du sens" was more thorough than theirs because it was not programmatic. The blessing at the end of the poem is the knowledge (very bitter knowledge) that the greatest felicity on earth depends upon a fixed antipathy of natures, that true love feeds on anxiety and betrayal. None of this is new to literature: what is purely Rochester's is the mixture of tones he uses to accomplish his vision. In the end the drinking songs, the lampoons, the extemporisations and variations on classical obscenity helped Rochester crown his lifetime's serious work — a description of the schizophrenic nature of love and of society.

About a dozen lyrics, another dozen lampoons and half a dozen satires may make a small arsenal with which to raid immortality, but Rochester's proportion of success to failures is very high, and he died almost as young as Shelley. In all his finest works there is a distinctive mixture of realism and restlessness, and especially an exasperation with the human condition, where godlike traits and vile impostures live side by side. Most poets feel this way, especially if they have any bent for satire, but Rochester seems to have been set off by an impatience with himself and with the art of poetry. He was Dorimant, but he was a lot more besides: he seems not to have been able to charm the misanthropist in himself. His satire is therefore wide-ranging and beyond faction. Sometimes he can be genial and occasionally he snarls, but generally his tone is made up of despair that human imagination takes people so quickly into pretence and folly, as though he is glossing Hamlet's ambivalent praise of the creature Man to Rosencrantz and Guildenstern.

His poetry offers one of the best opportunities known to me to study the chronic ambivalence of seriousness in a creative imagination. People being so little capable of reform, the satirist's railing must defend itself against the charge of self-indulgence. It often does this by going too far. Rochester will almost redeem mankind by making it heroically preposterous. But then his realism intervenes. His poetry, whether in the social form of the couplet, or in lyrics, strives towards a formal satisfaction which its author's restless imagination will not permit to prevail. His finest works snatch defeat from the jaws of victory, and do it in the name of truth.

Rochester's special quality as a poet is his pursuit of Nothing, his supreme adaptation of *sprezzatura* to a point where it anticipates the twentieth-century artist's concern for the purpose and value of poetry itself. This questioning of a calling in the calling's own highest attainment is at its most developed in his long poems, especially *Artemisia to Chloe*, *A Satyr against Reason and Mankind* and *An Allusion to Horace*. *Upon Nothing* itself, though a fine poem, is a mechanical development of well-worn philosophical tropes. *Artemisia to Chloe* shows morality as a house of mirrors, but its censure is very ambiguously placed. On the one hand, there is the famous encomium of love, seemingly (if its context weren't so equivocal) as serious as any written by a professional eulogist:

> That cordial drop heaven in our cup has thrown
> To make the nauseous draught of life go down;
> On which one only blessing, God might raise
> In lands of atheists, subsidies of praise.

In this manner, Fiordiligi and Dorabella croon in Act One of *Cosi Fan Tutte*, as they bid farewell to their lovers going to the wars — "Soave sia il vento". They are true, they are serious: it is the world which doesn't fit such sentiments. Later in Rochester's poem, experience suggests a more cynical form of husbandry, a variation on Daphne's response to Strephon — "Womankind more joy discovers/Making fools than keeping lovers". Fool-making is seen as woman's preferred business. It may be the only form of revenge readily available to women:

> A woman's ne'er so ruined but she can
> Be still revenged on her undoer, man;

But the cynicism is etched in lightly. Rochester seems to suggest that the world must go on, that its occupation is just to be itself. He would have sympathized with the smoothly sententious arguments of the auctioneer Sellem in Stravinsky's and Auden's *The Rake's Progress*: "Truly there is a divine balance in Nature: a thousand lose that a thousand may gain." Sellem calls the scavengers at his auction "Nature's missionaries". Under all the scars of its realism and its misanthropy, Rochester's satire still adopts the missionary position. After all, it has a clearer target than human folly — its belief in itself, the value inherent in writing poems well. The paradox is that the man who questions the very existence of art, or at least its usefulness, must, if his case will be heard, be a supreme practitioner of it. Setting out to discover what poetry is for, and what it can do, is a way of writing it, a legitimate source of inspiration. Rochester, the gentleman who must be seen to eschew professionalism (the one waylaid in *Timon*, who disclaims that he is the author of some verses which are the admiration of the town — "A song to Phyllis I perhaps might make/ But never rhymed but for my pintle's sake"), becomes in practice the disinterested poet, the writer, not above prejudice but free from faction.

It is possible to trace in all Rochester's finest work a virtuosity of disengagement — from the cordial drop, love, from fidelity, from the social order, from moderation and good sense, and especially from the claims of poetry itself. It is perhaps unwise to draw parallels between artists in ages widely separated from each other, but I detect in Rochester that taste for examination of language, for pursuing poetry into its own words, which is the mark of much verse written this century, especially that of Wallace Stevens and John Ashbery. By concentrating upon the impossibilism of poetry's high calling, Rochester achieves an art which will not serve, which is without utility, but which has more presence than that of its rivals.

The simplest way to demonstrate this is to put any Rochester passage up against one by Dryden or even by Pope. Rochester's verse has a quite different feeling: it is heavier and lighter at once; it upbraids without wishing to reform; it ignores good taste but is always elegant; it even eschews too much regularity of diction or prosody yet is rhythmically precise, fastidious as sound. It is the true voice of human despair lamenting that however great our attainments we must fall ludicrously below the gods. In the end it has no absolute to offer beyond its own existence. Stevens and Ashbery, as aesthetes, are self-conscious atheists. Rochester's atheism is equally profound. His goes beyond the Americans', and extends to a total distrust of reason and philosophy which they are too respectful of the academy to dare to make.

> Filling with frantic crowds of thinking fools
> Those reverend bedlams, colleges and schools ...
> And we have modern cloistered coxcombs who
> Retire to think, 'cause they have nought to do.

In the three hundred years since his death, Rochester has slowly come into his own. We hear that he was almost too celebrated in the 1670s when his most audacious pieces were circulating in the town. "One man reads Milton, forty Rochester", reports *Poems on Affairs of State*. Perhaps Milton might have enjoyed him, as Marvell did — Vieth records that the indecent song, "Have you not in a chimney seen" is attributed to Milton in *Oxford and Cambridge Miscellany Poems, 1708*. Rochester has always had devoted supporters, and just as vehement depreciators. He has never been entirely forgotten, so perhaps it matters less that today he is likely to be praised for the wrong reasons. He is not some wild outsider clamouring for clever people like ourselves to hear his voice: instead, he is a brilliant classical poet cheated of posthumous recognition by a combination of literary laziness and priggishness. He made the gesture in his lifetime of snubbing respectable fame, and the revenge taken has been a long one. Once encountered, however, his poetical presence is irresistible. However much or little he is studied, he is lovingly and repeatedly read.

What came after Rochester has done nothing to lessen the freshness and verve of his writing. And his appeal will always be in part his misanthropic exaggeration. Few poets as devoted to realism as Rochester have been so in love with form: even fewer masters of the high style of English verse have been willing to accommodate not just the vulgar but the life-denying. Rochester smuggles more unpoetic matter into great poetry than any other English master. Perhaps he was a true professional after all.

1980: Wadham College, Oxford. Tercentenary Conference on Rochester.
Included in: Spirit of Wit: Reconsiderations of Rochester, *ed. J. Treglown, Basil Blackwell, 1982.*

CHAPTER V

The Couplet's Last Stand

I think it is perhaps just as well that I am the last speaker in this series of lectures devoted to George Crabbe, since I am not an expert in his work, and my title alone will suggest that I shall be approaching him in a special way. It is seldom that a practising poet makes a very good critic of a distinguished past writer, but it is quite usual to encounter one who loves and is drawn to the work. Crabbe wrote a considerable body of poetry, and I have not read all of it; nor have I read much criticism of Crabbe; there is not a lot of it. But his verse has been in my mind for years, in a part reserved for special masters. He is high in my personal pantheon, that temple each of us erects for himself; and he exerts a pressure on my own way of thinking about and writing verse. Crabbe is often criticised for general low spirits, or for low-key realism. He is thought to be the least transcendental of poets, to be a sort of gas-and-water Fabian *avant la lettre*. Supporting this notion is not just his detailed reliance on surface reality, the describable world, especially in its thousand depressing aspects, but his persistence, long past its heyday, with the iambic pentameter couplet. According to lazy theory, the couplet was already superannuated when Crabbe's first important poem *The Village* came out in 1783. To go on then to write the vast majority of the rest of his copious output in couplets strikes commentators as deliberate neophobia, a temperamental turning of his back on Romanticism. Even as a view of Crabbe's technical make-up, this notion is not very interesting, but it has the worse effect of distorting our perception of the emotional and artistic force of his poetry. Without those numbing couplets — so I believe people's reactions go — Crabbe might have found some afflatus for his poetry; he might have taken off from facts into the realm of imagination.

For myself, I find him a highly imaginative poet. His great strength is his ability to flood the naturalism of his material with poetry. His is the gift of bringing together those two usually conflicting states that the Germans call 'Schein' and 'Sein' — appearance and reality if you like.

Crabbe's determination to 'paint the Cot,/ As Truth will paint it, and as Bards will not', is somewhat misleading. He serves the truth; he sticks to the observable reality of a life, both rural and social, which is generally grim; but he paints it with innumerable strokes of verbal magic. He is as much a believer in poetic revelation as Shelley or Keats. Beauty governs his use of language: he is a poet and not a Parliamentary Blue Book writer. The poor couplet has to take the blame for many people's failure to recognize this. In fairness, it should be said that people tend to be suspicious of Alexander Pope as well — and generally for his couplets. Pope's couplets in his masterpieces, especially *The Rape of the Lock*, the *Epistles* and *The Dunciad*, visit the wildest shores of grotesquerie, hallucination and fantasy. They are also pellucid, Mozartian, and Arcadian, on occasion. Crabbe finds the couplet no impedance to visionary writing. His couplets are far more filled with baroque and brilliant language than James Thomson's blank verse lines, for instance. But, before I get to the main matter of my talk, the degree to which Crabbe is a symbolist or self-contained poet, and not just a masterful realist, I'd like to permit myself a few words on the couplet in English, a history in nutshell of this misunderstood measure.

Most people seem to feel that English lines are at their best or, at least, most versatile, when they contain five feet. The iambus and its occasional inversion, the trochee, seem also to be the only feet practicable if you are not writing comic verse. Therefore poets' options come down to blank verse, couplets, or stanzas in five feet lines with rhymes in any number of different combinations. Indeed, these prescriptions cover all the finest poetry in the language up to the end of the last century — lyrics, translations, play texts, long poems, odes, romantic narratives, pastoral descriptions, satires — anyway, if you let in the three, four and sometimes six foot line as well. Only from the end of the Seventeenth Century until the birth of Romanticism did the heroic couplet dominate the writing of verse in English. Milton's blank verse is very different from Shakespeare's and Tennyson's, but it is even more remote from Pope's and Dryden's heroic couplets. Yet the rhyming couplet — and I confess that I don't like the term 'heroic couplet', since I think we import too much of the modern meaning of 'heroic' into the term — has always been with us. Sorts of things like it exist in Middle English. Surrey uses it and many minor writers of the Elizabethan Age, as well as Donne and Chapman. It picks up speed in the Seventeenth Century, until Rochester makes it the splendid social organ it became with Pope, and Dryden gives it force in satire and faction writing, as do hundreds of satirists and commentators thereafter; look to the thick volumes of *Poems on Affairs of State*. Everyone uses it in the Eighteenth Century, though Swift prefers four-foot couplets, the most primitive of all verse forms. But James Thomson returns to blank verse (very blank in his case) and Blake moves away, and then Wordsworth and Coleridge conceive *Lyrical Ballads*. The couplet survives, though thereafter it is most usually employed for public or social-commentary verse. Byron's *English Bards and Scotch Reviewers*, is as natural but as carefully selected a use of the couplet as is Auden's *The Truest Poetry is the Most Feigning*, or Clive James's *Peregrine Prykke's Pilgrimage*.

The couplet will never die, it is too useful. What it is unlikely to recapture, however, is its ascendancy as the ideal form for serious poetry, which it enjoyed with Pope and his contemporaries. No major poet employs it as his usual or chosen vehicle for his serious verse after the Augustan high noon, except George Crabbe. And that is why I chose my title for this talk. The couplet is a deathless actor, but after Crabbe it has been given no leading parts to play. And its last stand has led to underestimation of the man who handled it so affectingly.

Throughout what I have to say, I shall be referring to Crabbe's poetical feeling, and this will necessitate evaluation of his performance within the corset of heroic couplets. I have chosen five particular poems. His earliest masterpiece and perhaps his most striking work, *The Village*; then the Introduction to *The Borough*, then *Peter Grimes*, which I shall be examining because of its begetting of Benjamin Britten's great opera. Then, two poems from *Tales, 1812, Procrastination* and *The Lover's Journey*. I shall certainly refer to other poems in the course of discussing these, but I wouldn't want you to think that I am an authority on Crabbe.

When *The Village* was published in 1783, Crabbe was 28. There was to be a long gap before its successors appeared, and by that time, the advent of the nineteenth century had made his couplets seem old-fashioned to the literary world. This made him, of course, dear to the many reactionaries of his day — something no more advantageous to him than the contempt of the fashionable. Dr. Johnson had helped him polish *The Village*, and I suspect that it needed it in parts. The poem is in two sections, the second of which is almost worthless. In it, Crabbe presents one Manners, a noble and philanthropic sort, curiously similar to, and as solemnly unbelievable and wooden as Pope's 'Man of Ross' in the *Epistle to Bathurst*. Goodness comes down off the shelf ready packaged and the poet can do nothing with it but offer it to a fallen world with admonishings to go and do likewise. But the first of *The Village*'s halves is a very satisfying poem. Crabbe may have begun it to oppose the sentimental vision of Goldsmith's 'sweet Auburn', the deserted village of his title, but if so he achieved something much more than a successful debunking. Nor would such a debunking be fair to Goldsmith, who was remembering village life before enclosures and the Industrial Revolution. Still, Crabbe would hardly have found even Auburn as idyllic a place as Goldsmith did. Crabbe's anti-pastoral, for all its brilliant and sardonic realism, the parish poor, the hospital, the quack doctor, the appalling parson and the hideous labour of agricultural life, is fashioned as an emblem, in the full Renaissance sense of the term.

His realistic detail is worked into almost all his scenes with the care and love of a medal-maker. Before we get to the enumeration of the Village's inhabitants, we are shown its environs. This celebrated passage is often taken to be the epitome of Crabbe's anti-romantic sentiment. He is accused of seeing tares where other poets see orient and immortal wheat. Cyril Connolly, a literary critic who is usually underestimated in serious circles, saw better than this. He took Crabbe's carefully selected weeds and used them as headings under which he surveyed the snares which lie before the career of a young writer just down from University in our own age. This was in his *Enemies of Promise*. So Crabbe's hardy weed, the blue bugloss, becomes a Fleet Street gutter journal not a long way from the *Daily Express*. And he finds modern equivalents of the slimy mellow and the charlock's shade. Connolly was doing more than fixing his insights with a little clever metaphorical placing: he recognized that Crabbe's countryside stands for more than just itself, manifestly real though that self is. Crabbe saw the world clearly, but his leaf by leaf naturalism does not lead to Pre-Raphaelite innocence. Nor to a relish of horrors, the aestheticism which prevails in the German painters of the Neusächlichkeit and in Lucien Freud. Just as the world has a shape, so must art have a shape. All Crabbe's poems, even if episodic, are well-wrought. But we have heard too many of my words and too few of Crabbe's already. Here therefore is that celebrated passage from the opening of *The Village*. Nobody has used couplets in quite Crabbe's way. His verse has a sound instantly recognizable and entirely its own.

> Lo! where the heath, with withering brake grown o'er,
> Lends the light turf that warms the neighbouring poor;
> And thence a length of burning sand appears,
> Where the thin harvest waves its wither'd ears;
> Rank weeds, that every art and care defy,
> Reign o'er the land, and rob the blighted rye:
> There thistles stretch their prickly arms afar,
> And to the ragged infant threaten war;

> There poppies, nodding, mock the hope of toil;
> And the blue bugloss paints the sterile soil;
> Hardy and high, above the slender sheaf,
> The slimy mallow waves her silky leaf;
> O'er the young shoot the charlock throws a shade,
> And clasping tares cling round the sickly blade;
> With mingled tints the rocky coasts abound,
> And a sad splendour vainly shines around.

Now the agricultural land round Aldeburgh may not be the best in England, but it was probably not as bad as Crabbe paints it, even in the days before fertilisers. Crabbe is making his emblem, and what he wants at this point, is, as he puts it, 'a sad splendour'. If Crabbe's only intention were truth and not also art, he surely wouldn't have chosen to write poetry at all. There are better mediums for realistic descriptions of village conditions than rhyming iambic pentameter. His poetry in this passage takes on an unearthly menace, as though the very land were determined to exemplify the stunted life of its people. He had already countered the pastoral poets and their Arcadian shepherds.

> And shepherds' boys their amorous pains reveal,
> The only pains, alas, they never feel.

Now he moves into the village proper, and what he finds there is far removed from any picture of honest tradesmen, busy husbandmen, or caring pastors. His method is to describe the various inhabitants according to their occupations. Most are shown as wretched. For a while, he keeps up the device, begun as a strategy, of contrasting the real people with their poetic formulae, but the more he becomes involved with them, the less he bothers about convention. But forgetting to denounce the enamelled language of decayed Augustanism does not mean that Crabbe also forgets to style his poem properly. In a sense good writing is always its own style. He is, of course, in his element among the drunk, the sick and the dying. I'll have occasion throughout my talk to point to Crabbe's relish of those sides of life we might fairly call depressed. But he is not the occasion of depression in his readers. Take, for instance, his description of the parish poorhouse. As a documentary on the box, it would be heartrending. In the poem, it is a feast of language. The old paradox operates again: what should make us incensed (and perhaps still does) causes us also to wonder at the power of art to bring before our gaze the very 'thisness' or 'isness' of life.

Theirs is yon house that holds the parish poor,
Whose walls of mud scare bear the broken door;
There, where the putrid vapours, flagging, play,
And the dull wheel hums doleful through the day —
There children dwell, who know no parents' care;
Parents, who know no children's love, dwell there!
Heart-broken matrons on their joyless bed,
Foresaken wives, and mothers never wed;
Dejected widows with unheeded tears,
And crippled age with more than childhood fears;
The lame, the blind, and, far the happiest, they!
The moping idiot and the madman gay.
Here too the sick their final doom receive,
Here brought, amid the scenes of grief, to grieve,
Where the loud groans from some sad chamber flow,
Mix'd with the clamours of the crowd below;
Here, sorrowing, they each kindred sorrow scan,
And the cold charities of man to man.

Crabbe was both apothecary and parson in his time, but he had no high opinion of the general run of such men. He knew they neglected their patients and their parishioners and he portrayed them without mercy. Consider his picture of the village doctor at his work among the poor.

Anon, a figure enters, quaintly neat,
All pride and business, bustle and conceit;
With looks unalter'd by these scenes of woe,
With speed that, entering, speaks his haste to go,
He bids the gazing throng around him fly,
And carries fate and physic in his eye:
A potent quack, long vers'd in human ills,
Who first insults the victim whom he kills;
Whose murd'rous hands a drowsy Bench protect,
And whose most tender mercy is neglect.

The best friend any village inhabitant could have was death. Or so Crabbe suggests as he brings the first half of his poem to an end. Young men love to evoke death as a sort of moral purifier. They wonder why we older people want to go on living in this utterly cruel, deeply unreformable place, the world. Crabbe was young when he wrote *The Village*. He was

to go on invoking death all his life, but its benediction and its cleansing
power was never again quite so strikingly deployed as here. There is a
consolation: poetry is a way of obtaining pleasure from truth. Some
moralists think that truth is enough. It might be if we were certain what
truth was. Crabbe's poetry gives the blessing but goes on to report another
day. In the meantime, the end is portrayed unswervably.

> Up yonder hill, behold how sadly slow
> The bier moves winding from the vale below;
> There lie the happy dead, from trouble free,
> And the glad parish pays the frugal fee.
> No more, O Death! thy victim starts to hear
> Churchwarden stern, or kingly overseer;
> No more the farmer claims his humble bow,
> Thou art his lord, the best of tyrants thou!

What you've heard read so far, even in my UnEnglish intonation, will
give a flavour of Crabbe's special sound, that curious sado-masochistic
richness which floods the couplet with both energy and sadness. Crabbe's
relentless forward-moving versification is as personal as Racine's equally
remorseless Alexandrines. End rhymes make their due impression:
enjambment or not. I am sceptical of the very existence of the caesura in
English. Crabbe is cavalier with it, at least in Pope's sense, but he loves
the repetition of sentence structures, and all the rhetorical devices of
summoning attention, invoking absolutes and antithesising qualities. He is
sardonic and ironical, but also tender and reflective. Critics have been hard
on his rhyming. Leslie Stephen observed that 'when boy cannot be made
to rhyme with employ, Crabbe is very fond of dragging in a hoy'. But
why not? If Stephen had tried rhyming in English, he'd have had more
sympathy for Crabbe. Poets are less censorious in these matters than critics.
And Crabbe, at least, seldom resorts to feminine endings, which
automatically sound facetious in English rhymed poetry.

I don't intend to sketch Crabbe's biography, but will go on to the bulk
of his later work. After marriage, and the vicissitudes of several kinds of
work, he resumed poetry with *The Parish Register* in 1807. *The Borough* was
begun in 1804 and published in 1810. Britten called the village in his opera
'The Borough', since the tale of Peter Grimes appears in that book. And
indeed *The Borough* is *The Village* come of age. It contains some of Crabbe's
most powerful writing, and it amounts to an anatomy of English provincial
life in those hard years when the eighteenth century was turning into the

industrialised nineteenth, and England was poised on the verge of her final expansion into Imperialism. Not that Crabbe concerned himself with such high historical notions. He always took short views. If the jeer that he is a Parliamentary Blue Book writer among poets has any justice, then it might be seen also as a sort of praise. Later, I shall liken Crabbe to Jane Austen in his concern for the fascinating surface detail of genteel inanition, in his poem *Procrastination*, but I'll anticipate this now by asserting that Crabbe matches Austen in his love of the exact this and that, the very detail of how they lived then, pleated into the larger artistic fabric. *The Borough* is like *The Village*, only much more fully drawn. It is panoptic, with an introduction, almost 'as the hawk sees it or the helmeted airman', and then a sociologist's array of the types who go to make up this unimaginative but caustically alive community. But Crabbe is a poet, not a novelist, even an eccentric one like Dickens. So his Borough types are Theophrastian; they *stand* for more than they *stand up in*. It must be admitted that his fault of smooth summing-up came to him from the example of Pope, probably via Samuel Johnson. In general, Crabbe keeps the aesthetic ahead of the moral — in drawing his portraits, he is always the lover of language going about its task.

At the same time, his couplets prove to be better for realism than Wordsworth's lyrical reportage in stanzas and blank verse, since they restrict any impulse to 'the egotistical sublime'. *The Borough* is more certainly about real life and even 'the language of men' than *The Prelude* is. Up against Crabbe, Wordsworth appears a mystic. Crabbe pins things down, but if he is never transcendental, he is often close to extravagance. Describing boat-building he moves the fanciful world of *The Rape of the Lock* into the very different ambience of bourgeois realism.

> Near these, a crew amphibious, in the docks,
> Rear, for the sea, those castles on the stocks.

It has been alleged that *The Borough* was already out of date when it was composed, that Crabbe was remembering an Aldeburgh of thirty years previously. From the vantage of our own day, this seems a pointless observation, and, anyway, England changed most slowly in those East Anglian ports which Crabbe knew. Always behind the lineaments of the actual, Crabbe was working at his deeper map, the poetical ordnance survey of the English soul. A great sado-masochistic carnival! From the general description of the Borough come lines which Montagu Slater worked into the chorus's part in *Peter Grimes*:

> Where hang at open doors the net and cork,
> While squalid sea dames at their mending work;
> Till comes the hour, when fishing through the tide,
> The weary husband throws his freight aside;
> With ceaseless motion comes and goes the tide,
> Flowing, it fills the channel vast and wide;
> Then back to sea, with strong majestic sweep
> It rolls, in ebb yet terrible and deep;

and it is worth adding the next two lines which Britten and Slater do not include.

> Here samphire-banks and salt-wort bound the flood,
> Here stakes and sea-weeds withering on the mud;

These offer a pre-echo of the impassioned and visionary poetry when Peter Grimes surveys the estuary in his madness from his boat drifting on the river. Crabbe is always inspired by scenes of coastal waters. It is a great pleasure to me, a man for the littoral any day, to read Crabbe's description of the East Anglian coast. Few English poets, despite national pride in marine achievement, bother with the coastline. Of those who do, after Shakespeare's aerial description of Dover's cliffs, Crabbe takes pride of place. In such lines as those which follow, Crabbe attains a pantheism which is stronger for being such accurate depiction.

> Nor angler we on our wide stream descry,
> But one poor dredger where his oysters lie;
> He, cold and wet, and driving with the tide,
> Beats his weak arms against his tarry side,
> Then drains the remnant of diluted gin,
> To aid the warmth that languishes within.

From the detailed mass of couplets itemising the Borough folk — The Vicar and Curate, the Clubs and Social Meetings, Inns, Alm-Houses, Prisons etc — I have chosen to look at just one section, that devoted to Peter Grimes, listed by Crabbe as one of the poor of the Borough. Crabbe designed Grimes to be a realistic and cautionary tale of the dangers of a violent temperament. By the end of the poem, though, he had created, unusually for him, a doomed character of extra-terrestrial proportions, a Romantic sufferer looking forward to the types which throng nineteenth century literature. Benjamin Britten, homesick for East Anglia in California in 1941, hit upon Grimes as hero for the opera he wanted to write. In this, he proved faithful to what I believe was Crabbe's original intention. Britten's opera is a masterpiece, but if fails in one direction, namely in the depiction of Grimes himself.

The very Romanticism of Grimes's alienated character, the individualist whose desire to excel is frustrated because the Borough suspects any such aspiration, was clearly both Montagu Slater's and Britten's intention, but instead it is the Borough itself which is the hero of the opera. In Crabbe's poem, Peter begins as a brute. We are shown his scoffing and deriding of his dying father, though his scorn for the old man, who will appear as an apparition to him in his madness, has its rational side —

> 'It is the word of life', the parent cried,
> 'This is the life itself', the boy replied.

Clearly, no good can be expected of a person who thus scorns the Bible. Then, as Peter comes into his own fisherman's kingdom, his cruelty and brutality, usually for its own sake, brand him an emblematic villain, someone a good moralist can get mileage out of. Yet even here a warped idealism begins to make itself felt.

> And hoped to find in some propitious hour,
> A feeling creature subject to his power.

The prentice boys whom Grimes mistreats are the attendant angels of his fallen state. His blows and violence towards them might even be deemed his technique to get them used to the notion of reigning in Hell and not serving in Heaven. And Grimes's misanthropy is a proper match for the Borough's small-minded respectability. Three of the boys are listed as dying in his service, but he does not murder them. Neglect, despair and accident dispose of them. And the Borough, willing enough to disparage and hunt Grimes down in its own turn, cares little enough for the fate of the apprentices, though Crabbe is never as explicit as the libretto is. There Balstrode, the retired sea captain and chief of the goodies, says 'Something of the sort befits/ Brats conceived outside the sheets'. Crabbe asks rhetorically why the Borough worthies did not raise a hand to help Grimes's workhouse slaves, but comments that all they ever say on hearing the cries of the tormented children is 'Grimes is at his exercise'. This line becomes one of the key passages in the opera, the Sunday morning ensemble after church when the Borough is roused to track down Grime to his hut. But once Grimes is ruined, after the last boy's death, Crabbe picks up that tone of poetic rebellion which I have suggested was mooted much earlier in the poem. Now, in the last part, he writes some of his greatest poetry, a real vision of despair, freed of right and wrong, as Peter, fallen into madness, finds no consolation but the contemplation of Nature at its most implacable, as he drifts in his boat among the unlovely reeds, mudflats and backwaters of Aldeburgh and Slaughden Quay.

Slater and Britten were writing an opera, and had to have more plot than Crabbe affords. Slater, in my opinion, did a marvellous job, and I am happy to speak of him so warmly here, now that both he and Britten are dead, since the composer was given to accusing his collaborator, in later days, of penning many solecisms in the libretto. It is in Britten's music that the character of Peter Grimes fails finally. I say this fully conscious of Britten's greatness as a composer. It is just that the *poète maudit* aspect of Grimes won't fit with the circumstances of the plot. He cannot both be the brute fisherman and the lost dreamer of his song in the pub the night of the storm, 'Now the Great Bear and the Pleiades'. In the opera Grimes's madness is a direct result of the death of his latest apprentice who falls down the cliff under Grimes's hut while preparing the boat for a shoal which his master has seen, the revenging cordon of villagers meanwhile approaching led by drum and law. In the poem, Grimes dies in the poorhouse, fearful of the avenging angel. Britten's view of the madness of the individual opposed by society is softer than Crabbe's.

But the triumph of the opera is in the marvellous picture it builds up of the Borough itself. It is as though Crabbe's personal inspiration, which lays a benediction on Grimes in verse, becomes one part of Britten's musical work; and the whole series of poems which make up the Borough become the rest of the opera. Because Britten is working within a different convention, where Crabbe's deliverance seems at variance with the story, he is not able to convince us of Peter's thwarted humanity. Crabbe is, in poetry, more musical here than the composer can manage to be in sound. But the characters who fill up the magnificent cast-list of the Borough, many of them, or at least their names and activities, taken from the poems, bring to the stage a web of life almost the equal of the great nineteenth century European folk operas. *Peter Grimes*, pioneer work of the English musical renaissance, is also the English *Boris Godunov*, *Mastersingers* or *Forza del Destino*. Here Britten realises (to use a musical term) Crabbe's essential representative quality as a poet. Crabbe the portraitist is also Crabbe the epic depictor of his country. And never more so than in this work which his genius inspired. Slater's Ellen Orford, the widowed teacher, Bob Boles, the lay preacher, Need Keene the Quack, the gentle Parson, the pompous Lawyer, even Auntie and her nieces, who run the pub and comfort with booze and sex the hard-pressed denizens of the Borough, are verismo pen-pictures deriving from Crabbe. And the superb choruses which Britten writes, picking up, as they do lines from various Crabbe poems, inherit the point-of-view of Crabbe's editorial stoicism. Perhaps I should close this brief analysis of Grimes by quoting from the one section where Britten did not equal Crabbe — Peter's merging with Nature in the gentle regalia of his madness. This is quiet and more moving than the Macbeth-like visions of father and victims Crabbe also provides for Grimes.

> When tides were neap, and, in the sultry day,
> Through the tall bounding mud-banks made their way,
> Which on each side rose swelling, and below
> The dark warm flood ran silently and slow;
> There, anchoring, Peter chose from man to hide,
> There hang his head and view the lazy tide
> In its hot slimy channel slowly glide;
> Where the small eels that left the deeper way
> For the warm shore, within the shadows play;
> Where gaping mussels, left upon the mud,
> Slope their slow passage to the fallen flood;—
> Here dull and hopeless he'd lie down and trace
> How sidelong crabs had scrawled their crooked race;
> Or sadly listen to the tuneless cry
> Of fishing gull or clanging golden-eye;
> What time the sea-birds to the marsh would come,
> And the loud bittern, from the bullrush home,
> Gave from the salt-ditch side the bellowing boom;
> He nursed the feelings these dull scenes produce,
> And loved to stop beside the opening sluice;
> Where the small stream, confined in narrow bound,
> Ran with a dull, unvaried, saddening sound;
> Where all presented to the eye or ear,
> Oppressed the soul with misery, grief or fear.

But which, as verse, consoles us with its beauty. I think it as mellifluous as any passage in Pope.

I am going on so long that I shall be more expeditious in my presentation of the two other poems I have chosen. I picked them out because they represent sides of Crabbe's character not mentioned so far. Each is a study in social characterisation, rather than a version of realistic pastoral, as even *Peter Grimes* might be held to be. But we are not straying from the couplet. It is still vehicle, ground-breaker and delineator of Crabbe's sense of decorum. We are now with *Tales, 1812* — a less boisterous Crabbe, but perhaps the repository of his best writing. Mr. Howard Mills, in his Cambridge University selection of Crabbe's poetry, suggests that *Procrastination* may have given Jane Austen the idea for *Persuasion*. Certainly, not only is the tale itself Austen-like, but so is the tone it is told in, with a savagery beneath the ordered and ironical surface. *Procrastination* relates how Dinah and Rupert are betrothed but cannot for the moment marry. Dinah must attend an ageing widow from whom all her expectations come. Rupert has no expectations beyond some sort of work in the town they both inhabit, though he is not too lowly born, and is entirely respectable. We watch their love grow inwards like malign fingers or toenails, as prudence lends weight to a procrastination honoured, Crabbe seems to suggest, not just by village economics and good sense but by some failure of nerve in their characters, especially in Dinah's. Dinah has the stronger will, and is the first to find the waiting more pleasant, and to banish any urge to hurry marriage's pleasures. Rupert goes to sea to make his fortune. Crabbe sends him off with all the automatic flourish of a seasoned novelist in need of a turn of plot, and the reader is pretty certain that he will come home empty handed.

Crabbe is much more interested in Dinah. His unfolding of the corruption of her character, as she moulds her life in service to the possessions which will soon be hers and to her new higher station in life, is masterly, and entitles Crabbe to a place with other masters of pre-Freudian psychological insight. It is, of course, all done with familiar objects, names and notions: there is no spooky atmosphere, no neurasthenia beyond descriptions of mental states licensed to writers in Crabbe's day. Even before the widow dies and Dinah inherits, we see her learning to enjoy the inanition of possessing, her willing service to inanimate objects.

> In small but splendid room she loved to see
> That all was placed in view and harmony;
> There, as with eager glance she looked around,
> She much delight in every object found;
> While books devout were near her — to destroy,
> Should it arise, an overflow of joy.

Crabbe's own years in the church may have goaded him to sharpen his claws for that last couplet. We are told that Crabbe had small success with his sermons. They bored his congregations, but he persisted with them. Perhaps they may be likened, as burdens, to the modern poet's journalism. Not dishonest, not untrue, not illiberal, but undertaken to live rather than as literature. Without private means, a poet has to find work, and all sorts of work may be harmful to his talent. But lacking necessity may prove injurious also. Who knows where poetic inspiration comes from? This little aside does have relevance to Crabbe, since the main distrust of him in modern minds springs from his apparent lack of a poetic temperament. One is forced back on the important truism: a poet is a person who writes good poetry. In all other matters, there is no uniformity of poetical signs. Even beautiful, haunted, poetical young men may turn out to be poets.

But back to Dinah and Rupert. Dinah comes into her inheritance, and it is far too late to contemplate sharing her wonderland with anyone, let alone a Rupert returned middle-aged and as penurious as when he departed. His service against the king's enemies has left him washed-up with nothing, as such service so often does. Dinah is in service herself, but to more glittering and ultimately more demanding gods:

> A silver urn with curious work was fraught;
> A silver lamp from Grecian pattern wrought;
> Above her head, all gorgeous to behold,
> A time-piece stood on feet of burnished gold;
> A stag's-head crest adorned the pictured case,
> Through the pure crystal shone the enamelled face;
> And while on brilliants moved the hands of steel,
> It clicked from prayer to prayer, from meal to meal.

There is an interview where Dinah rejects Rupert absolutely. Love has cooled, love which was never permitted to become really warm. Yet Crabbe has been judicious in seeking the cause of Dinah's callous rejection of life's possibilities. He must have known so many merely mercantile and unhappy marriages that he wasn't tempted to pronounce upon anything like Auden's 'foiled creative fire', or some version of psychosomatic depression. Dinah falls in love with possessions: by her procrastination, she has learned to esteem only the unreciprocal joy of ownership. Year by year, she becomes more withered and more stately, and ever less human. At the end, Crabbe shows her crossing the road to avoid even having to acknowledge Rupert, who now is a pensioner of an alms-house and is

sunning himself in the road after church. This becomes her custom
whenever she goes out.

> Thence as she walks the street with stately air,
> As chance directs, oft meet the parted pair:
> When he, with thickset coat of badge-man's blue,
> Waves near her shaded silk of changeful hue —

Crabbe's poetry is a very refined instrument in *Procrastination*, as refined as
Miss Austen's prose. The last line I read — 'Waves near her shaded silk
of changeful hue' is surely as unexpected and beautiful a bonus as one of
the flowers which sprang from the weeds in Crabbe's village wilderness.
And, in these later poems of his, the social and fictional plant is as strong
as any mallow thistle, or bugloss.

   Another of the poems included in *Tales, 1812* is *The Lover's Journey*. This
is a light poem, not without shadows of fate, as I doubt that any poem
by Crabbe could ever be, but not set in poverty nor in the miseries of
genteel frustration. Yet it is a very extraordinary work, and reveals Crabbe
to be capable of a sort of metaphorical planning entitling him to the label
symbolist — something I did earlier on, and have hardly justified till now.
The poem has a simple plot, but a peculiar performance. Orlando sets
out to ride from one parish to another where his inamorata Laura lives.
Crabbe, though, is very conscious of his role as narrator/strategist of the
events to hand. He tells us that this is to be a tale with a structure and
a purpose. And he states plainly that if we knew them we would also
know that Orlando and Laura are really christened John and Susan. We
are to be shown a landscape-reflecting attitude. In a way the whole poem
might be thought of as pathetic fallacy before the term was invented, but
Crabbe seems to be pointing in almost the opposite direction. Rather than
say that the way events will fall out is prefigured in the world about us,
he suggests that what we see reflects our mood in viewing it. Yet not
even that — that is a simplification of Crabbe's performance. His poem
offers us a choice of landscapes and activities. The world is not a fixed
state; nor is it even something which changes according to our involvement
with it. Instead, we and the world are players in a dream: the dramatis
personae and the sets of our acts and scenes are unforecastable. And we
must forever be faring forward.

   I am getting in so deep that it is time I described roughly what happens
in the poem. Setting out full of expectation of seeing Laura (in whose
house incidentally he is expecting to stay, so presumably he has proper

title to be her fiancé or some accredited suitor), Orlando passes country and town scenes which are described in the light of his happiness. Not necessarily in an Illyrian mode, but according to the felicity of Orlando's canon. So the gypsies he passes are not given the sympathetic portrayal they get from John Clare. Admiring them would not be one of Orlando's visions of contentment. When he gets to his destination, Orlando discovers that Laura has gone away, leaving only what he considers a curt message, 'Gone to see a friend!' He then sets out on his return journey, and the same scenes which cheered him on during his earlier ride now seem to mock him. He envisions them as full of hateful pictures, just as before he had found them redolent of promise and human warmth. When he gets home, however, he finds Laura waiting for him. She had set out for his place at the time that he departed for hers. The poem ends happily, if equivocally. The ending is still enigmatic: it inclines towards the peace of exhaustion, not the calm of contentment. What makes *The Lover's Journey* such an interesting poem is not the rather mechanical contrast of the fair vision against the dark vision, but Crabbe's implied sense that our world really knows neither fair nor dark in nature. His text might be Hamlet's to Horatio, 'Nothing is either good or bad, but thinking makes it so'. This has become a cliché of conversation, but Crabbe gives it a very sharp focus in his poem. For instance, Crabbe's beloved weeds are here openly admired. Since Orlando is happy, he can perceive their beauty. But the reader suspects that Crabbe has loved them all along.

> See! wholesome wormwood grows beside the way,
> Where dew-pressed yet the dog-rose bends the spray;
> Fresh herbs the fields, fair shrubs the banks adorn,
> And snow-white bloom falls flaky from the thorn;
> No fostering hand they need, no sheltering wall,
> They spring uncultured and they bloom for all.

Set this against lines from the return journey. They are strained perhaps, but they are a pretty representative example of what one sees if one looks in the negative half of Nature's magic mirror.

> And these vile beans with deleterious smell,
> Where is their beauty? Can a mortal tell?
> These deep fat meadows I detest; it shocks
> One's feelings there to see the grazing ox;—
> For slaughter fatted, as a lady's smile

> Rejoices man, and means his death the while.
> Lo! now the sons of labour! every day
> Employed in toil, and vexed in every way;
> Theirs is but mirth assumed and they conceal,
> In their affected joys, the ills they feel;
> I hate these long green lanes; there's nothing seen
> In this vile country but eternal green;
> Woods! waters! meadows! Will they never end?
> 'Tis a vile prospect — Gone to see a friend!

When he encounters a wedding party en route to church, Orlando's vision is clouded even more.

> Each by some friends attended, near they drew,
> And spleen beheld them with prophetic view.

It must be admitted that it is not true just of Crabbe but of most artists that prophecy is a great promoter of gloom — perhaps never more so than in our century of Doomwatch. But Crabbe keeps his sense of proportion. He knows that artists (and in this they are only representative of mankind in general) give themselves up entirely to the moods they are possessed by. And that such moods alter and are replaced by others, and often better ones. For a poet his hope and his benison will usually be his energy. What he has to say is often possessed by gloom, but he becomes of the party of hope if he pronounces it with energy and art. How he does so is a great and unexplained mystery. It is too tempting to tell the history of literature as a series of style wars. Was Crabbe right to stick to the couplet? The future lay with Wordsworth. Everyone is agreed about that. But is not Wordsworth as strange to us today as Crabbe? Perhaps not, since he is much more widely read. We need some way of measuring talent which is not at the mercy of history, morality and style. Early in *The Lover's Journey*, Crabbe writes a couplet which could be his house motto.

> Ye hours of expectation, quickly fly,
> And bring on hours of blest reality.

But, after Orlando's deliverance from despair, he rides back without Laura, a third time past the familiar scenes. Now he is not happy, because he does not expect much. But he is not miserable either.

Then could these scenes the former joys renew?
Or was there now dejection in the view?—
Nor one nor other would they yield — and why?
The mind was absent and the vacant eye
Wandered o'er viewless scenes that but appeared to die.

And there, in the no-man's land between appearance and reality, I am
prepared to leave George Crabbe and the couplet.

1982: Loughborough University. Bi-centenary Lecture Series, "Crabbe in Context"

CHAPTER VI

Rhyme and Reason

A suggestion of the untheoretical background to
the greatness of the poetry of Alexander Pope

With a poet of such unchallengeable standing as Pope, the usual thing for a commentator to offer in any talk or lecture will be some interesting textual byway or penetration of a scholarly arcanum — general comment will seem as otiose as making a value-judgement of Shakespeare would. Not that Pope has always been so far to the front of the Pantheon. He was in his own time — even his enemies conceded that. And he stayed pre-eminent for the rest of the Eighteenth Century, the obligatory role model for aspirant poets. The Romantics changed this, though it was the Victorians who were most revisionist. Byron championed him in letters and articles back to England from Ravenna, but, even as late as the early manhood of W.H. Auden, Pope could appear as a major talent in need of backers. In *Letter to Lord Byron*, Auden rhymes

> For many a don while looking down his nose
> Calls Pope and Dryden classics of our prose.

Well, things have changed. It is the dons now who wave the flag of Pope so high, and learned books pour from the academic presses dealing with every aspect of Pope, at any one of 360 degrees to his centrality. Some of the new preoccupations are interesting: for instance, Pope and the landscaping of gardens as practical preoccupation, and as metaphor. I even thought of making this talk an investigation of Pope and music, a vein nobody to my knowledge has attempted yet — though I'm sure I'll be proved wrong on this, so wide would anyone's acquaintance with learned journals have to be to be certain of accuracy on such a matter. I'd always presumed that, like most literary men, Pope knew little about music, and would have praised it in the usual clichés had he bothered to interest himself in it — the sort of received opinion which so angered Igor Stravinsky when he heard Proust warbling on about the profundity of the late quartets of Beethoven. But Pope took an interest in the practical side of libretto-making, and he seems to have genuinely respected Handel although Handel on several occasions was under the protection of Pope's political enemies. Apart from The Scriblerus Club, and Pope's encouragement of Gay's forays into the musical theatre of his time, the main evidence of Pope's musical involvement is the quotation from his pastoral "Summer" interpolated into the libretto of *Semele*, in that opera's most famous air — 'Where e'er you walk, cool gales shall fan the glade/ Trees where you sit shall crowd into a shade,/ Where e'er you tread, the blushing flower's shall rise,/ And all things flourish where you turn your eyes." There is some reason to think that he also lent a hand in the arrangement of Racine's biblical play *Esther* into Handel's oratorio of the same name. Handel is praised in the final version of *The Dunciad* in resounding terms — the writer of oratorios, not the opera composer.

> If Music meanly borrows aid from Sense:
> Strong in new arms, lo! Giant Handel stands,
> Like bold Briareus, with a hundred hands;
> To stir, to rouze, to shake the Soul he comes,
> And Jove's own Thunders follow Mars's Drums.
> Arrest him Empress; or you sleep no more — "
> She heard and drove him to the Hibernian shore.

The Empress, of course, is one of the many manifestations of Dullness. For Pope the Italian opera was a domain of excesses, and of those perversions of art he associated with Dullness.

> O *Cara! Cara!* silence all that train:
> Joy to great Chaos! let Division reign:
> Chromatic tortures soon shall drive them hence,
> Break all their nerves, and fritter all their sense:
> One Trill shall harmonise joy, grief and rage,
> Wake the dull Church and lull the ranting Stage;
> To the same notes thy sons shall hum, or snore,
> And all thy yawning daughters cry, *encore*.
> Another Phoebus, thy own Phoebus, reigns,
> Joys in my jiggs, and dances in my chains.

Pope explains in a footnote that this second Phoebus is of French extraction
— married to the Princess Galimathia, one of the handmaidens of Dullness,
and an assistant to Opera, here a personification of artificiality. He rather
quaintly believes that Handel was forced to flee England for Ireland, since
his music was unappreciated in London. *Messiah* was given its first
performance in Dublin, and Pope seems to have been one of the first to
express the very English preference for Handel's oratorios over his operas
— a preference the business-like Handel bowed to, but by no means
endorsed.

In case I seem to be devoting too much time to a theme I said I wasn't
going to follow, I ought to return to the track by stating that for Pope
music had most value as a demonstrable proof of the place of order in
the universe. The very technical terms used in music — melody, harmony,
rhythm, concord, dissonance etc — are also a poet's compressed metaphors.
The mellifluous, the singing, the musical — these are the very clichés of
literary men's encomia. Too many ecstatic wordmen forget that music can
be harsh and jagged as well as sweet and legato. Pope's poetry, especially
The Essay on Criticism, written when he was only 21 and still, I believe, his
most brilliant and finished single composition, employs musical terms in
just this common metaphorical way. Throughout the eighteenth century
the art of music was seen as a public manifestation of the divine harmony
of God's creation.

But Pope is unrivalled among poets since Shakespeare at filling his verse
with pictures of the real world, of the activities of society in all its multiple
facets — 'business and desire', the bright-surfaced planet we actually live
on. So the concert hall, the opera, the theatre, the everyday business of
musicians' lives get into his poetry, as well as the grand similitudes which
music can offer to aesthetics. Here, in another passage from *The Dunciad*,
generalisation is fleshed out with those touches of what might be called
morning-newspaper actuality, so that we see the proper concerns of art
embellished with confirming warts.

> Till raised from booths, to Theatre, to Court,
> Her seat imperial Dullness shall transport.
> Already Opera prepares the way,
> The sure forerunner of her gentle sway:
> Let her thy heart, next Drabs and Dice, engage,
> The third mad passion of her doting age.
> Teach thou the warbling Polypheme to roar,

And scream thyself as none e'er scream'd before!
To aid our cause, if Heav'n thou canst not bend,
Hell thou shalt move; for Faustus is our friend:
Pluto with Cato thou for this shalt join,
And link the Mourning Bride to Proserpine.
Grubstreet! thy fall should men and Gods conspire,
Thy stage shall stand, ensure it but from Fire.
Another Aeschylus appears! prepare
For new abortions, all ye pregnant fair!
In flames, like Semele's, be brought to bed,
While op'ning Hell spouts wild-fire at your head.

So, like reading the review section of a Sunday paper, we are reminded
of Congreve's opera, *Semele*, set by both Daniel Purcell and Handel. This
very *Semele*, which ends with the heroine's incineration as Jove reveals his
godlike presence, contains those four of Pope's lines I quoted earlier.
Polyphemus gives Pope the chance of a jibe at Colley Cibber but also
conjures up John Gay's text for Handel's *Acis and Galathea*. *Faustus, Pluto*
and *Cato* are the names of farces which had been hits on the stage. We
also hear of Congreve's tragedy *The Mourning Bride* (which incidentally
contains the famous line, 'Music hath charms to soothe a savage breast').
The effect of Pope's poetry is not to secure assent to satire but to clothe
his powerful constructions of language with appropriate reflections of
reality. His poetry always runs deeper than its paraphrasable meaning. The
spectacles for which the London theatre was renowned are mocked,
together with the foibles of fashionable taste.

And so to my title — *Rhyme and Reason*. This coyly familiar phrase
contains the essence of Pope's greatness as a poet, and also hints at why
he is still not quite acceptable, or perhaps I should say moving enough,
for those who are at home with Shakespeare, Milton and Blake. *Rhyme*
stands out not just for itself, but for his overall mastery of prosody: *Reason*
for the strategy with which he confronts his subjects. In both departments
he is the most consistent master in all of our literature. However, I intend
a little later to develop what I mean by *Reason*. I don't consider Pope's
argument in his more developed pieces particularly convincing as argument.
Poetry probably developed out of rhetoric as much as it did out of pastoral.
Rhetoric, that is, in the Roman sense, as deployed by a barrister in a court
of law — putting the best case in the most persuasive words. But a case
argued in court is not necessarily true, and is seldom deep enough to be
termed philosophy. It's my own belief that philosophy is death to poetry.

They are set implacably in opposition to each other. Very few poets can stand up as philosophers, if only because they are called by the nature of their art to use different systems from those of philosophy. Poetic systems are open-ended, subject to as many exceptions as confirming instances, and work on irrational elements, such as coincidence, passion and the oddity of language itself. Philosophical systems have to be inclusive and seamless, and obey reason in defiance of feeling. I am prepared to admit that the profession of philosophy, of the unified pursuit of reason to see an explanation of the universe is a higher calling altogether than that of poetry. But poetry is older and more basic. Probably Plato was right to keep poets out of his ideal republic. He would have had the example of the Greek playwrights before him. They were essentially emotional and religious, and the arguments they offer their audiences in justification of some action or other are as threadbare of logic as they are passionate of conviction.

This doesn't mean that poets can't think. Has there ever been as great a mind working with words as Shakespeare's? All great poets are extremely clever. That may sound a banal thing to say: but it is important, as we have encountered this century an emphasis on the deliberate avoidance of invention in favour of direct expression of feeling. We can answer, of course, with Touchstone's observation to the country folk, 'The truest poetry is the most feigning', but there are still going to be many theorists who prefer either the true voice of feeling (whatever that is) or 'no ideas but in things'. Poets' inveterate love of play rules them out as serious and consecutive thinkers. In fact, looking right down the long vista of English poetry, I can't see anyone who might be called a philosopher as well as a poet. Milton might make a theologian, Blake a psychoanalyst and Wordsworth a faith-healer, but we have to come to the twentieth century and to the United States to discover poets who are at least partly philosophical. Wallace Stevens and John Ashbery are two such. Yet even here no philosophy department would be satisfied. Stevens declared that 'the greatest poverty is not to live in a physical world' and Ashbery employs techniques of non sequitur to upset our expectations of significance and our love of received ideas.

No, my category of *Reason* stands for the poet's sense of the dramatic in the strategy of his verse. And for no poet more wholeheartedly than for Pope. In many of his longer poems (and he was the pioneer of a form which has become the richest in English literature, the medium-length social poem) he prints advertisements in prose before the poem proper. The *Epistles* (or *Moral Essays* as they are sometimes called), for instance, announce what the course of argument of the poem is going to be. Leaving aside whether Pope actually follows these advertisements or not, I think we may agree that, as examples of developed reasoning, they are not very impressive. In fact, it seems to me, the main force of a Pope poem is similar to a speech in a play — it is headlong, idiosyncratic, full of personal detail — indeed, what I like to call 'warty'. His concern for the logical flow of his argument grew less as he matured. *The Essay on Criticism* has a more consistent and sequential argument than *The Essay on Man,* and, by the time Pope was writing his late masterpieces, *The Imitations of Horace* and the revised version of *The Dunciad,* he had more or less abandoned logical development in favour of nightmare vision. *The Dunciad* is a sort of acid trip or bad dream, and the *Horace Imitations* are like Surrealist studies into which Pope pours an extraordinary bundle of disparate notions. These are extraordinarily rich poems, which make me think of those crowded demonic paintings which the Netherlandish masters loved to compose: Bosch and Brueghel, and, if one reaches down to Italy, Orcagna, Piero di Cosimo and Dosso Dossi.

When I say Surrealistic, I don't imply any lack of formality in the mechanics and technique of the poem. In this, Pope is always immaculate. Though one might fault him perhaps, every now and again, on his rhymes, you can never do so on his prosody. In Pope's poetry, English verse attains for the only time in its history the mellifluousness which Italian poetry enjoys nearly always. I have tested Pope's verse on almost every page of his complete works, looking for improper scansion, clumsy enjambement, unattractively inverted word order and brusque alignment of caesurae, and have always failed to find such things. Indeed, if I wanted to mount a hostile foray on Pope, I would claim that he is too much of a good thing — the marvellously oiled machine moves forward with a boring grace, the perfect word placing lulls one into complacency. It is like Mozart in the key of E Flat: such euphony can be wearing. Oh for a little of Beethoven's and Haydn's abruptness and bad manners.

It is here that Pope's wilfulness and scatological way with subject matter comes to his aid, and prevents the perfect versification from stultifying the reader. And, as an aside, I would stress that Pope should always be read headlong, with no glancing down to the footnotes. Scholarly editions of his poetry should be consulted only after you have got to know it in unannotated form. The thin trickle of verse at the top of the page, running through rich sediment of critical prose (I think the image is Dr. Leavis's), is especially defeating in Pope. He is the liveliest and least pedantic of poets and should be read as you would listen to the best conversation.

It is with the vital subject of versification that I must amplify the first of my categories — *Rhyme*. As I said, it stands for all the tropes and resources of poetical technique. Immediately, we come up against a hard option — namely the preponderance of rhymed couplets in Pope's output. Not that he always employs his couplets in five-feet units. There is a fair quantity of verse in Swift's preferred tetrameters, and not only when Pope is imitating his friend. There are also some poems in quatrains and other stanzas, and there are metres beside iambics. But ninety percent of his greatest poetry is cast in what is called, for better or worse, heroic couplets. I must admit that while supporters of Pope can point to a thousand felicities in his placing of the caesura, in his management of end-stopping, in his scrupulous marriage of sense and syntax, there is something a little defeating in the unstoppable progress of these five-feet couplets. Whether this is due to the rhymes (of which English is deplorably or beautifully deficient — according to your taste) or whether it is the mechanical repetition of iambic metre, relieved occasionally by a neat inversion — I am not certain. I find that I have nothing to criticise directly in Pope's versification, but that I am sometimes driven to seek relief from it in the more imperfect but more various metric of Shakespeare, Browning and Marvell. Blank verse is undoubtedly more flexible than the rhymed couplet, and the metaphysical lyric in complicated stanzas of unequal line length offers scope for greater surprises and coups. Yet, Pope's case is similar to that of Domenico Scarlatti in music — 555 sonatas, almost all of them for keyboard in binary form. No more extraordinary and wide-ranging sound world exists in eighteenth century music. Something pushed these men — Scarlatti and Pope — into the constant effort to refine and yet expand the one form until it was capable of including everything they wanted to say. To diversify into more mixed forms might have been for them to decompress their imaginations, to lose the full force of their often wild invention in a delta of indirect and meandering courses.

It's a while since I've quoted any poetry so this is the right place to pick a passage of Pope's which illustrates the musical beauty and the convincing feeling of his verse under full sail. This time I've selected a well-known excerpt from his most admired poem, *The Rape of the Lock*. In Canto Four the mock-heroic desperation is mounting fast. One of Belinda's attendant spirits in the search for the lost tress penetrates to the underworld, to the gloomy cave of the goddess Spleen, and Pope is inspired to conjure a vision of a light-hearted Dantesque Inferno — as though Michaelangelo's Last Judgement had been repainted by Tiepolo.

Swift on his sooty Pinions flits the Gnome,
And in a Vapour reach'd the dismal Dome,
No cheerful Breeze this sullen Region knows,
The dreadful *East* is all the Wind that blows.
Here, in a Grotto, sheltered close from Air,
And screened in Shades from Day's detested Glare,
She sighs forever on her pensive Bed,
Pain at her Side, and *Megrim* at her Head.

   Two Handmaids wait the Throne: Alike in Place,
But diff'ring far in Figure and in Face.
Here stood *Ill-nature* like an *ancient Maid,*
Her wrinkled Form in *Black* and *White* array'd;
With store of Pray'rs, for Mornings, Nights and Noons,
Her Hand is fill'd; her Bosom with Lampoons.

   There *Affectation* with a sickly Mien
Shows in her Cheek the Roses of Eighteen,
Practis'd to Lisp, and hang the Head aside,
Faints into Airs, and languishes with Pride;
On the rich Quilt sinks with becoming Woe,
Wrapt in a Gown, for Sickness and for Show.
The Fair-ones feel such Maladies as these,
When each new Night-Dress gives a new Disease.

   A constant *Vapour* o'er the Palace flies;
Strange Phantoms rising as the Mists arise;
Dreadful, as Hermit's Dreams in haunted Shades,
Or bright as Visions of expiring Maids.
Now glaring Fiends, and Snakes on rolling Spires,
Pale Spectres, gaping Tombs, and Purple Fires:
Now Lakes of liquid Gold, *Elysian* Scenes,
And Crystal Domes, and Angels in Machines.

   Unnumbr'd Throngs on every side are seen
Of Bodies changed to various Forms by *Spleen.*
Here living *Teapots* stand, one Arm held out,
One bent; the Handle this, and that the Spout:
A Pipkin there like *Homer's Tripod* walks;
Here sighs a Jar, and there a Goose-pie talks;
Men prove with Child, as pow'rful Fancy works,
And Maids turned Bottels, call aloud for Corks.

You can feel, towards the end of this passage, that Pope is going into overdrive; his fantasy has stoked up his language until traditional devices like personification, metaphor and alliteration begin to live a life of their own. And he is frequently at this pitch throughout his best poetry. Far from being a mincing poet, a namby-pamby one (to appropriate the name he bestowed upon Ambrose Phillips) or even a classically restrained poet, he is baroque and grotesque. But the poise of the verse never slips: the more violent the vision, the more exquisitely phrased the language will be. Perhaps we should moralise and consider what purpose is served by a mock-heroic poem such as *The Rape of the Lock*. W.H. Auden saw *The Dunciad* as performing a genuinely heroic act, of identifying in the dullness of bad writing a real threat to civilisation. In a lighter way, *The Rape of the Lock* purges its readers of epic falsity, and banishes fustian from poetry — that fustian which was likely to attend all ranting writers. Pope did not believe that modern poets could aspire to the classical heroism of Homer. They weren't even up to the propaganda patriotism of *The Aeneid*. But 'mock-heroic' would blow away exaggerated feeling, and yet enable people whose experience of life was more to do with elegant drawing rooms than sea-tossed voyages or ten year sieges to experience the larger forms of poetry. He took over the apparatus of the past — not just the obvious parallels with classical epic, but all the medieval panoply of ghosts, spirits, sorcerers, fairies, dreams and chivalric champions. He lightened the Gothic and he put a smile on the face of allegory. Metamorphoses quieter than Ovid's accrue until society is seen at variance with its own decorums. The world is upside down in this sublime comic-strip or day-dream out of Lewis Carroll. And all is to restore the world to its senses. This mannered mock-epic turns out to be his most natural poem, and the one which illustrates most clearly his divine good humour.

He wrote *The Rape of the Lock* while still a young man, of course. And much that happened to him subsequently did produce bitterness. His late verse is often satirical, and biting. Satire, however, I hold to be only another version of pastoral, a way poets have of managing to relish what they dislike. They have cause to bless their enemies for existing. Pope must have had Sporus waiting in the wings before he saw that Lord Hervey would be the perfect impersonation of him. And Pope's hatreds are not as petty as some critics assert. Though the Scriblerus Club — Pope, Swift, Gay and Arbuthnot — did look down their noses at the hacks too much, each of its members was capable of courageous and disinterested philippic. The great lines against Addison in *The Epistle to Dr. Arbuthnot*, had been on ice for some years, but it took courage to write them at all. It's one thing to hit at a Sporus — quite another to challenge the very epitome of clubland, Atticus, the smoothest law-giver of them all.

I have still not come to terms with my desire to moralise about the direction of Pope's poetry. What is it drives any poet to force his way through thickets of thought at the behest of formal rules, which can be heartbreaking in their demands on his time and skill? Somehow a great poet must hear the dual voice of morality and pleasure. Though Freud addressed himself to the problem of getting beyond it, his invention of the Pleasure Principle has been a boon to aestheticians wrestling with the subconscious impulses of art. If I now compose a vignette of a poet's setting out to write, I do so knowing that this may be a presumption if I apply the case to a great writer like Pope. Nevertheless, here is how it goes. There is a challenge to create a made object of beauty, a Promethean imitation of the gods. We have a hole in our natures the exact size of some Platonic template. The artist attempts to make that imagined object and the reader or consumer to use it. The craving to make the work of art is a form of satisfaction of the Pleasure Principle. But there is a second party to the exchange — at least in practice. Something in the world out there annoys the artist — yet more imperfection, dispute, cruelty, wrongdoing, and so on. The only way the work of art can get made is for it to pass through the shaping force of entertainment. And one of the great extruding pressures on entertainment is indignation.

Perhaps I should abandon these paradoxical figures before they tangle me up utterly. But thinking like this is the only way I can reconcile what happens in great poetry. It must have an object intensely felt by the poet, and it must satisfy the artificer's desire for beauty. With *King Lear*, the reforming principle is less obvious than with Pope's *Moral Essays*. Shakespeare shows us good and evil in action. We can draw the moral for ourselves — don't behave like Regan, Goneril, Edmund etc. And don't expect virtue to save you if you're unimaginative and silly, like Cordelia. But crude morals are less important in *Lear* than the richness of the study of human behaviour. We can hardly nourish a true morality if we don't know how people behave. Shakespeare would have been attracted initially to the story — not to the opportunity to lecture us on human conduct. With a poem which is constructed like a single long speech in a play — and Pope's poems resemble soliloquies — the story, the details from more than one person's point of view have to be fitted into a single linear progress. I incline to see all poems of medium-length which are in one voice, even an editorial voice, as dramatic monologues *avant la lettre*. The most personal of Pope's poems even sound sometimes like pre-echoes of

Robert Browning. It's true that Pope was a natural moralist; he had his
interfering, busybody side. But then so did his age — Dryden before him,
Swift and even Rochester were given to flaying the conduct of their
contemporaries. But did he expect people to reform as a result of reading
a poem full of brilliant surfaces? Wasn't their reaction more likely to be
that of a member of the audience leaving an opera house. Their heads
would be full of pleasurable detail, Pope's skill in versification and his ability
to coin memorable lines being the equivalent of a composer's tunefulness.

Writing poetry came to Pope as naturally as breathing. As he put it in his
famous lines

> I left no Calling for this idle Trade,
> No Duty broke, no Father dis-obeyed.
> The Muse but served to ease some Friend, not Wife,
> To help me thro' this long Disease, my Life.

He states also, 'I lisped in Numbers for the Numbers came'. But, as I
said at the beginning of this talk, Pope was no philosopher. He had
opinions in plenty and could map out the real world with extraordinary
skill. His choice of the heroic couplet, and of the townsman's scene for
his great poems, meant that he had to construct scenarios for his poems
which looked like consecutive arguments — which imitated the progress
of the logician. But a poem is a world, not a homily. I think this can be
demonstrated by looking at Pope's most 'argufying' poems — to use a
favourite word of William Empson's. The *Epistles to Burlington and Bathurst*
both on the proper use of Riches; the *Epistle to a Lady on the Characters of
Women*; and *The Epistle to Dr. Arbuthnot*, which is basically an
autobiographical sketch, as well as a portrait of London literary life. *The
Essay on Man* is divided into four *epistles* also, but this, the most generalising
and least personal of Pope's poems, seems to me also his thinnest, and
the one most stocked with received ideas. I love the *Imitations of Horace*,
but they are essentially in the same mould as the *Moral Essays*, and are
slightly less self-contained, being variations on their Roman Models, as
well as having picked up hints from The Earl of Rochester.

I'll content myself with looking into the *Epistle to Bathurst* to see what
sort of a moral universe Pope is evoking. And make forays into the poems
which are its neighbours. The Use of Riches was a personal as well as a
suitable subject for Pope. His friends included some of the richest noblemen
of his day, and he was not afraid to advise them on how best to spend

their money, and equally important, how to justify their good fortune. Pope was no leveller, of course, but neither was he an advocate of what is called these days 'enterprise culture'. He is better at conjuring a scene into life than in creating a picture of moral goodness. The poem ends with his extended portrait of 'The Man of Ross'. This rather insipid paternalist is inflated into an emblem of good works. He hardly comes to life, despite Pope's fervent advocacy. Nor is there much proportion in the poem's argument up to his appearance; rather, there is a natural progression of poetic ideas lamenting mankind's habit of falling into one of two extremes, Avarice or Profusion. It is the mean between the two which Pope exalts. He surveys his own age in considerable detail, listing many absurdities arising from the abuse of wealth — people leaving their money to cats or to sons they hate; the fear the rich entertain of the poor, the hypocrisy of the clergy. Behind all these and many other perversions lies the one dreadful curse — mankind's lust for money.

> But thousands die, without or this or that,
> Die and endow a College, or a Cat:
> To some, indeed, Heav'n grants the happier fate,
> T'enrich a Bastard, or a Son they hate.
>   Perhaps you think the Poor might have their part?
> Bond damns the Poor, and hates them from his heart:

(I leave the presence of Pope's selection of one entrepreneur's name to be noted by you all, without further emphasis).

> The grave Sir Gilbert holds it for a rule,
> That 'every man in want is knave or fool:'
> 'God cannot love (says Blunt, with tearless eyes)
> The wretch he starves' — and piously denies:
> But the good Bishop, with a meeker air,
> Admits, and leaves them, Providence's care.
>   Yet, to be just to these poor men of pelf,
> Each does but hate his Neighbour as himself:
> Damn'd to the Mines, an equal fate betides
> The Slave that digs it, and the Slave that hides.
> Who suffer thus, mere charity should own,
> Must act on motives pow'rful, tho' unknown:
> Some War, some Plague, or Famine they foresee,
> Some Revelation hid from you and me.

> Why Shylock wants a meal, the cause is found,
> He thinks a Loaf will rise to fifty pound.
> What made Directors cheat in South-Sea year?
> To live on Ven'son when it sold so dear.
> Ask you why Phryne the whole Auction buys?
> Phryne foresees a general Excise.

It's immediately apparent that the City of Pope's day was much like it is today. There were monopolies, take-overs, fraudulent issues, and insider dealing. What Pope fears is the destruction of society, the triumph of anarchy. Money is society's cement, so the miser and the profligate equally threaten the security of the state. Pope is serious about this — his moral centre is utilitarian rather than Christian. Moderation for him is not a pallid virtue but a full-bloodied one. His poetry attains its greatest power whenever he imagines the disintegration of society, as he does in the final lines of *The Dunciad*.

A similar passage occurs in this epistle. It is a vision of the evil wrought by the pursuit of wealth and property.

> At length Corruption, like a gen'ral flood,
> (So long by watchful Ministers withstood)
> Shall deluge all; and Av'rice creeping on,
> Spread like a low-born mist, and blot the Sun;
> Statesman and Patriot ply alike the stocks,
> Peeress and Butler share alike the Box,
> And Judges job, and Bishops bite the town,
> And mighty Dukes pack cards for half a crown.

This is not the snobbish fear a modern misunderstanding might deem it to be. It is not the levelling of ranks which threatens society, it is the willingness of those born into security to match, in their cheating and conniving, those made villainous by necessity. Pope would probably have agreed with Bernard Shaw that poverty has no virtue in it, but that the cupidity of the fortunate is especially dangerous. You could go through this Epistle and put modern names to those who earn Pope's opprobrium — perhaps starting with Guinness's Ernest Saunders to replace Francis Chartres. Yet the course of the poem is more passionate than reasoned: it reminds me of the conviction of many rationalists that reason is itself a passion.

Riches — money, property, power — are subjects worthy of any moralist's invective. Turn then to the *Epistle to Burlington* and you find that the use of riches is approached from another, and to our way of thinking, much less serious angle. When, in the early seventies, I made a short selection of Pope's poetry intended for popular reading, I excluded any passage from this Epistle, but included all of those to a Lady, to Lord Bathurst and to Dr. Arbuthnot. I now feel that this was a mistake. I recognized, even then, that the famous lines in *Burlington* describing Timon's Villa was brilliant poetry, but I suppose I must have valued the overall approach less than that of the epistles I included. In *Burlington*, Pope is concerned with Taste. It's still hard for a modern sensibility to care much about Taste — certainly we don't place it centrally in our moral universe as Pope did in his. But the poem is wholly serious, and I can see now, well into the brutal and opulent eighties of this century, that grossness and vulgarity are sure signs of bad faith towards humanity. We are in thrall to millionaires whose rapacity is as all-consuming as any Roman slavemaster in Petronius, or American Nineteenth century Stock Exchange pirate.

If I may leave England, for a moment, and speak of Australia, the only other social democracy I know from personal experience, I must say that the worship of material success has reached alarming proportions in that country, and the Australian suspicion of fat cats and tall poppies has given way to sedulous admiration. The behaviour of the Bonds, Murdochs and Elliotts is like that of the tasteless demonstrators of their wealth whom Pope deplores. The curious psychology of these men makes them naturals for bad taste. They wish to possess everything in the world merely for the sake of possessing it. A few subscribe to absolutist theories of government or to programmes of autocracy, but most are rootless and restless persons who wish to own the world's riches merely because they are there. Consequently when they spend their money their displays are overweening and pointless. Pope always denied that Timon's Villa was based on The Duke of Chandos's Hertfordshire mansion. Considering that Chandos kept a chapel and commissioned Handel to write his first great compositions to English texts, Pope would have had little reason for attacking him, however magnificent his estate. Pope was not against nouveaux riches on principle, and did not prescribe to the snobbery of preferring old money to new. Waste, false magnificence, and corruption were his targets. Ridiculousness in wealthy men may be a way to unmask their viciousness. Certainly, there is passion as well as sardonic humour in Pope's painting of Timon's Villa.

At Timon's Villa let us pass a day,
Where all cry out, 'What sums are thrown away!'
So proud, so grand, of that stupendous air,
Soft and Agreeable come never there.
Greatness, with Timon, dwells in such a draught
As brings all Brobdingnag before your thought.
To compass this, his building is a Town,
His pond an Ocean, his parterre a Down:
Who but must laugh, the Master when he sees,
A puny insect, shiv'ring at a breeze!
Lo, what huge heaps of littleness abound!
The whole, a labour'd Quarry above ground.
Two Cupids squirt before: a Lake behind
Improves the keenness of the Northern wind.
His Gardens next your admiration call,
On ev'ry side you look, behold the Wall!
No pleasing Intricacies intervene,
No artful wildness to perplex the scene;
Grove nods at grove, each Alley has a brother,
And half the platform just reflects the other.
The suff'ring eye inverted Nature sees,
Trees cut to Statues, Statues thick as trees,
With here a Fountain, never to be play'd,
And here a Summer-house, that knows no shade;
Here Amphitrite sails thro' myrtle bow'rs;
There Gladiators fight, or die, in flow'rs;
Un-water'd see the drooping sea-horse mourn,
And swallows roost in Nilus' dusty Urn.

I mentioned in passing that Pope's contribution to versification in English was not just his standardising of the heroic couplet, but his invention of the medium-length social poem. There are, of course, many precedents which he will have known: some of Donne's Elegies, poems by Ben Jonson, Marvell, Milton and especially Rochester's *Tunbridge Wells* and his *Letter from Artemisia in the Towne to Chloe in the Country*. But before him the greatest achievements in English poetry had been in the theatre, in the long romance from Italian, and lyrics and songs. Skelton alone treated the middle-length non-allegorical poem. Pope contented that part of himself which looked to the classics and to *Paradise Lost* by translating Homer. By the time he came to write his great poems in the first years of the new century, English prose had begun to take over much of the territory occupied by English poetry. Shakespeare's plays, even his comedies, are predominantly in verse. The Restoration dramatists work in prose, other than in their tragedies, which are markedly inferior to Jacobean tragedies. The quality of prose in the best of Wycherly, Etherege, Congreve and Farquhar is so high, that poetry was forced to tool up to meet the challenge of this new, fast-moving, referential, allusive style. What Pope had to do was to illuminate the prosaic imagination of the Restoration, to find in verse an equivalent to the new literalness, which might be represented by the almost 'touchable' quality of dialogue in Vanbrugh's plays. By now, too, the country possessed a whole class of literary persons — there was a literary life, and writing had become a profession in a sense different from that which Shakespeare knew as script-writer for a company of actors. The Restoration also saw the founding of The Royal Society — all these factors made Pope the pathfinder of a new sensibility in English poetry.

It's scarcely going too far to suggest that the tone which Pope established then has remained the dominant one in our literature ever since. It even survived the Romantic Movement and Wordsworth's revolution of sensibility. And it has to do with Pope's approach to subject matter, to his subsuming of everything tragic, magical, irrational and psychological to the norms of social intercourse. What seems like artificiality stems from the couplet, and perhaps from the special diction which the Augustan age affected. But if you look into the poems you see that specifically poetic words are outweighted by the larger number of everyday words from social intercourse, business, science, and even gossip. There are sylphs, muses, classical heroes and personifications in Pope's verse, but there are also London streets, Windsor Forest, drawing rooms, gardens, dead dogs in the Thames, theatre boxes, bookshops, and coffee houses. There is friendship and rivalry; conversation and dinner-parties; country vistas and town comforts; sickness, gambling and death; action and desuetude; business and desire; the gamut of life from joy to pain. For many people, but not for Pope, poetry subsists in transcendence, not of quality and perception but of subject. Thus, for them, a poem should distance itself from what Freud called 'Alltagsleben' — ordinary life. The mystical was not Pope's domain. He makes the living world seem more marvellous than we knew it to be, by dressing it in definitive orders of itself. With Pope, poetry steps out of the shadow of myth and into the modern world.

I began this talk by dragging in the red herring of music. I tried to cover my trail by discussing Pope's obsessional technique under the heading of *Rhyme,* and his natural ebullience under *Reason.* I want to end with a repetition of what I said about the Pleasure Principle. No poet can be great who is not memorable, unmistakeable and a virtuoso. He must give pleasure. Reading him must surmount any tendency to theorise and any signposting towards historical necessity. Maynard Mack's exhaustive *Life of Pope* will help fill in all the lacunae of your knowledge of the world he lived in, and the causes he espoused. It is your own love of language which must make Pope come to life for you. The beauty of his language, the justice of his imagery, the musicality of his versifying — these you can taste on your tongue and prove on your ear. And there is so much more of Pope than you think. The one volume Twickenham Edition is almost a thousand pages long, and it doesn't include his Homer. When Maynard Mack wrote his *Life,* he remembered a poem written by the American poet, James Wright. It came about after Wright had attended a literary conference in an American University: He wrote it in a colleague's volume of Swift. Wright conjures up the ghosts of those great and exemplary friends, Pope and Swift. Wayne, in the poem, is the Christian name of the American professor in whose book Wright inscribed his poem.

> Only, when Swift men are all gone
> Back to their chosen fields by train
> And the drunk Chairman snores alone,
> Swift is alive in secret, Wayne:
> Singing for Stella's happiest day,
> Charming a charming man, John Gay,
> And greeting, now their bones are lost,
> Pope's beautiful, electric ghost.
>
> Here are some songs he lived in, kept
> Secret from almost everyone
> And laid away, while Stella slept,
> Before he slept, and slept alone.
> Gently, listen, the great shade passes,
> Magnificent, who still can bear,
> Beyond the range of horses' asses,
> Nobilities, light, light and air.

I know that we are not such 'horses asses'. We can hear these works of art nourished by great friendships. But to make assurance doubly sure I'll finish by reading an occasional piece of Pope's composed as a loving variation on Gulliver's Travels. It has a long, mocking title — *The Words of the* KING OF BROBDINGNAG, *as he held Captain Gulliver between his Finger and Thumb for the Inspection of the Sages and Learned Men of the Court.*

In Miniature see *Nature's* Power appear;
Which wings the Sun-born Insects of the Air,
Which frames the Harvest-bug, too small for Sight,
And forms the Bones and Muscles of the Mite!
Here view him stretch'd. The Microscope explains,
That the Blood, circling, flows in human Veins;
See, in the Tube he pants, and sprawling lies,
Stretches his little Hands, and rolls his Eyes!

Smit with his Countrey's Love, I've heard him prate
Of Laws and Manners in his Pigmy State.
By travel, generous Souls enlarge the Mind,
Which home-bred Prepossession had confin'd;
Yet will he boast of many Regions known,
But still, with partial Love, extol his own.
He talks of Senates, and of Courtly Tribes,
Admires their Ardour, but forgets their Bribes;
Of hireling Lawyers tells the just Decrees,
Applauds their Eloquence, but sinks their Fees.
Yet who his Countrey's partial Love can blame?
Tis sure some Virtue to conceal its Shame.

The World's the native City of the Wise;
He sees his Britain with a Mother's Eyes;
Softens Defects, and heightens all its Charms,
Calls it the Seat of Empire, Arts and Arms!
Fond of his Hillock Isle, his narrow Mind
Thinks Worth, Wit, Learning, to that Spot confin'd;
Thus Ants, who for a Grain employ their Cares,
Think all the Business of the Earth is theirs.
Thus Honey-combs seem Palaces to Bees;
And Mites imagine all the World a Cheese.

When Pride in such contemptuous Beings lies,
In Beetles, Britons, Bugs and Butterflies,

Shall we, like Reptiles, glory in Conceit?
Humility's the Virtue of the Great.

We live in this same Britain, still. A peculiar self-conscious country, but it did nurture Swift and Pope. I hope it may nurture such generous spirits today.

1985: Loughborough University. Open Lecture.

CHAPTER VII

News from the Front

I always find it instructive to look at authors' manuscripts. Not because I am interested in their emendations, the evidence of their struggle to bring their inspiration to light, or because I presume to haruspicate their personality from their handwriting, though Lord Byron's secondary modern scrawl, plus his punctuation being confined to dashes, tells us something about his up-to-date spirit, but to be reminded of the origin of so much of that material which textbooks and conferences elevate to solemn proportion. I know that many people now believe that literature is language writing itself, but ironically that doesn't prevent such persons from subscribing to a narrow pantheon of authors and books worth discussing, plundering or categorising.

Like all writers who have been asked to say something about topics like "What is the fate of the Modern?" I have coined the odd phrase myself. "We are in a permanent museum" is one such. But the museum in your head is less daunting than the massive structure in the city square. The only way to deal with such places is to be possessed by the spirit of irreverence. How badly the Uffizzi is hung; what a lot of junk has got into the Louvre. The justification of the irreverence is this: hundreds of masterpieces have left their birthplaces and are bedded down in one spot. Beauty and truth have. been washed up in a sargasso of their own; each noble essence has joined a quintessence. Somewhere there is a road leading back to the place where each of our acknowledged masterpieces was made. Some of us are jockeying to admit new faces to the company of the gods. Others are hoping for the Curator's job, so we can show our originality by arranging startling vistas, ironic silhouettes and witty confrontations. One thing is certain: in our institutions — universities, museums, training colleges, conservatoria and the rest, we are grappling with the task of passing on a tradition of masterpieces extraordinarily varied in origin, almost none of which was or could have been made inside the institutions themselves.

I like to remind people of this when I hear them propounding views such as the late Dr Leavis maintained: that the highbrow newspapers, the Sundays (or in Australia the Saturday review sections), the weeklies, the monthlies and the BBC, are the real enemies of a properly humane culture. They are accused of compromising with fashion, of pandering to readability, and of overestimating the present. This makes them worse than the ordinary rubbish which makes no pretence at seriousness, the argument goes. I admit that such notions are not heard so much nowadays. Attacks on literary journalism come from different quarters — insufficiently theoretical would be the cry now. I continue to be surprised that people are so attached to the concept of a stockade culture that works of art conceived outside the walls must be mustered, brought inside and saved from the dangers of an indifferent or hostile environment. At the same time, I admit it makes sense. If you can gather the best which has been done, preserve it, analyse it and prepare it for the instruction of new generations, you can ask the state to support your good work, bring masterpieces to the attention of those whose chances of encountering them for themselves may be less than good, and so promote seriousness in a climate unpropitious to it.

The analogy to the place of monastic orders in the body of the church has often been made. If monasteries are spiritual powerhouses, then universities may be cultural ones. In America, of course, this analogy can be pushed a very long way. Take music. Avant-garde scores which would frighten away audiences in concert halls are regularly composed and performed on the campus, as, no doubt, at one time exercises in theology were presented in the security of abbeys. Some of the art which is created out in the world can indeed be made in the Parnassian academy but this is much more often done in music and the plastic arts than it is with literature. To return to Leavis for a moment: I am baffled by his belief that Cambridge University represented at least the possibility of an organic society unspoiled by the alienating organisms which have accumulated since the Industrial Revolution. Are people made more humane and cooperative by constant exposure to great poems and novels? Especially if they are obliged to distinguish among them, on pain of accusation of heresy? To state, as Auden did, that poetry makes nothing happen is to exaggerate. But what it makes happen may well be outside the canons of enlightened behaviour. I prefer to think that literature is dangerous stuff — it is sometimes worked out of the human spirit by forces which the writer cannot resist. It must justify itself in the end by its being a universal impulse, though not one possessed by every person. The consequences will be good and bad, but its moral force is not literature's chief justification.

Therefore, it will not scorn the newspapers, the publishing house and the television studio, in order to keep itself pure in the university. Some of its patrons will be very sleazy, and almost none will have only its welfare at heart. But the serious writer must find ways of getting round his employer's desires, and somehow manage to satisfy his own. I doubt that today we can hope for such prodigious triumphs of genius over box office as the plays by Shakespeare and his contemporaries, but we have before our gaze many fine and innovative writers who have made good livings in the commercial world. The late Philip Larkin once described the poet in the university as being like the cow that turned up at the headquarters of United Dairies. It was his little joke and a nostalgic one at that. But it will do to point us in another direction: the hard-to-describe outside world where new works of the imagination are first presented to the public.

Before settling down to my metaphor of the front-line, it might be worthwhile to touch on the matter of how the centrepieces of the existing Pantheon were first made available to their readers. A few examples will do. Pope issued his poems usually by subscription: for that he needed a wealthy and interested public. His social activity, while not detracting from his seriousness, helped guarantee his success. His translations of *The Iliad* and *The Odyssey* (the second not all his own work) were great publishing triumphs. The commercial theatre made the fortunes of early playwrights, or at least some of them, and continues to do so for their successors today: but Shakespeare did not see his texts into print. Dickens preferred to publish in installments, though the journals he issued his novels in are not what we call literary magazines today, being popular papers read by a wide public and spanning many different classes. They were thus in the public mind as entertainments long before they could be held up to admiration as part of a literary pantheon. With poets, it's hard to determine quite how their works were promulgated, at least to decide on any one dominant pattern. In the nineteenth century, their books sold bountifully. Byron, Tennyson and a host of lesser figures were widely circulated. And here we begin to notice the importance of magazines and journals as places where new names might be spotted and dry runs of well-known works carried out. Even poets who didn't publish could expect to be collected after their death in book form, sometimes in unauthorised editions, as with Donne (collected by his son) and Rochester (pirated). By Wordsworth's and Byron's time, there was a mass-market for poetry, but in earlier epochs a reputation as a poet was a more confined thing. From the middle of the eighteenth century novels had settled into much the same pattern as today — sold in bookshops and reviewed in journals of news and opinion.

The real difference between (say) the year 1800 and today is the very Pantheon I spoke of before. Then the inheritance, including the classics, had not been claimed, stored, and diffused by educational establishments. Each informed person was capable of making up his own Pantheon. Therefore magazines and journals then were not excessively preoccupied by the past. Contemporary literary magazines are not so much filled with reassessments of the established canon as daunted by its existence, to such an extent that they both present and judge fresh work almost apologetically, in an attitude of unbecoming deference. Each new writer is seen as a wagon or carriage potentially able to be hitched to the train of the heritage. This self-consciousness is new, though it was perhaps prefigured by such nineteenth century apostles of tradition as Jeffreys' *Edinburgh Review.*

You will notice from the title of this essay, "News from the Front," that my chosen metaphor is an out-of-date one — trench warfare not tank encounters, Polaris submarine patrols or Star Wars. This is because I come from a generation whose sensibility was formed by pictures of the Somme and Passchendaele. I was born in 1929, but my mind's epicentre is 1917. The idea of a continuous war may not be the happiest one for literary production but it fits much of the detail. There in the front-line are the troops of this battle of attrition. What these literary frontliners are fighting for and who their opponents are can be filled in by each person to his or her satisfaction. The lines straggle and criss-cross as much as the trenches in France. And there is not just one enemy and one alliance — writers shoot it out in an anarchy of artistic loyalty and ambition. But whatever their allegiance, they share the camaraderie of the front-line and can, at moments of reflection, see the critics or Headquarters men as the real enemy. Writers seldom know why they are writers, and may well feel that, against their will, they have been conscripted to serve. In this metaphor the danger of being killed refers to the authors' productions. In some generations, their works suffer casualties equivalent to the first day of the Battle of Arras. Behind the lines at GHQ the critics are planning campaigns, but they seldom venture near the front. Perhaps, like a famous First World War general, they might burst into tears if they saw what they were sending the troops into. What the literary magazines print is news from this front-line. There are always pushes, the network of trenches is changing, veterans are lying low but making sudden successful forays, renowned snipers keep a whole line on the defensive, and some salients prove so costly they have to be abandoned. This warfare is, of course, noisy and disorganised. It lacks the strategy of a real battle. But from its deeds, after the smoke has cleared, a few solid gains will be incorporated into the inheritance of the language.

How are we to know, not just what is going to be important ultimately, but even the most commanding of the actions of the moment? We need bulletins, communiques, reports by accredited correspondents. These are what we get when we read literary magazines. Their responsibility is twofold: they must print as much of the good new material as they can find space for, and they must act as a monitoring force on the whole contemporary campaign. This is why we need so many of them. Much of this assessing suffers from the same topicality as the material it reports on. Looking up a copy of a literary journal of forty years ago can be like consulting a correspondent's report of the German push in the Ardennes. We must read it in the light of history: we now know, or partly know, the outcome. Yet we will always owe a debt to those who brought us the news in the first place. And some of it may never need to be amended. Pound said that art was news which stayed news. No wonder so much that has been tidied away into definitive corners of the Pantheon, and which is today the mainstay of the academic curriculum, first saw the light of day in the apparently flimsy pages of a literary journal — these were signals passed down from the front at the very moment of their happening.

I think I have milked this metaphor for as much as it is worth. It would be distortion to try to play it out through the rest of my paper. But I shall stick to its main purport: it is no use looking to academic critics for news of the latest productions of the age. Editors of magazines and literary journalists must be our guides, over and above the writers themselves, many of whom we are bound to encounter (also in the role of journalist) in the periodicals I am speaking of. For example, Leavis's *New Bearings in English Poetry* was an influential book in its day. But did Dr Leavis discover Eliot and Pound and Lawrence? By no means — each had been taken up and expounded in many different quarters long before *New Bearings* was conceived. Leavis gave many critics the chance to write in *Scrutiny*. Some of these were creators of verse and prose in their own right, but he did not, to my knowledge, encourage or identify one new novelist or poet. I suppose we may say, as Larkin did, that the present is always overvalued, but it is natural in us to go on overvaluing it. The magazine contributor (that is, the frontline liaison runner) may progress to become a fully fledged critic at Headquarters. Years ago, in a polemical piece in Ian Hamilton's *New Review*, I tried to identify what I called "the Klemperer Syndrome". This takes its name from the conductor who, in his turbulent youth, plays just-composed pieces of music, but, after he has become a great and legendary figure, confines his programming to Beethoven and Brahms, and reads Goethe before going to bed. I extended the notion to literary critics, once lean figures prowling the pages of literary journals and assessing all the new volumes of poems as they came from the press, but who abandon the here and now, once they attain academic promotion, for a contemplation of the fixed great — for Tennyson and Keats. One critic, who took umbrage at this and threatened to cancel his subscription, was indeed in my mind, but he was by no means the worst offender. He is well known to be devoted to a modern American balladeer.

Naturally, people deserve to be brought out of the trenches when they have served several seasons. It is very impressive, however, when they volunteer to go back into the line. I find myself well disposed to Terry Eagleton, for instance, despite not sharing his enthusiasm for Marxism and his many ways of stealing the clothes of the bathers — notably adopting bits of deconstruction and feminism for his own argument. The reason why is simple: throughout a long career as an academic critic, he has gone on reviewing contemporary poetry, usually in long compendious round-ups, in Jon Silkin's magazine *Stand*. In the literary war, he is one of the top brass who volunteers to go on commando raids. And I should have been more impressed by Leavis's Puritanism if I had ever seen him directing it to books not yet established in The Canon. Some who sat at his feet followed his principles more closely than he did. Philip Hobsbaum, who studied at Downing, was one. Hobsbaum encouraged a generation of poets, including Peter Redgrove, Ted Hughes and Seamus Heaney. Hobsbaum believed that Leavis's principles would stand up when applied to texts as yet unpublished and unscrutinised.

The whole notion of what a literary magazine is and what it does remains to be explored. Perhaps I can speak for those who are not experts, and for the "users" of literary magazines. My experience of literary journals is almost entirely at the receiving end. Once, during the period from January 1973 to June 1974, I was Fiction and Poetry Editor of the *Times Literary Supplement* (*TLS*), that is in the last months of Arthur Crook's editorship and the first weeks of John Gross's. I discovered that I lacked the first requirement of a good editor: I was too lax. If a review looked halfway decent and seemed fair, I would let it go in. I had little notion of a house style. Mine was only a one day a week stint, and that is too short. Most of the time I simply sent books out, hoping that those who received them would review them. It was not easy then, and I believe it is not easy now, to get people to take on the task of staple reviewing — novels, poems, biographies, books which are not in specialist disciplines and form the bulk of the parcels which pour into an editor's office. In those days *TLS* notices were anonymous. I remember that when by-lines appeared, Kingsley Amis shook his head and muttered "Ah, yes, *names*, *names*, now we shall have *names*!" I think he believed that the danger of reviewers showing off beneath a by-line outweighed the possibility that an anonymous writer might indulge in spite with impunity. That battle is long since over, and has been decided fairly, though I hanker after anonymity from time to time. I was the unnamed reviewer who wrote a front on Larkin's *Oxford Book of Contemporary English Verse*. I think it was a reasonable notice, and I remember how surprised I was when a well-known authority on Larkin asked me, "Who wrote that bloody awful piece in the *TLS*? It must have been some don trying to be with it." I didn't volunteer a guess at the reviewer's identity. It was the younger Amis, Martin, who got fed up with my not being severe enough with our reviewers. He was my assistant but he came into the office every day. Accepting poems, however, was not something I took lightly. I returned several pieces by renowned authors, and achieved notoriety by refusing Derek Mahon's poem, "A Disused Shed in Co. Wexford," considered by many to be one of the finest poems of the last twenty years. I don't know whether I did right or wrong in stalling Martin's insistence that we publish some poems by his Oxford tutor, Craig Raine, whose work had not been seen outside the university at that time. I did print one, and now look what has happened: Martianism has spread across the globe.

I have also been the regular radio reviewer of the *New Statesman* and poetry reviewer of *The Observer*, and have contributed notices to dozens of periodicals and newspapers. Here my insider dealing ends. At no time have I been a policy maker or editorial guide to any journal. My real relationship with literary magazines has been that of consumer. Even my contributions are a form of consumerism, since undertaking to write a notice of a book has made me read hundreds of volumes I would have been too lazy or biased to bother with otherwise. If the topic is contemporary poetry in English, I can at least talk shop with almost anyone, and I believe that this is as worthwhile an accomplishment as being able to give a learned paper on Jonathan Swift. Many critics who write on Lowell or Hill or Seamus Heaney had never heard of these poets when their books were first reviewed in magazines and papers by G.S. Fraser or A. Alvarez or Ian Hamilton. And further back, before the poems were gathered into books, the public was being introduced to them in dozens of publications, the majority of them probably qualifying for the title "little magazine". Almost all of us got our start in little magazines. The first poem of mine to be published was in the Cambridge undergraduate magazine *Delta*, and I wasn't an undergraduate. If you were to look through the outstanding books of poems issued in Great Britain each year, you would find, from the acknowledgements, the names of hundreds of periodicals and papers. And we read many that we don't publish in. My house is rendered nearly unlivable in by the accumulated mass of back copies of such things. Just to reel off the names of the most eminent of them would use up the rest of my time. Perhaps I may be permitted to list a few, to demonstrate how widely the generic title literary must be stretched if it is to bring everything to account.

A great number are defunct. *The Nineteenth Century and After*, which became the *Twentieth Century*; *Perspectives*; *Botteghe Oscure*. Then there are those famous periodicals whose back runs we keep beside us and whose reprint editions are in demand: the *Criterion*, *New Verse*, *Horizon*, *Poetry London*, *Scrutiny*, *Listen*, the *Review*. My bias is British, not American; the roll call from the United States would be even longer. Literary magazines are like Ted Hughes's thistles; they die and then a new generation fights back over the same ground. At this moment someone somewhere is starting another one. It may be in the obscurity of a small town in Wales or New South Wales; it might have a name like *Cadwallader and all his Goats* or *Toss Me a Tinny*, on the one hand, or *Interface* or *Iconolatre* on the other. It may survive for one or one hundred and one issues. You may feel that such a magazine has little in common with the famous journals I've mentioned, some of which have entered the canon in their own right, but it is quite possible that a new Seamus Heaney or Les Murray will have his first poem published in its pages.

Is the modern literary magazine more a begetter of taste and opinion than the instigator of original writing? Immediately, you have to distinguish what sort of publication it is. It is the duty of severe academic journals to act as a forum for scholars. *Essays in Criticism, Notes and Queries*, the many specialist quarterlies devoted to the classics, to textual commentary and research are not my concern. I don't read them: I don't know what they contain. I'm sure that they sometimes bring forward fine work previously obscured, and clarify attitudes to the past which had got out of date. It would be nice to think that in the pages of one of their number a great lost poem, like Smart's *Jubilate Agno*, might soon be scheduled to appear. The minutiae, the small print of literature is their concern. Perhaps such specialist journals are chiefly rungs on the ladder of academic preferment. But scholarship must always be respectable, and most of us have observed the university lecturer who writes and publishes experimental novels but continues to send impeccably scholarly articles on fugitive topics to the appropriate journals. In a way these are trade papers, and will always be read by those in the trade. Less severe but still scholarly journals have certainly come my way, and I often read them with concern. *The Critical Quarterly* is one such intended for the non-professional but informed reader. This is a genre which is really no genre. Here the *dernier cri* and the old-fashioned rub shoulders; interviews with Kathy Acker appear side by side with discussions of Coleridge's *Abyssinian Maid*; politics outfaces strategy; poems are printed which are subsequently damned in the magazine's review pages.

It will be in the purer specialist journals that the new orthodoxies of criticism will be launched. If Yale can be credited with the dissemination of the new theory, it was nevertheless in magazines of small circulation that the French originators of these theories first presented them to the world. The French have always been keen practitioners of uncompromising journalism, and only a few of their periodicals such as *Cahiers du Cinema* have attained wider public readership. In the sixties the phrase "global village" was often heard: it sounds quaint today, at least in its hopeful "flower power" sense. But it is pertinent to the way critical theory has come to dominate literary debate. The news has passed rapidly round the academic and even the wider writing community like rumour in a village, its exciting nimbus easier to perceive than its more demanding detail. The carriers of the news are the magazines which live in the shadow of the university departments where such topics are promulgated. Much of it has been gathered into books, especially in America, but the latest break-outs will still come in the journals. I've even heard that in Sydney some of the cognoscenti have a landline to Paris, so that print-outs of the latest developments there can be rushed to their own bulletins almost as soon as they are on the bookstalls in Paris. The casualties of this battle continue to mount. I saw the other day that *M/F*, the journal of Marxist-Freudian radical feminism, had ceased publication. But where one fails another is sure to appear.

I have hardly attempted to answer my question, whether most magazines are begetters of taste rather than instigators of new writing. Perhaps some sort of answer might come if I turn now to the sort of literary magazine I know best, and which, in truth, I enjoy most. For want of a better term I shall call it "the general literary journal". In this number you will find some whose bias is toward politics; some towards fiction and poetry; and some towards sociology, history and so on. But to qualify all must be directed at the general if informed public, and must carry articles on what is going on today, must print new stories and poems, and must follow, chiefly in reviews, the new works coming from the publishing houses. The reliance on reviewing will vary from journal to journal. *The London Review of Books* (*LRB*) and its New York namesake both chart the climate of opinion by commissioning long articles usually attached to a book or sheaf of books. Thus overall think pieces are launched in the form of reviews. The *TLS* does something of the same, but it covers a wider range, and carries more short notices. It also has a Commentary section, which amounts to a brief resumé of what is going on in London and to some extent the provinces, rather like the entertainments reviews in the English Sundays and Australian Saturdays. These newspaper review sections have an important role in the presentation of cultural attitudes. *The Observer, Sunday Times, Guardian,* the *Age,* the *Sydney Morning Herald,* the *Times on Sunday,* the *Australian* — in all these, freelance journalists and academics alike prepare dossiers of the latest names and opinions week after week. Most of us read these reviews though many of us say that we don't. Many of us actually write them. Whether they do good or bad is not for me to say, but without the reputations bestowed on their subjects by these widely diffused reviews, a playwright might not get his new play accepted, a novelist her novel, biographers their next blockbuster, and so on. Even more important, the public, which is as idle as it is easily led, would not buy anything like the quantity of books it does. So I may smudge the issue and declare that affecting taste is one way of promoting new writing. It has its negative side, of course, but universal praise would ruin the market rather than enhance it. To this category of the general should be added many of the other supplements, the weeklies, like the *New Statesman* and *Spectator,* including chapters from special sources, such as the *Listener,* and journals such as the *London Magazine, Scripsi, Meanjin, Overland, Westerly,* and I could go on.

Is a magazine with a strong polemical basis more likely to be influential than one with an eclectic approach? A sort of answer is suggested by one undoubted fact — every journal which has made its mark on the history of literature has been edited by a person of strong views and powerful personality. There are different orders of polemic. Some are tied to a world-view — Marxism, Anti-Communism, Freudianism, left or right, but others reflect an equal rigour which is the individual taste and perception of the editor. Thus *New Left Review, New Society, Encounter* and *Quadrant* are committed to a kind of evangelism different in kind from *Scrutiny, The Review* or *The LRB.* The latter group take their power from the vision of excellence held by their editors, whose convictions may include much which derives from established orthodoxies but which remains highly personal. Theirs is a dogmatism of taste and instinct. Its chief intolerance is of bad writing, something which would not matter particularly at the editorial desk of a committed journal. A corollary of this may be a narrowing of their acceptance of much of the new writing on the scene. Thus they can seem to the literary world's many aspirants ruthless and dismissive. It often appears a precondition of preparing the stage for the as-yet-only-perceived good writing of which they are Baptist-like forerunners that they must be voices crying in the wilderness. Clearing the decks is invigorating. It makes exciting reading.

The quarterly founded in Oxford by Ian Hamilton, *The Review*, is, in my view, the locus classicus of the brilliant journal which takes its tone and toughness from the personality of its editor. There is not a dull issue, but there are several where I did not agree with a single contributor's animadversions. Such a forum is bound to have a limited life, since it is extremely unlikely that the hour of the Messiah will come. When *The Review* expanded into *The New Review*, its policy changed, and it became much more a "general" magazine. It is interesting to note that some of the old contributors stayed behind and some went on to different triumphs in the new format. Clive James was one such. James wrote brilliant serious reviews of poetry and prose in *The Review* (as he did anonymously also in the *TLS*), and *The Review's* satirical section gave him his chance as one of the voices of the parodist Edward Pygge. In the *New Review*, however, he first developed his highly successful technique of making pot-pourris of popular culture by captioning pictures. The whole career of Clive James can be plotted by following his contributions to a range of journals — *The Review*, *The Listener*, *The Observer*, *The New Statesman*, *The New Review*, and the *LRB*. It is a pattern of high culture melding with popular culture. If I prefer the high, I also suspect that his popular culture contributions may prove more important in the long run. I would not necessarily say the same of many of the dons who have also written in general periodicals, though what Christopher Ricks and Frank Kermode have done as journalism stays in the mind as readily as any of their more formal critical essays. Some of the polemical severity I have been talking about might be called backward-facing. It is a well-recognised phenomenon that memorable journalism is often hatchet-work, and savage articles against new art make more attractive reading than balanced appreciations. Clearing the decks will frequently appeal to the brilliant and embattled critic as work more worth persevering with than the ushering-in of new talent or preparation for some literary annunciation. There is an avant-garde form of the same thing, though the magazines which promote it are more fugitive and disappear more quickly.

Since I am both a poet and a freelance journalist, I embody all the difficulty which a divided loyalty implies. One part of me listens sympathetically to the cry of the world's unloved and unrepresented — that is the poets. Last in the queue for fame and money, they bunch together in dozens of magazines for which the adjective "little" might seem a form of gigantism. Even the critical theorists are more in the public eye. In fact, I've noticed at universities that theory is "sexy". Put on a series of lectures on the varieties of theory and you won't be able to get a cat through the door. Announce a parallel series on authors, even admired ones, and the house will be pretty thin. Are the poets doomed to the ghettos of their trade magazines and to their posts as column-fillers in larger and more general periodicals and newspapers? Well, no, not necessarily. Quite flatteringly large displays of poetry appear in many literary magazines; poetry is widely reviewed, though this is tailing off; the poet is always being asked to contribute to the temperature-taking of his own discipline, in dozens of "state-of-the-art" symposia and questionnaires. His condition is probably easier than that of the short-story writer and possibly the novelist, outside a few renowned figures. Yet he hungers to be considered as a formative figure like the playwright, the TV series writer and the political commentator, when portraits of the times are being compiled. The journalist in me rebukes this wishful thinking, and the sceptic looks suspiciously on such notions as "an early warning system for the psyche," "the wound and the bow" and "the human spirit under pressure." We are looking through the wrong end of the telescope: the problem is that people don't read books of poetry; not that they ignore poems when they encounter them in journals.

When preparing this essay, I imagined that I would finish with a prescription for my ideal literary magazine, one which would include every feature which I admired of all those already existing. But now I appreciate that this would be ridiculous, and any such journal would be a monstrous excrescence, and as thick as an American newspaper. All those good things could not go in the same pot. I see now that it is the enormously wide variation in literary magazines which is the most valuable aspect of them. Horses for courses: we can all obtain satisfaction. But that mountain of back copies which fills my study in London may serve to distil a nostalgic essence of fifty years' literary journalism — I say fifty since I read journals issued before my time with the same avidity I do the latest arrival on the bookstall. So I conjure up the whole of Waugh's *Loved One* in *Horizon*; the Auden double number of *New Verse*; Colin MacInnes on Notting Hill Gate from the *Twentieth Century*; Nigel Dennis's versions of Giuseppe Giusti, and with even greater affection, Auden's lyric, "The Willow-Wren and the Stare", which I cut out of an early *Encounter*; the issue of *Listen* with Larkin on Betjeman; the Empson interview in the *Review*; a copy of the *Colorado Review* which contained J.V. Cunningham's Martial translations; a *Paris Review* with Henry Green's revelations of his working methods; Larkin's *The Old Fools* in the *Listener*; Stevie Smith excoriating the new translation of the Bible in the *New Statesman*. It is a wholly wilful and instant biopsy of an extraordinary body of work. It comes from the mass of material which the literary historians must consult for their official versions. All of it was brought down the communications trench to the waiting public. But the war goes on. Let me end therefore with two snippets from my observation post. After all, I write myself and shouldn't miss a chance to get into the picture. Two short poems: let me call them tangentially relevant texts. Firstly, a rendering of Martial's Epigram Book 2, no. 86. Martial was an undoubted provincial, like myself.

> Because I don't attempt those modern poems
> like lost papyri or Black Mountain lyrics
> stuffed with Court House Records, *non sequiturs*,
> and advice on fishing; and since my lines
> don't pun with mild obscenities in
> *The Sunday Times*; nor yet ape Ezra's men
> in spavined epics of the Scythian Marsh,
> The Florentine Banking Scene, or hip-baths
> in Northumberland; nor am I fully-fledged
> in the East European Translation Market
> whose bloody fables tickle liberal tongues;
> despite this I make my claim to be a poet.
> I'm even serious — you don't ask a runner
> to try the high-jump, and if my trade is words
> I'd be a misfit in the People Show.
> From Liverpool to San Francisco, poets
> are tuning to the Underground, a pop-
> ulous place where laurels pale. My pleasure
> is to please myself and if the Muses listen
> I may find an ear or two to echo in.

That was written in 1970. The detail is out-of-date, but the sentiment may still apply. The second and more recent poem is called "Throw the Book at Them". Since we are living in highly forensic times, it admits freely that we live in a cultural museum, but tries not to be too embarrassed about the fact. Robert Browning is not only the poet of "A Toccata of Galuppi's" but the hero of a Shaftesbury Avenue romance, *The Barretts of Wimpole Street* (viz Flush, Elizabeth's dog), and even the great hermeticist himself, Flaubert, is now legend as much as literature. So, perhaps the writer is the books he reads as well as those he writes.

Where do we go to live? We're born ticking
on the page and from the first disclosure on
we sense that time is useless without fear.
So here must gather all those claques of fact
we make good use of, and what are they
but words? Imagine the tight nucleus we know
is true inheritance: we find nothing more
to do with it but turn it back to chaos.
Proust could get ten thousand lines from
one night at a party and Robert Browning
knew he was in love only when he found he'd
said so on the page. How Elizabeth
loved his profile when it hovered over her
in trochees. Personification's special dangers
outweighed Daddy's growlings and the bladder
weakness of poor Flush. Rochefoucauld
spoiled things with his fully-frontal maxim:
it's all much cooler really, exile under cypresses
and chatting at the well, but never far
from the cherished self-immersing diaries —
no matter how fast they fill, white paper presses
on the eyes of nightmare and the black dog
barks defensively. There are mornings
in the bathroom when a wonky razor seems
pons asinorum of responsibility,
but don't despair, a brush with life's not final
till it's found a way to do the rope-trick
with dependent clauses. Dying's a book
with uncut pages: the pentel scurries and the tea
grows cold, and back in London a publisher
announces a burnished tome on Tuscany.
To get through life, just join the dots up, they
may prove a subcutaneous punctuation.

Today in Rouen there is an Avenue
Gustave Flaubert, but nothing spoils the stillness
at his desk. The D.P.P. has all he needs
to start the trial — the boys in blue, the talkative
punk witnesses slurping from chipped cups.
The rules remain: you are the books you write.

1987: Canberra. Humanities Research Centre Conference.
Collected in Outside the Book, *ed. David Carter, Local Consumption*
Publications, 1991.

CHAPTER VIII

Browning's's Important Parleying
Stylistics across two centuries

It will not have escaped anybody's notice that the name I have given my talk is a twisting of the words in the title of Browning's penultimate book of poems, issued in 1887, *Parleyings with Certain People of Importance in Their Day*. I happen to like this book of poems very much; I also think it constitutes a late summing-up of the special genius of utterance which is Browning's gift to English poetry; and it suits the theme of this seminar in being a fine fruit of his last years, the Veneto years, though the poems were mostly written in London. It's entirely appropriate that we should be here, one hundred years after Browning's death in the Ca' Rezzonico, to pay our respects to him, his achievements and the territory which harboured him at the end, the whole man and the full range of the poetry he wrote, and in doing so, we must look back, not only at the remarkable England which nurtured him, but at other parts of Italy, from which he derived so much inspiration. It's a fact that, once he left Florence after Elizabeth Barrett's death, he never set foot in Tuscany again — indeed, it was many years before he ventured back to Italy. None the less, no vision of Browning could underestimate the effect of time in Florence on his work. The Tuscan years must take precedence when one is looking at Browning's poetry — this was high season of his genius, and, consequently I shall refer throughout this talk to the great poems which he wrote in and about Florence, as well as the "late Browning", the Indian Summer culminating in *Asolando*.

This very word "parleying" offers a key to the understanding of Browning's style. It is perfectly comprehensible, meaning talking to a person or persons, but it is also slightly archaic — not exactly formal but smacking of discursiveness, of a tendency to holding forth, perhaps even of not listening very carefully to any reply. For a writer not actually composing dramatic poetry, parleying won't always be colloquy. The many voices have to be contained in the one voice, though the *Parleyings with Certain People of Importance* begin and end with exchanges in the style of Goethe and Arthur Hugh Clough; a form, I suppose, of the eclogue. Apollo and the Fates exchange words whereby the god hopes to persuade the sisters to let Admetus off his call-up by death. Thus, at the start, Browning is thinking of the death of his friend Milsand and possibly looking forward to his own demise. At the end, we have another Goethean criss-crossing with John Fust revealing his printing press to a school of doubters. It's interesting that there is an anticipation here of Umberto Eco's device in *The Name of the Rose* whereby the murders in the monastery are intended to prevent Aristotle's lost book on laughter being released, so corrupting the seriousness of a fallen universe. Browning too, amid much difficult-to-accept boisterousness, suggests that the invention of printing (credited to Fust and not Gutenberg) will aid the damnation of mankind as readily as help in its redemption.

> I hailed Word's dispersion: could heartleaps but tarry!
> Through me does Print furnish Truth wings? The same aids
> Cause Falsehood to range just as widely.

But the burden of the parleyings is, of course, hopeful — though hopeful in that strenuous vein which was always Browning's manner. He seemed temperamentally to need difficulties, despairs even, to triumph over. The often asserted criticism of his poetry as being full of an unattractive muscular Christianity (or do I mean Deism?), of a sometimes insensitive optimism and triumphalism, is, if you consider both the bulk of his work and its finest moments, simply not the case. Indeed, I find in Browning as much as any poet since Shakespeare, a willingness to admit the existence of evil in the world, plus a readiness to do battle with it. As late as *Asolando*, he looks this problem in the face

> Head praises, but heart refrains
> From loving's acknowledgement.
> Whole losses outweigh half-gains:
> Earth's good is with evil blent:
> Good struggles but evil reigns.
>
> Yet since Earth's good proved good —
> Incontrovertibly
> Worth loving — I understood
> How evil — did mind descry
> Power's object to end pursued —

> Were haply as cloud across
> Good's orb, no orb itself:

He makes, as indeed he was seen to right from the start, a good comparison with Tennyson. Tennyson is melancholy, you might say, while Browning is always overcoming a tendency to despair. Out of melancholy comes lyricism, and nobody had a better ear for the dying fall in English verse than Tennyson. Auden was wrong in thinking Tennyson brainless, but he is not interested in the moral wrestlings which pre-occupied Browning and which are given their most prolonged outings in *The Ring and the Book*. I've always believed that poetry and philosophy are natural enemies, but Browning gives this belief pause. It is the very need to find room in the not always spacious forms of English verse for the angles and arguments of his dramatic dilemmas which makes him a symphonic poet, an achiever of whole edifices rather than of arresting details. Of course, he is a phrasemaker — no major poet is not. And he has many famous lyrics in the anthologies. But, unlike Tennyson, it is not his party pieces which we think of when we remember his finest poetry. We think of the situations and the people in the poems: we know they are clothed in brilliant and idiosyncratic language, but we rejoice in the creation of a whole world, its elaborate though dramatically chosen furnishings. Only Shakespeare and Pope in English poetry inhabit so highly-lit yet palpably real a cosmos as Browning does. So much of Browning is paradoxical, and I am happy to support a well-known paradox of his art which states that he failed as completely in his plays as he succeeded in his dramatic monologues.

A small caveat must be entered here in favour of *Pippa Passes*, which is actable — at least on radio. But the pattern is clear: *A Blot i' the Scutcheon* is dead and *Caliban Upon Setebos* is pulsingly alive. To claw back the great attainments of English poetry from the drama, where Shakespeare had deposited them, and give them to verse revelling in the extra attractions of dozens of forms, quirks, complications and secondary styles, is a very considerable achievement. It had to be paid for at a price and later I shall try to point out some of the heavinesses and stalenesses of the dramatic monologue — but almost unaided Browning made poetry interesting again. He made poetry concern itself with people. He didn't abandon the lyric — instead he humanised the editorial voice. These are simplifications, of course. Even Wordsworth lifted his eyes from mountains and lakes to parley with leech-gatherers. But it is with Pope and Browning that poetry comes on course again — a Shakespearean course after too much epic and lyric. And Browning, while a lesser poet than Pope and a much less perfect one, has more variety, especially in the forms he chooses. It is a miracle that Pope can be so wide-ranging in one poetic form — the couplet. I can think only of Domenico Scarlatti in music as an equal genius similarly self-confined to one sort of structure. But Pope doesn't take Browning's risks with human character, and has the satirist's perfection-seeking in typology, the Theophrastian roundness. Browning is cruder but wider.

At this point, I propose to generate a second paradox. Browning and Tennyson are the leading poets of an age which nowadays we say was best represented by its novelists. Each, though Browning the more so, has novelistic qualities. Parts of *Bishop Blougram's Apology* could go into George Eliot; similarly there is some flavour of Henry James in *Mr. Sludge the Medium*. Those two poems are rare instances of Browning's taking his own times as subject matter. And here is the paradox. Although we read them nowadays mostly for their lyrical interpolations, Tennyson's *Maud* and *The Princess* are serious studies of contemporary Victorian dilemmas — human psychology and the education of women. Browning mostly roams the Italian Renaissance, and rarely engages with the mechanical realities of Britain in the Industrial Age. (There is, I know, a factory in *Pippa Passes*, but it is for local colour, like the tobacco factory in *Carmen*). It is a commonplace that his Italian painters, monks, soldiers, harpsichord players, grandees, gondoliers etc are robust Victorians in character and voice, but they are conspicuously South British voices. Orwell pointed out that Dickens was not happy with characters north of Yarmouth unless they were aristocrats out of stock: much the same is true of Browning — the people in his poems have a feeling of the Camberwell Library about them, rather than the Clapham Omnibus. They are spirited, tough, worldly and wide-ranging but they tend to be bookish people invented by a bookish imagination. This suits persons from the Italian Renaissance pretty well. I've always thought that the speaker in *My Last Duchess* sounds a note familiar from the letters we have from Renaissance Courts (Browning sets the poem in Ferrara). Change the sex, and you have Isabella d'Este corresponding in terms of realpolitik all over Italy with her stewards, on the lookout for a bargain painting or conducting ruthless personal campaigns. Browning's Andrea del Sarto is seen, however sympathetically, through Vasari's eyes — a wonderful technician but a bit of a wimp. And this fits many Tuscans of the Quattrocento.

We are used, in English-speaking countries, to imagining Italians of the Middle Ages and the Renaissance as so many condottieri — picture-book Hawkwoods and Castruccios and Machiavellis. Then, later, we see a very different Italy through the eyes of the romantic poets of a period of English ascendancy, the early Nineteenth Century — through Byron's and Shelley's and ultimately Landor's and Browning's. Byron certainly understood the Italy he encountered: two centuries of the Counter Reformation had depleted its confidence and laid waste to its art, other than to music. But Browning, arriving in Italy in the tumescence of the Risorgimento, was able to imagine the Italy of the great days of the New Learning, which were also the less great days of the decline of the Communes into signorial despotism, as no English poet, except Shakespeare, had done. I find, reading Browning's many different approaches to his Italian subjects, a convincing small-town worldliness, a conspiratorial scribblers' ambience, a freshly-coined opinionatedness. It is the Paradise of the Word. Almost at once, and certainly strangely, that soot-stained Capitalist Century — the Nineteenth — attains a clarity it otherwise can only be nostalgic about. Browning, in Tuscany, was able to enjoy the contentious idealistic England into which he was born by re-setting it in an imaginary Renaissance world. Had he stayed in England, the reality there would have drained his freshness and his fervour. But he had to invent his Italy: his poetry had to feed, like an orchid on a rock, on its own detritus. And so we have that remarkable gallery of talkative figures who constitute Browning's tribute to his adopted country, and who are, for us, an artificial senate where self-justification never stops, and language holds all the aces.

Thus, I have no hesitation in offering Browning to you as the best case in English poetry of the old/new oxymoron; he "made it new" by looking back at the old and that, in turn, was the single greatest nudge Modernism received from its poetic predecessor. Consider once more the word 'parleying'. As I have said before, it has an archaic ring to it: it also suggests a truce called in the middle of a battle, or a sortie under a white flag from a besieged town. By the time Browning wrote his *Parleyings*, he had to point out that his interlocutors were people of importance in their own time, but practically unknown in his. This was to be his last essaying of his role as Hermes, the bringing together of the living and the dead, the bridging of the past and the present. Auden once suggested that we value poetry because it enables us to speak with the great dead (and perhaps he might have added the ordinary dead). And what do we listen for when the dead are talking to us? Their pitch, their tone of voice, the inflections of singularity which breathe life into their discourse. Browning's dramatis personae are the most determined in English verse to insist on the voice as the vehicle of life. By "parleying" in so many voices and with so many imagined listeners, Browning opened up a channel down which modern literature went with alacrity.

The change from the Nineteenth Century to the Twentieth in literature is usually discussed in terms of style. It has, of course, its own massive hagiography, and, like all good triumphs, tends to be told in terms of heroes and villains. I have long believed however, that we live in a perpetual artistic present, where all styles cohabit naturally a sort of museum. Each creator is a prince of anachronism. The model for this might be a concert. You start with an overture by Weber, go on to a concerto for several instruments by Vivaldi and end the first part with a Haydn Symphony. After the interval we listen to a Prokofieff symphony. The mind has no difficulty adapting immediately to the very different presumptions of style in each piece. The longer we live and the more art piles up, the more opportunities we have to choose from the complete range of the past those qualities we judge to be most effective for us, and therefore most helpful to our contemporaneity. This has always happened — think of what the Renaissance made from the classics, including the advantages of misunderstanding and of partial knowledge. What Robert Browning gave so providentially to the poets who came after him was the example of the "leading voice" as the way through the wood. Diction, subject matter, poetic form — these are less important than tone, than utterance, the Edenic identification which never goes out of fashion.

On occasion, Browning's poetry may strike us, not least in his later works, as quintessentially Victorian. But it does not seem dated. The medley of voices which we know as poetry can be indifferent to editorial up-to-dateness or aesthetic theory. Poems might be regarded as the least perishable of signs in a universe of deciduous signs. The bearer of the sign is a voice, and behind the voice is a person. Browning, a legend in his day for obscurity and modernity, came to be seen, towards the end of his life, as dangerously prosy. Yet it was precisely his refusal to let prose have all the interesting matter, to confine verse to lyrics which could dance on the surface of literary pond life, that he handed down to poets today. Sir John Mandeville, in his travels to Arctic latitudes, found that all the words which had ever been spoken froze in the air and then lay about in heaps, or gathered on sills, or hung from the branches of trees. Thus every sentence pronounced since the beginning of speech was potentially recoverable. Appalling as this might be to think about, it offers us a formula to escape the stop/go of fashion, the replacement of style generation by generation. Browning, so much in some ways a product of his time, pointed the way forward. Mandeville's words existed once in sentences. Someone spoke them. Poetry, even apparently objective poetry, is made up of voices speaking to us. Since Browning's example, the predominant mode in English poetry has been the monologue in some form or other, the sounding of speech and not the rustling of nature.

Browning's immediate influence was negligible. Despite the Browning Societies and the flurry he made in literary circles, he had no immediate followers, other than Eugene Lee-Hamilton. His effect was like a time bomb. His great influence began to manifest itself only after the Nineteen Twenties. To give what may strike you as an over-pitched example — it is the voice of Robert Browning which I hear in the poetry of John Ashbery. The official line on Ashbery makes him the last word in experimental chic — and where it looks intensely at him, it does so through the lens of pictorial art — contemporary painting mainly. But Ashbery, who never writes anything but a proper syntactical sentence, has precisely that Browningesque garrulity and lucubration, that incorrigible talkativeness which is the mark of modern humanism. In Ashbery's poems, which are deliberately impure and mixed, the monologue is absorbed into the passing parade. The direct voice of feeling which Browning signposts is dissolved into a solution of words. The seeing of all sides of the case which Browning pioneered in the voices of his self-justifying characters becomes in Ashbery a cancelling out of certainty, a very elaborate distrust of statement and assertion, when not modified by copious codicils. Looking back at (say), *Mr. Sludge*, or the *Parleying with Charles Avison*, one begins to see Ashbery-like ectoplasms in Browning. Everything is dissolving into language — people have become words themselves.

I may be pushing my luck too far, but once equipped with the Browningesque model, I find it easy to see his fluid Tarnhelm-like mind in many modern masters. In T.S. Eliot, whose voices in both *The Waste Land* and *Four Quartets* are deliberately ambiguous, and whose *Gerontion* and *Prufock* are celebrated monologues — to say nothing of the Sweeney exchanges, which have a Browning-like rumbustiousness. In Pound, obviously, who acknowledged Browning's influence. The *Cantos* are almost *The Ring and The Book* cut-up and sprinkled about Mandeville-fashion. It is interesting, too, that Pound needed exemplary figures from the past to embody his convictions about the present. He went further back than Browning, preferring the Provencal poets who were Dante's predecessors to Browning's Renaissance worthies. And Pound, whose control of

Modernism was masterfully self-promoting, ensured that a kind of stained-glass medievalism imposed prismatically on both Browning and Swinburne, became one of the main jargons of twentieth century experimentalism. But I would be wasting my time and yours to multiply examples of direct Browning influence on poetry in English this century. There is hardly a poet in the past fifty years who has not written monologues or composed frescoes of words into and out of which tribal voices come and go. If anyone is interested, I undertake to locate Browning's method in Lowell and Berryman and David Jones and a host of lesser figures. I can condense my notion by stating that, while I relish Tennyson's prelapsarian lyricism, I feel in Browning the wind of that other planet, the Twentieth Century.

It remains only for me to essay a few movements towards defining the monologue, as pioneered and perfected by Browning, and, out of a desire to esteem neglected poems and as a gesture towards the theme of 'Late' Browning, to comment on two poems especially — *The Parleyings With Certain People of Importance* and *Of Pachiarotto, and How He Worked in Distemper.*

From Horace and Juvenal, and from medieval times onwards, poets have couched their verses in other men's and women's voices, but it was with Robert Browning that the dramatic monologue assumed the centre of the stage. There are many different kinds of Browning Monologue, and some of them require more elaborate supporting machinery than others. In *Up at a Villa, Down in the City*, subtitled "As distinguished by an Italian Person of Quality", you hear about Italian life, but it doesn't matter who you are. "Soliloquy in a Spanish Cloister", on the other hand, seems to be addressed to another and sympathetic colleague, who might be expected to share the speaker's distaste for Brother Lawrence. The reader then becomes the second listener. Because "Up at a Villa" is a better poem, we shouldn't miss that the Soliloquy is a more complicated structure. Almost every Browning monologue has some special co-ordinates appropriate to it and it alone. Where the speaker is named, the interlocutor may come from the same background and even be part of the mise-en-scène. The ideal listener might be God: in "Caliban Upon Setebos", the monster appears to be talking to himself, imagining his God and finding that presence everywhere. The subtitle is important once more: it is 'Natural Theology on the Island'. But Caliban wants to be overheard by this God — he's almost asking to be congratulated on so likely an hypothesis. Thus his conjecture grows ever more fervid and contorted.

> Well then, supposeth He is good i' the main,
> Placable if His Mind and ways were guessed,

But rougher than his handiwork, be sure!
Oh, He hath made things worthier than Himself,
And envieth that, so helped, such things do more
Than He who made them! What consoles but this?
That they, unless through Him, do aught at all,
And must submit: what other use in things?
'Hath cut a pipe of pithless elder-joint
That, blown through, gives exact the scream o' the jay
When from her wing you twitch the feathers blue:
Sound this, and little birds that hate the jay
Flock within stone's throw, glad their foe is hurt:
Put case such pipe could prattle and boast forsooth
'I catch the birds, I am the crafty thing,
I make the cry my maker cannot make
With his great round mouth; he must blow through mine!'
Would not I smash it with my foot? So He.

"Caliban Upon Setebos" is about as far removed from a confidently Christian or progressive world-view as it is possible to get. It's interesting, too, that a poet not normally thought of as one of Browning's epigoni, W.H. Auden, follows a similarly agonised line of self-reasoning in his Caliban fantasia, the Henry James imitation in *The Sea and the Mirror*. The same sort of theological introspection inhabits Auden's soliloquy for King Herod in the oratorio *For the Time Being*.

Browning's tropes are often legal ones — I put it to you, he says, like a prosecuting attorney — and what he puts via Caliban is an exercise in the higher doubt. London's rationalists were asking just such questions in Browning's time and instancing Darwin's discoveries in examples like Caliban's — though Browning numbered himself among the opponents of Darwin. The material on which the poem's voice must build is gently and beautifully established. The given notion extends initially little beyond our memories of Shakespeare's play. Thereafter, Browning avoids too many obvious signposts on the one hand, or too arcane a build-up on the other. The worst fault in dramatic monologues will always be obviousness — a mass of information necessary to understand the poem's point which becomes unpalatable and which destroys the sense of a real voice speaking to us. In life we seldom recapitulate our histories all in one speech, though people in plays frequently do. Many monologists accordingly choose situations where a great deal of information might seem appropriate — deathbed confessions are a favourite, as in Browning's "The Bishop Orders his Tomb at St. Praxed's Church". This poem is pure invention, though the Bishop is a recognizable Renaissance type, if of the sort which makes for a TV series. The church of Santa Prassede in Rome, always the first place I head for when I am in the city, lends nothing in atmosphere to the poem, and fortunately the Bishop doesn't regale us with an excess of circumstantial detail.

Elsewhere in Browning, one may be reminded of Max Beerbohm's famous parody of Jacobean drama, *Savonarola Brown* — "Enter Leonardo da Vinci, Lorenzo il Magnifico, Filippo Brunelleschi, Pope Alexander the Sixth etc, all making remarks highly characteristic of themselves!" At one point the stage directions even say "Pippa Passes". However, Browning can be fastidious and almost parsimonious with atmospheric detail in his monologues. Two devoted to Florentine painters, both poems of genius, demonstrate the width of his range. "Fra Lippo Lippi" is a masterpiece of exuberance. The lecherous friar, creator of ethereal Madonnas painted from life in the persons of his mistresses, is caught by the city watch sneaking home. Browning fills in every detail of the situation: Lippi tells us about himself at the drop of a pikestaff. It is a rich poem, but not a particularly subtle one. You would not praise it for its mystery or suggestiveness: it is a wide-canvas night-scene floodlit by poetry. But the later and more problematic painter, "Andrea del Sarto", receives very different treatment. His is a sombre monologue, another nocturnal study but worked up from the melancholy thoughts of Sarto as he hears his wife's young cousin whistle for her. He loves her and he knows she will never care for him. He is resting away from the hurly-burly of Florence on the hill of Fiesole. The subtitle once more is suggestive: "Andrea del Sarto, called the faultless painter". Sarto compares himself with Michelangelo and with Raphael. His is the better technique, his the more settled and moral personality, his the aspiration — why have the masters from Caprese and Urbino always surpassed him? Browning mixes the themes — sexual betrayal, envy of a greater talent, the intransigence of patrons, despair at man's imperfection and the remoteness of God. The poem is subdued, vesperal, and has none of Lippo Lippi's fireworks, and unlike Lippi, is composed in the smoothest of lucubrative blank verse. No composer of dramatic monologues can afford to be entirely cryptic, but the degree of information needed for each poem depends on the mood adopted.

The heart of Browning is his 1855 volume, *Men and Women*. Almost every poem in it is a sort of dramatic lyric or monologue, or is pervaded by that 'cult of personality' which is the mark of the dramatic writer. Flanking *Men and Women* are the *Romances and Dramatic Lyrics* of 1845 and

Dramatis Personae of 1864. Then there is *The Ring and the Book*, that wonderful but interminable Rashomon of a poem which elevates the monologue almost to a Summa Theologica of ancestral voices. Put all these books together and the protagonists run all the way from kings of Israel to bogus American spiritualists. A mysterious sub-ballad such as "Childe Roland to the Dark Tower Came" (incidentally, Browning made good use of Shakespeare in a tradition which goes back to Dryden and Pope and forward to Auden) is a further sort of dramatic monologue and so is "How It Strikes a Contemporary". In his copious and generous output, Browning satisfies the unquenchable haranguer which is in each of us. We are born, we talk and we die. But chiefly we talk, and when we meet a good talker we listen. Browning is the talker non pareil.

And this brings me to the collection of parleyings which was Browning's farewell to his lifetime's practice (not his last book, but *Asolando* is a collection of much more occasional pieces). The surprise here is a change in Browning's tactics. While he was always a poet to include plentiful bits of himself in the wrappings of his assumed personae, it is only in the *Parleyings* that he corrals all his people as listeners and not as speakers. This collection of addresses is Browning's sketches for an autobiography. Writers, ever egocentric, are drawn to autobiography at the end of their lives. The *Parleyings with Certain Persons* are as close as Browning ever got to a *Praeterita* — Ruskin was engaged on his book at about the same time. Framed by the two eclogues which I described at the start of this talk, the volume draws up on the parade ground a platoon of artists who had been part of Browning's education, figures whose opinions and whose art had been influential in his youth. They are hardly bywords for fame — witness the second part of his title. I must enter a private observation at this point. I was first drawn to these late poems by my having a fondness for two of the cast whom Browning parleys with — Christopher Smart and Charles Avison. I was amazed that such a complete Victorian should have been attracted to these artists — proof, it seemed to me, in the smug way we have with the taste of our own time, that Browning was really very sharp indeed. But it was not quite like that. Browning loved Smart's *A Song to David*, but he had never encountered *Jubilate Agno* which was not published until 1939. For me, *Jubilate Agno* is one of the greatest poems of the English language. Browning takes an altogether less elevated view of Smart. His interest in the mad poet is as a corrective for false doctrines of art. In Bedlam, Smart, freed of any art for art's sake obligations, can compose a kind of Benedicite on the wonders of God's creation. Browning may not get Smart right but he sees the point of poetry doing what it does best — praising what exists.

The technique of 'strettoing' the poetic entries at the end of Smart's hymn is one which Browning also employs in his own poetry. Like Smart, he was drawn to poetic formulae analogous to musical ones. Charles Avison is probably a more fugitive figure than Smart. An organist in Newcastle in the middle of the eighteenth century, Avison was, in fact, one of the supreme masters of the Italian 'concerto grosso'. He esteemed Geminiani well above Handel and was responsible almost single-handedly for establishing the reputation of Domenico Scarlatti in England, a country where he has always been more highly esteemed than elsewhere — witness his only publication, the keyboard Esercizi in London in 1738. Avison is also a fine composer in his own right. I advise anyone who has not done so to listen to his Concerto Grosso in E Minor Op. 6 No. 8, the "amoroso" of which is the noblest melody in all English Georgian music. Browning knew a march in C major of Avison's and prints it with his poem. Browning loved music but he also envied it its power of reaching directly to human emotion, its freedom from the distorting lens of opinion and meaning. So he argues with Avison and rather meanly evokes a sort of Elgarian procession of the roast-beef British sort as an appropriate conjuration of Avison's art. Avison was also a theorist of music, following the rather arcane principles enunciated by Geminiani, and Browning had read his *Essay on Musical Expression*.

Yet, this parleying, even more than its companions, shows Browning in the full flight of his own theorising. Music arouses in him a disputatiousness (so I suppose does painting) which takes on a tone of "vanitas vanitatem". The best known example of this, of course, is "A Toccata of Galuppi's", another instance of Browning's off-centre taste. Galuppi was an opera composer par excellence, but Browning equips him with a Lisztian keyboard demonism. It is true that Galuppi was as close to the *empfindungs* style of the North Germans as any Italian composer could be, but it is still strange to find him marshalling a Venetian opulence more suited to Veronese or Tintoretto. Music showed Browning a world in harmony with God, but it also offered a vision of materialism and degeneracy. The first of these outlooks pervades "Abt Vogler", perhaps Browning's single most profound poem, and the second fills the Avison piece. I feel that Browning remained somewhat ill at ease with music, precisely because the art will not cooperate with words but insists on them serving it. Music is always likely to overwhelm its collaborators.

It is wholly characteristic of Browning that when he came to write autobiographical poems, and to look back on his formative youth, he should recall the impact of ideas on him more than of people or places. His bookish childhood and training in Camberwell is now at the forefront of his mind. His interlocutors are stalking horses for his puzzlement and for the persistence of his aesthetic creed. Who are Bernard de Mandeville, Daniel Bartoli, George Bubb Doddington, Francis Furini and Gerard de Lairesse? I do not think it matters much; nor what they did or believed in. And if they stand in for Browning's friends and enemies, as Doddington does for Disraeli, and Furini for Pen Browning's nudes, that too is not of great consequence. We are back in the auditorium of Browning's mind. He is old now and more tired than his exuberance suggests. But life must be lived through words — an old man's version of "airy nothing" must get its "local habitation and a name". The poetry machine is set in motion, the rhyming virtuosity cranks the progress of the philosophical conjecture, and the flamboyance lasts to the end. Above all, the phrasemaking, the sloganising for hope, never falters. "Nothing has been which shall not bettered be/ Hereafter", he declares. Again, looking at populist politicians, he pronounces "The multitude means mass and mixture .../ Dive into Man, your medley: see the waste!". His optimism never neglects the fallen world — to Gerard de Lairesse he says "point me out which was it of the links/ Snapt first, from out the chain which used to bind/ Our earth to heaven". It is amusing to interpret one of his sayings anachronistically and deduce that he might think modern literary theory a case of just such a snapped link. He asks us to "Look through the sign to the thing signified". Immediately before this he employs a striking phrase, "Flesh composed of suns,/ How can such be". But the finest moments are in the old Browning vein, the earnest wrestling with judgement and its final resolution, a dipping of the mind in syntax, the conversion of everything into words.

> O, yes
> The other method's favoured in our day!
> Master the heavens before you study earth,
> Make you familiar with the meteor's birth
> Ere you descend to scrutinise the rose!
> I say, o'erstep no least one of the rows
> That lead man from the bottom where he plants
> Foot first of all, to life's last ladder-top:
> Arrived there, vain enough will seem the vaunts
> Of those who say — 'We scale the skies, then drop
> To earth — to find, how all things there are loth
> To answer heavenly law: we understand
> The meteor's course, and lo, the rose's growth ...

...

> ... But reverse
> The order, where's the wonder things grow worse
> Than, by the law your fancy formulates,
> They should be? Cease from anger at the fates
> Which thwart themselves so madly. Live and learn,
> Not first learn and then live, is our concern.'

But I do not want to end on an analytical note. I can only bring a poet's appreciation to Browning, not a scholar's. How better salute his hundredth anniversary than by looking at his technique and celebrating his virtuosity, and his peculiarity. Unlike Byron, his compound rhymes are not primarily satirical and facetious. For him, rhyme was a robust challenge — almost as if he despised flat races and only esteemed hurdles. Take "Pachiarotto", probably the most notorious of his poems with outrageous rhymes. I will not pretend it is a good poem; I just assert it is an enjoyable one. The plot is not so much obscure as invisible. I tracked down a couple of Pachiarotto's paintings in Siena, and they are duly as insignificant as Browning suggests. Ostensibly "Pachiarotto" is Browning's attack on Alfred Austin. As an experience it feels more like the middle-period Browning one knows and loves scurrying round Siena and filling his poem with that bustle and surface detail which is a measure of life. Yet I am sure that the only way to read it is to watch for Browning to come unstuck — the rhyme and metre work like a top — should they stop spinning for a moment, the whole thing would fall over. It is in trimeter — and I can assure you that the three-foot line is almost impossible to prevent collapsing into doggerel. And its iambics are, as Browning liked them to be, liberally spiced with trochaics, the more urgent of the two metrical units. The rhymes are feminine throughout. It is ridiculous but enjoyable.

> Nay, here shall my whistling and singing
> Set all his street's echoes a-ringing
> Long after the last of your number
> Has ceased my front-court to encumber
> While, treading down rose and ranunculus,
> You *Tommy-make-room-for-your-Uncle* us!
> Troop, all of you — man or homunculus,
> Quick march!

In this farrago I hear a more moving note that Browning struck years before. The headlong enthusiasm of his verse is welcome in an art too frequently judged to be at its best in the languorous cadence, or the solemn stride. I think of that great poem which ends *Men and Women*, "One Word More", Browning's love tribute to his wife and his celebration of a remarkable literary partnership. The vitality of lost Tuscany, the Keatsian robe of language, buoy up a sad heart, but a brave one. The metre is self-confident trochaics, the feminine endings swagger. As much as the famous Epilogue to *Asolando*, energy is seen shaping up to death, and English poetry is made richer by it.

> Raphael made a century of sonnets,
> Made and wrote them in a certain volume
> Dinted with the silver-pointed pencil
> Else he only used to draw Madonnas:
> These, the world might view — but one, the volume.
> Who that one, you ask? Your heart instructs you.
> Did she live and love it all her life-time?
> Did she drop, his lady of the sonnets,
> Die, and let it drop beside her pillow
> Where it lay in place of Raphael's glory,
> Raphael's cheek so duteous and loving —
> Cheek, the world was wont to hail a painter's,
> Raphael's cheek, her love had turned a poet's....
>
> Dante once prepared to paint an angel:
> Whom to please? You whisper 'Beatrice'....
>
> Dante who loved well because he hated,
> Hated wickedness that hinders loving,
> Dante standing, studying his angel, —
> In there broke the folk of his Inferno,
> Says he — 'Certain people of importance'
> (Such he gave his daily dreadful line to)
> 'Entered and would seize, forsooth, the poet'
> Says the poet — 'Then I stopped my painting'....
>
> You and I would rather see that angel,
> Painted by the tenderness of Dante,
> Would we not? — than read a fresh Inferno....
>
> This I say of me, but think of you, Love!

This to you — yourself my moon of poets!
Ah, but that's the world's side, there's the wonder,
Thus they see you, praise you, think they know you!
There, in turn I stand with them and praise you —
Out of my own self, I dare to phrase it.
But the best is when I glide from out them,
Cross a step or two of dubious twilight,
Come out on the other side, the novel
Silent silver lights and darks undreamed of,
Where I hush and bless myself with silence....

Oh, their Raphael of the dear Madonnas,
Oh, their Dante of the dread Inferno,
Wrote one song — and in my brain I sing it,
Drew one angel — borne, see, on my bosom!

1989: Venice: Browning Centenary Conference
Collected in Browning and Venezia, *ed. Leo S Oldaki, Serenze: A Ciuria di*
Sergio Perosa, 1991.

CHAPTER IX

Recording Angels and Answering Machines

OURS IS AN AGE dominated by brand names and logos. It's surprising therefore to discover that some of the most famous of these identity signs hark back to the very beginning of the century. On second thoughts, perhaps this isn't so strange — the nineteenth century brought nationalism out from cover, and what is a flag or a national anthem but a working logo. It has been left to our own century (on its last millenial legs, so to speak) to give such code signs an international significance once more. The multinational corporation might be considered the reincarnation of the eighteenth century's universalism, best represented by the frontier-passing style of Italian music. 'Va, pensiero' is still sung at Italian football grounds but we are far from the time when the name Verdi suggested 'Viva Emmanuele, Re d'Italia'. This is the age of Mozart, of Italia in Germania, international casts, Salzburg Americans and discs of Herbert von Karajan on special offer from Kidderminster to Kamchatka. I bring music into this since music is even more metaphorical than literature, and because the most potent signs I know are the celebrated logos owned by the great recording companies. They, too, date from the beginning of the century, being typical entrepreneurial oddities of a bustling new mechanical age. First there is the Dog and Trumpet, the most idiosyncratic of all, with Nipper the fox-terrier, his head in the gramophone's trumpet, listening to His Master's Voice. Then The Recording Angel, a rather Kensington Gardens putto sitting on a disc and tracing its grooves with a stylus. Finally, there are two large-scale tied semi-quavers, called Magic Notes.

All these now belong to EMI, but they were rivals at one time, serving The Gramophone Company and the strangely-named Columbia Graphophone Company. I forbear to extend this musical signposting to other recording firms, to Decca, Deutsche Grammophon, Hyperion etc. The ones I have mentioned will suffice for my purpose, which is to help me focus on poetry in what one might describe, violin-like, as its first position.

That is, on the human voice itself. We have come a long way since poetry was the province of the bard, harp-accompanied, relating stories of war and honour. I, for one, admit to being relieved that the poetry I care most about is anchored firmly on the page. Though the paradox of oral poetry's having invented highly elaborate forms apparently *sui generis* has to be faced, I feel confident in believing that the flux of excitement in Donne, Browning and Wallace Stevens owes much to the complication permitted by unimprovisational methods and the mass-printing of the result. Nevertheless, to a greater extent than prose, poetry has not succeeded in purging itself of its shadow cabinet of voices. Much which seems objective is, in an unproveable sense, subjective.

If we concentrate for a moment on Nipper and His Master's Voice, we may approach one of the mysteries of poetry as performance. The dog is responding to a familiar tone, but being a dog he can't know what his master is saying to him unless it is something he has learned to respond to before. Although we, more than Nipper, want to learn new things from the literary voices which speak to us, we cannot do so unless they tell us what we already know and so give us a point of departure for the new. Poetry has always shown a fondness for the aphoristic mode, the parcelling-up of information and feeling in structures easily remembered and shaped by the Pleasure Principle. Where does the authority of literary utterance lie? Or, to put it another way, why are we like Nipper in not fully understanding what is being said while immediately recognizing the annunciating voice? I exaggerate, of course, but do so to stress that shock of recognition precedes enlightenment by cognition. Eliot's suggestion that a poem may communicate before it is understood might be extended to proposing that it is never completely understood at all. It only becomes more familiar. Also, paradoxically, the power of the arbitrary — and I am certain that part of the authority of poetry resides in its arbitrariness — is heightened by the way it deflects expectation from the known and wanted pattern. Sonic art where all the coordinates are unfamiliar, however, would not be art but noise. What Nipper listens to are sounds, not noise — you can tell that by his concentration and the poise of his ears. At the beginning of childhood, we learn the meaning of language largely through the attractions of the rhythmic and melodic patterns which words make.

I'm not suggesting that nursery rhymes for instance are just mnemonic devices; many of them were conceived for now-forgotten satirical and political purposes, and survive as attractive sequences. Time alters literary signposts and demotes even sententiousness to the minor duty of reassurance. Only the generalized satire in *Gulliver's Travels* is recognized by most modern readers, and Lilliput has become the domain of children. What is unchanged is the voice of Jonathan Swift. But children, once past the amniotic delights of words as sound patterns, go on to school and learn meanings. They usually start to read poetry some way into their formal teaching, and this means that they either wonder why it isn't straightforward ideas-carrying stuff, or they sanctify it as if it were essentially liturgical or perhaps some species of deep-thinking like philosophy. In fact, what they are hearing are their ancestral voices, not invariably prophesying war. It would be happier for all of us if we could continue to respond to poetry as Nipper did to His Master's Voice. I find that there is a voice inhabiting every poem in some way or other: from the apparently 'given' tone of description or proverbial wisdom (the Voice of God perhaps) to the identifiable voice of the speaker in a Browning monologue.

Before attempting a few light classifications of the voices which that sharp-eared listener, Caliban, might have heard on his island wired for sound — familiar reminders stand out, 'recondita armonia' and 'Hearing Secret Harmonies' — I should like to explore my other record logo a little, the Recording Angel, and merge it with the second device in the title of this lecture. When he was anxious to reassure himself and the ghost that he was truly serious about vengeance, Hamlet announced he would wipe from his mind 'all trivial fond records', though he remained the most haunted of analysands throughout the play. When he or any of us tries to find out what the Recording Angel has filed about us, the answer may be a brush-off or an oracular message on which not even the most anxious penitent could act. Everyone here must have winced when the click comes soon after the ringing tone, and our hoped-for interlocutor's voice pronounces 'I am not in at the moment, but if you would leave your name and your message, I'll get back to you as soon as I can. Please speak after the pips.' Such friendly monstrances underlie much poetry as well. From the Bible on to modern American Language Poetry we are frequently in receipt of highly sophisticated signals stored in answering machines. It is one of the responsibilities of poetry to discourage certainty, to act against the generic conveniences of philosophy. How much more attractive than snatches of The British Grenadiers or echoic arpeggiated chimes are the beautiful evasions of poetry.

I said before that we go to poetry to be told what we know already, but if the vaunted phrase 'Make it New' has any meaning beyond a polemical call-sign, it indicates that the familiar has another dimension, like the far side of the moon. Take, for instance, mankind's oldest habit — that of likening things, the method of metaphor. 'Odd that a thing is

most itself when likened', as Richard Wilbur put it. What happens when
the search for assurance is answered in poetry? I could give a thousand
answers in as many poems, but Wallace Stevens' 'The Motive for Metaphor'
is as good as any. The poem goes like this:

> You like it under the trees in autumn,
> Because everything is half dead.
> The wind moves like a cripple among the leaves
> And repeats words without meaning.
>
> In the same way you were happy in spring,
> With the half-colours of quarter-things,
> The slightly brighter sky, the melting clouds,
> The single bird, the obscure moon —
>
> The obscure moon lighting an obscure world
> Of things that would never be quite expressed,
> Where you yourself were never quite yourself
> And did not want nor have to be,
>
> Desiring the exhilaration of changes:
> The motive for metaphor, shrinking from
> The weight of primary noon,
> The A B C of being,
>
> The ruddy temper, the hammer
> Of red and blue, the hard sound —
> Steel against intimation — the sharp flash,
> The vital, arrogant, fatal dominant X.

The things we shrink from are the things we make poetry out of. In
another poem, Stevens asks 'How is it that/ The rivers shine and hold
their mirrors up,/ Like excellence collecting excellence'. This collecting of
excellence is the Recording Angel's work; it is going on everywhere in
nature and occurs in special ways in poetry. The millions of poems the
world has so far given rise to are all intimations which the steel of reality
is set against. Intimations are made in many different voices, and I shall
devote most of my time this afternoon to checking on them, trying to
find the locus from which various sorts of being may speak. If we would
listen carefully we should be able, as Caliban was, to hear all the island's

frequencies, not just the official announcements, the public concerts and the beguiling confessions.

In the play which contains to my mind Shakespeare's most orthodox achievement in blank verse — the epitome of iambic pentameter — *King Henry the Fifth*, some of the finest poetry is found in the speeches of the Chorus. A Chorus is an old and easily understood device. It is the equivalent of the editorializing voice of the author in a novel or set of essays. Shakespeare used the Chorus to enrich the paucity of his stage scenery, and to cover shifts in time and place. 'Think when we talk of horses that you see them/ Printing their proud hoofs i' the receiving earth' ... etc.... 'Turning the accomplishment of many years into an hourglass' ... and so on. But is it just that the Chorus insists that ''tis your thoughts that now must deck our kings', or is this out-in-the-open mouthpiece up to something else? Isn't he really giving us a glimpse of what happens all the time in poetry (and in much prose as well) — namely, language pretending that its choice among the available epithets of reality is reality itself, free of the bias of the observer and compiler? I don't want to rush this into absurdity: in practice we experience little difficulty in responding to the Chorus's evocation of the eve of the Battle of Agincourt. Yet we might ask ourselves, 'What is the point of view of the speaker?' I'll quote a part of the opening of Act Four, since I think that lectures usually include all too little poetry and because I relish this richest of blank verse, even if it has to be in my own voice.

> Now entertain conjecture of a time
> When creeping murmur and the poring dark
> Fills the wide vessel of the universe.
> From camp to camp, through the foul womb of night,
> The hum of either army stilly sounds,
> That the fix'd sentinels almost receive
> The secret whispers of each other's watch.
> Fire answers fire, and through their paly flames
> Each battle sees the other's umber'd face;
> Steed answers steed, in high and boastful neighs
> Piercing the night's dull ear; and from the tents
> The armourers, accomplishing the knights,
> With busy hammers closing rivets up,
> Give dreadful note of preparation.
> The country cocks do crow, the clocks do toll,
> And the third hour of drowsy morning name.
> Proud of their numbers, and secure in soul,

The confident and over-lusty French
Do the low-rated English play at dice;
And chide the cripple tardy-gaited night
Who, like a foul and ugly witch, doth limp
So tediously away. The poor condemned English,
Like sacrifices, by their watchful fires
Sit patiently, and inly ruminate
The morning's danger, and their gesture sad
Investing lank-lean cheeks and war-worn coats
Presenteth them unto the gazing moon
So many horrid ghosts.

That is half the Chorus's speech. He goes on to praise the king, telling of how cheering the English soldiers find a visit from this paladin, with his liberal eye, universal like the sun, giving them their 'little touch of Harry in the night'. This last almost Monty Python phrase crowns the partisan tone of the second part of the speech, but it's worth wondering what the first section does to our sense of expectation. The partisanship here is not predominantly that of English versus French, but of a Cecil B. deMille-type producer expending a lavish poetical budget on a nightpiece whose reality might well put the theatre patrons off. Shakespeare's command of realism misleads us beautifully: in telling the truth to our senses, he lies to our understanding. I wouldn't have it any other way — if you want the truth about war, you must fight in it and discover that any words further than the blankest and most communique-like will misrepresent it. Whatever one thinks of Yeats's attack on Wilfred Owen's war poetry — 'all blood, dirt and sucked sugar-stick' — there is no good reason to believe Owen's own assertion that the poetry is in the pity. He would have written very differently had that been the case. The poetry is in the language. And we are seeing at this moment, sadly, that the language of poetry cannot match computerized technology. High Tech wars drain all poetry from the world; they become video games leaving only charred bodies behind. Even Shakespeare could do nothing with Baghdad and smart bombs. The hard rule is that poetry has to be loyal to language, to Stevens's 'essential gaudiness.' Poetry was one of the consolations offered Adam and his partner after their expulsion from the garden. It was the rainbow of lies over Eden when the natural vision faded. Laertes, looking at mad Ophelia, noted that 'Thought and afflictions, passion, hell itself/ She turns to favour and to prettiness'.

At this point I can hear the voice of George Herbert, a poet whose genius might be said to derive from his passion for truth — and then also of Samuel Beckett whose progress was from an almost Yeatsian extravagance (I think Joyce is not to the point here) to the nothingness of his last-breath last works. Yet what all these have in common is a falsification which is built into language, and each knows that beauty alone will justify their efforts — or, if not beauty, at least some sort of pleasure in the shaping of truth beyond its commitment to right behaviour. It is exactly if not precisely the voice inside the words which we believe in, and which gives us the satisfaction we call art. A poem quite as much as a painting, a piece of sculpture or a musical composition is a made object — its difference from these other artworks lies in the raw material it is made from — language, words and their couplings, mere symbols, not their own creatures. Right from the start poetry has had to put up a fight against meaning which painting and music have hardly been bothered by. In our century we have made this battle the very subject of poetry. It isn't easy to take sides honestly: just as you are about to rejoice in a juicy collection of non sequiturs in one of John Ashbery's poems, the voice of conscience calls you back to the obligations not just of meaning but of emotional congruity. The long poetic career of W. H. Auden reveals a steady tug of conscience away from Edenic arbitrariness to a dour reticence made up of short views and trust in God. But the Old Adam isn't suppressed so easily — witness Auden's habit of fitting up his later verses with a special camp or nonce vocabulary. His lexical sweet tooth remains in danger of becoming carious, to borrow a phrase of Stravinsky's. But he loves to warn us of the dangers of poetical independence, which can so readily lead to showing-off and smugness. His poem 'September 1st, 1939' quickly became one of his most popular. Almost equally quickly it earned its author's distrust, especially the stanza which everyone loved to quote, and which Auden excised from the poem as soon as he could.

> All I have is a voice
> To undo the folded lie,
> The romantic lie in the brain
> Of the sensual man-in-the-street
> And the lie of Authority
> Whose buildings grope the sky:
> There is no such thing as the State
> And no one exists alone;
> Hunger allows no choice
> To the citizen or the police;
> We must love one another or die.

Ostensibly it was the last line which so offended the poet. That 'or die' should have been 'and die', he stated. I wonder though whether it wasn't the admission that all he had was a voice which stuck in Auden's throat. It is one of those boastful confessions poets love to make: we want to be contradicted or to be allowed to assert shyly that our voices are more important than Authority's buildings or the duties of citizens and policemen. The suppressor of this stanza is the Auden who found Pacifism dishonest and insisted on taking seriously his democratic duties of voting and doing jury service. But a poet can't turn his voice into that of a divine or a philosopher without surrendering his older oracular powers. The young Auden was certainly oracular — who is this new guy who's got into the landscape? Wyndham Lewis asked. The older Auden too reverted from time to time to warnings of a more paradoxical sort, as in the coda to his poem 'The Truest Poetry is the Most Feigning'.

> For given Man, by birth, by education,
> Imago Dei who forgot his station,
> The self-made creature who himself unmakes,
> The only creature ever made who fakes,
> With no more nature in his loving smile
> Than in his theories of a natural style,
> What but tall tales, the luck of verbal playing,
> Can trick his lying nature into saying
> That love, or truth in any serious sense,
> Like orthodoxy, is a reticence.

So, we are to attain Christian reserve by being playful — perhaps the only time Auden and Wallace Stevens might be thought to be speaking to the same text.

I said earlier that the battle between poetry's atavism and literature's responsibility has hotted up this century. Both Modernism (a fairly unclear concept) and Post Modernism (a desperately unclear one) seem to me centred on the problem of meaning — Voice versus Meaning is an aesthetic current running through poetry since Robert Browning. It may even be glimpsed in Pope's medium-length essay-poems: compare the prose advertisements which Pope sometimes appends to them. The poetry flows with the brilliance of a sonata-form exposition: it feels utterly convincing, the sound leading the sense by the hand. It is, however, as the advertisement makes plain, a daisy-chain of argument put forward with little logic beyond its rhetoric. I find this the case with the *Moral Essays* and *The Essay on*

Man, though not with the very early, perfectly crafted *Essay on Criticism.*
In Pope's mature poems it is the Voice of The Master to which the dog
is devoted, rather than the Master's message. Such anxiety can produce a
kind of poetic paralysis. Perhaps I may justify my quoting two lines of
my own poetry, by pleading my envious bafflement when reading modern
virtuosi of the opulently oblique.

> Wonderful for those who keep away
> from meaning, living somewhere better

That 'somewhere better' has always been with us, but only since Robert
Browning has it appeared in its secular self-sufficiency, not serving a larger
cause. So many elaborate contrivances, often wreathed in tendrils of
erudition, have been handed down to us by poets whose concern was to
promote a theology, a world view or a commanding orthodoxy. I admit
the case could be put the other way round: *Sir Gawain and the Green Knight*
and *Orlando Furioso* might appear to serve Christianity in order that they
can indulge in poetry. We have been warned very severely about this —
'don't read the Bible for its prose', we're admonished. Attitudes like Neville
Cardus's, who said that if he knew that his Redeemer liveth it was because
Handel had asserted the fact, seem very outdated and Manchester Liberal.
Yet I'm sure many of us wonder when we look at Pontormo's *Deposition*
in Santa Felicita, Florence, or listen to Josquin's setting of *Psalm 51* whether
their depth of feeling must of necessity spring from dogmatic conviction.
It is the service which counts: the reward for that service is a whole
society, vocabulary and range of reference from which artistic constructions
can be properly made.

   The voice of poetry up until the nineteenth century was a Christian
voice. It didn't matter too much how seriously the artist believed in his
theology; he had no alternative but to employ Christian language and
symbols. I don't think we should be nostalgic about this — I mean about
some of us having lost such certainty. I deplore the sort of seriousness
T. S. Eliot uses to reprimand Shakespeare's lines in *King Lear,* 'As flies to
wanton boys, are we to the gods;/ They kill us for their sport', when set
beside Dante's 'la sua voluntade è nostra pace'. To be fair, Eliot does not
make his comparison on poetic grounds but on philosophical ones. Even
so, I smell a sort of snobbery in his and Pound's elevation of Dante's
allegiance to an organic Christendom over Shakespeare's local and
proverbial loyalties. In practice, Shakespeare's plays rely on Europe's
classical inheritance and on the Bible as much as *The Divine Comedy* does:

think of the passage in *The Merchant of Venice* beginning 'When Jacob grazed his uncle Laban's sheep.' One could go on and cite Dante's Florentine spite as being more parochial than anything in Shakespeare. Shakespeare's fault for Eliot is his unwillingness to be prescriptive: he hears too many voices and speaks in too many accents to be trusted.

From the beginning of our verse, English poets have couched their poems in other men's and women's voices, but it is with Robert Browning that the monologue became dramatic and assumed the centre of the poetic arena. His practice tried not only to pack a whole play's dramatis personae into one usurping voice but also to allow that singleton to editorialize as it saw fit. This is to put a gloss on that view of the Browningesque monologue (and since Browning these have sprouted up everywhere) urging that it should be thought of as a key speech in a play which doesn't exist but which it creates around itself as ectoplasm. In his cruder moments we can see Browning lifting the stage directions up into the text — 'put up your torches .../ No more wine, then we'll push back our chairs and talk' ... and so on. But usually his technique is much subtler: he has led whole generations of poets to experiment by fitting analysis and criticism marsupially in their poems; Byron's 'Every poet his own Aristotle' almost achieved.

Browning's separation of the key speech from its context, implied or immersed, is, I believe, the basic technique which many contemporary poets employ. There is fairly general critical agreement that, despite his fondness for archaic diction and 'poetical' word-order, Browning is the father of Anglo-American Modernism. Pound thought so: Eliot kept off the subject, but relied heavily on Browning in poems such as *Prufrock* and *Gerontion*. However, the real revolution wrought by Browning was quieter than the noisy manoeuvrings of Pound. It wrested scope and seriousness from novel, play and biography — even from natural history — and gave it back to poetry. There was something to be done in poetry beyond satisfying the lyrical impulse, the sub-division of a whole landscape into its song lines, a task entrusted to *The Golden Treasury*. When the modern poet sits down to write he has Browning to thank for several circumstances which he probably takes for granted. Firstly, he can use any voice he pleases, and not necessarily have to identify it. Secondly, he can assume that the reader does not think that the world he evokes will be taken for objective reality. Thirdly, he can find his material anywhere, and weave it into his poem and so make it his own. The voice in modern poetry is tantamount to instant baptism: it makes poetical whatever it incorporates. It has no attitude to poetic stock; no preferred diction; and no prescribed ethical or aesthetic duty. Browning changed the coordinates by which poetry is recognized. Out went recitative and aria; in came the style the Germans call 'durchkomponiert', through composed, continuous melody. The chief gain was poetry's escape from a ghetto of appropriateness. The poet ate further down the table from the salt, but he ate more voraciously.

In Browning's hands the monologue becomes a Protean device, a path poetry may adopt to open the whole world to its investigations. There is no subject for which the poet cannot establish a relevant voice. From the one voice in charge of revelation come many voices, as Browning diversifies into highly complicated shapes. With his Tarnhelm on, Browning slithers into the various genres: 'Andrea del Sarto' (Vasari versified); 'Childe Roland to the Dark Tower Came' (bonsai ballad-opera); 'How It Strikes a Contemporary' (literary criticism); 'A Grammarian's Funeral' (literary theory); and the later 'Parleyings' (self-education as autobiography). One thing which strikes the reader of Browning each time he goes back to the poems is their bookishness. This is another reason for considering him the Father of Us All. Browning's English and Italian characters alike exhibit a convincing small-town worldliness, a conspiratorial scribblers' ambience, a freshly-coined opinionatedness. The world has been metamorphosed into talkative figures obliged to get everything down, and from all points of view. Apotheosis arrives with *The Ring and the Book*, that twelve-part *Rashomon*, suggesting that truth belongs to the garrulous. Browning satisfies the haranguer who is in each of us. The world turns into words. The Recording Angel becomes our Chief Soliloquizer, and the message on the Answering Machine is 'Keep Talking'.

Fashion has changed since Browning's day. So when we look for his influence in poetry written this century we might miss it, thwarted by his Victorian love of inclusiveness, of preferring connections to cryptic omissions. Even here we should note that a poet may be mysterious to the point of eschewing Victorian accountability and yet preserve a Victorian opulence — I am thinking of John Ashbery's extended poem, 'Self Portrait in a Convex Mirror'. This is the very model of the modern monologue, though its talking heads are hydra-like. They all sprout from one art-historical, philosophical neck. For all his shining New York stylishness, Ashbery might be called 'Le Browning de nos Jours'. He is as fond of writing about artists as Browning was. In 'Self Portrait', Parmigianino, for me and I guess for Ashbery as well the most technically accomplished painter who ever lived, is in and out of Ashbery's own distorting mirror. The I of the poem is that modern I (not spelled eye) which we are certainly not to conclude is the poet, but which must include him. The other pronouns are likely to fail an identity parade as well. As the self breaks up in dreams, so in Ashbery's poem the true voice of feeling becomes a feast of ventriloquism. Everything is explained, but then we add another word — *away*. One American critic has referred to the 'Self Portrait' as a mysterious and beautiful response to Whitman's invitation to American poets to loaf and invite their souls. But Parmigianino is more intellectual and more European than that and Ashbery's poem is too dandified to be Whitmanesque. What the mirror is to Parmigianino, the oil slick of associations is to Ashbery. You cannot get any deeper, you can only go wider. The soul can't accept all its invitations.

> The soul has to stay where it is,
> Even though restless, hearing raindrops at the pane,
> The sighing of autumn leaves thrashed by the wind,
> Longing to be free, outside, but it must stay
> Posing in this place. It must move
> As little as possible. This is what the portrait says.
> But there is in that gaze a combination
> Of tenderness, amusement and regret, so powerful
> In its restraint that one cannot look for long.
> The secret is too plain. The pity of it smarts,
> Makes hot tears spurt: that the soul is not a soul,
> Has no secret, is small, and it fits
> The hollow perfectly: its room, our moments of attention.
> That is the tune but there are no words.
> The words are only speculation
> (From the Latin speculum, mirror):
> They seek but cannot find the meaning of the music.
> We see only postures of the dream,
> Riders of the motion that swings the face
> Into view under evening skies, with no
> False disarray as proof of authenticity.
> But it is life englobed.
> One would like to stick one's hand
> Out of the globe, but its dimension,
> What carries it, will not allow it.

What I called the fight between Voice and Meaning is neatly placed in this passage (a characteristic of Ashbery is the way the passage seems self-sufficient but in fact is a small part of a long poem). In imagination and in inspiration — in the head or in the dream — you will find what Ashbery calls the tune. But on the page there are only the words. The meaning of the music will never, in any easy sense, be the meaning of the words. Which is why poets go on writing. They are musicians by other means. I have always been suspicious of analogies in the arts — poet as sculptor, frozen music, unacknowledged legislator etc. — but I do find a useful parallel in poetry's and music's use of thematic development. Also, I feel in my bones that music is the 'Ur-Kunst', the one from which all the others spring, despite its apparent late development as Europe's premier art. The bias in any sort of scale, even in a twelve-note row, is a musical strait-jacket equivalent to the poet's, who has to use symbols (words) invented for purposes more utilitarian than his. Both poet and musician have to put up with the paradox that their opportunities for extravagance are less good in these free-thinking times than they were when every artist had to appear to serve a cause beyond himself. But as Ashbery, Stevens, and a whole range of modern poets show, the need for disguises is as great as ever. Today's inquisitors, however, are the aestheticians and theorists.

It may seem to many who have followed me so far that I have been playing about irresponsibly with serious matters — nothing less than poetry's power to move its readers and listeners, and its duty to promote good and demote evil. Anybody on his feet on an occasion like this should try to imagine what Milton would think of the course of his argument. But that would be Milton the law-giver, moral revolutionary and republican polemicist. Milton the poet is another matter. Though they hold strong views, like any other member of the public, poets do not necessarily keep those views in sight when they sit down to write. They look to criticism to help them follow their own track, to trace the voices in their words. Critics, of course, would rather grade them like eggs. There is no help for this. Another poem of Ashbery's makes it clear that a poet may be aware that his performance sets up difficulties of tone and language. It's titled *Paradoxes and Oxymorons*.

> This poem is concerned with language on a very plain level.
> Look at it talking to you. You look out a window
> Or pretend to fidget. You have it but you don't have it.
> You miss it, it misses you. You miss each other.
>
> The poem is sad because it wants to be yours, and cannot.
> What's a plain level? It is that and other things,
> Bringing a system of them into play. Play?
> Well, actually, yes, but I consider play to be

A deeper outside thing, a dreamed role-pattern
As in the division of grace these long August days
Without proof. Open-ended. And before you know
It gets lost in the steam and chatter of typewriters.

It has been played once more. I think you exist only
To ease me into doing it, on your level, and then you aren't there
Or have adopted a different attitude. And the poem
Has set me softly down beside you. The poem is you.

Many people, myself included, find it tiresome that modern poets make
'the poem' the hero of their productions. But then we find ourselves doing
it. The reason is that we have so many voices in our heads and levels of
responsibility in our understanding, that we cannot be innocent listeners.
The very art we practise has taken over the role of nascent reality. It
would be good to see and hear things freshly, and perhaps we can only
do that if we recognize all the programmes we've been listening to, whether
we wish to recall them or not. As Stevens wrote, 'Tell X that speech is
not dirty silence/ Clarified. It is silence made still dirtier.' In Ashbery's
quatrains the poem which sits down next to his up-to-date Miss Muffet
will certainly frighten her away. To learn about the self is usually frightening.
It is hard to imagine any authorial disdain friendlier than Ashbery's. What
distinguishes him from many fellow domesticated Surrealists is the
authenticity of the material he makes his poems from. They are never the
sayings of a man in an isolation ward, though they do insist on being
heard in their own voice — that is, as interim statements, messages perhaps
intended for bottles. Behind his highly aesthetic surface, the real muddled
world of America lurks. But reality is judged as no more real than any
other verbal manifestation. If imagination, rather than reality is to be
celebrated, then the number of possibilities is limitless, and Ashbery is
deliberately inclusive, though not in the Victorian mode. He is unworried
by the most hair-raising of non-sequiturs. In another poem he reminds us
that the artist 'often ... finds/ He has omitted the thing he started out
to say/ In the first place ...'. To the eager anticipator of truth and beauty
the answer on the machine is likely to be something completely different.
The only thing a poem shouldn't be is less generous than its questioner.

One of the difficulties in talking about contemporary poetry seldom
gets aired in serious quarters. It is too close to the bone. Namely, that
we are too many, as Yeats observed. Reference books exist which list
more than 2,000 poets living and working in the English-speaking world

alone. The usual, perhaps the humane, if not the generous, reaction to this is to narrow the field to a workable canon, and to neglect everything else. After all, Jonathan Swift observed long ago, 'Say, Britain, could you ever boast/Three poets in an age at most.' The combination of intense competition among poets and an absence of any universally agreed style greatly emphasizes the individual voice. Again — and this will be the last time — I'd like to quote from one of my own poems:

> the trouble is the shock,
> too much talent in the world, it can't absorb
> its own creation; there are queues in Heaven
> as the million dreams fight to be born
> and troop before the face of vindication —

It was all very well for Auden to say that originality was the last thing he looked for in poetry — in practice he was not so reactionary. It might even be worth asking whether the craftsmen who carved the face of Chartres Cathedral were as anonymous in their own time as historians sometimes say they were. A lingua franca may help a great artist find his individual voice, not bury him beneath its uniform outlines. The point remains, though, that as the next millennium approaches, we have no way of authenticating new verse beyond the resonance set up in us by its personal accents. Discussion of technique, of historical necessity and of prevailing theory will continue, but the critic will have to be more of a talent-spotter than a quality control inspector.

In attempting to delineate the way voice underlies and subverts meaning in poetry I have found it easier to traverse what one might call the flats and maynes of the twentieth century than to dwell on the larger achievements of the past — other than one foray into Shakespeare and a dip into Browning. (As a momentary aside, it is worth stressing that Shakespeare has the most compellingly individual voice of all, despite his shadowy biography and his indifference to publication. The more cryptic his utterance the more personal his sound. Compare his sonnets with Sidney's *Astrophel and Stella*. The difference is between the gamiest Freudian case-history and Amateur Night in the Petrarchan Academy. Shakespeare's poet-hero is the Rat-Man of the High Renaissance.)

I want to end by examining two well-known poems from the past where I believe some enlightenment may come from considering the voice or voices which inhabit them. First, one of Wordsworth's lyrics, 'A Complaint.'

There is a change and I am poor;
Your love hath been, nor long ago,
A Fountain at my fond Heart's door,
Whose only business was to flow;
And flow it did; not taking heed
Of its own bounty, or my need.

What happy moments did I count!
Blessed was I then all bliss above!
Now, for this consecrated Fount
Of murmuring, sparkling, living love,
What have I? Shall I dare to tell?
A comfortless and hidden WELL.

A Well of love — it may be deep —
I trust it is, and never dry:
What matter? if the Waters sleep
In silence and obscurity.
Such change, and at the very door
Of my fond Heart, hath made me poor.

Not being a Wordsworth man, I first encountered this poem when a student in Perth Western Australia brought it to me and asked me what it meant. At first, it didn't seem difficult. I was sure that it was not a love poem in the usual sense. Nevertheless, it borrowed from that well-tried convention. I decided it was an affecting example of the love poem directed to a side of life all too little explored in poetry — collegiate loyalty, masculine sodality. Which gave it a pleasant irony if you considered that Browning was to set Wordsworth up as 'The Lost Leader' some years after this was written. But I was too lazy to discover who Wordsworth had in mind.

The tone and some of the locutions interested me, however. A sort of selfish grievance pervades the poem. There is no examination of why the fountain played for him in the first place. In this the similarity to an erotic love poem is strong — how dare you take away the bounty I've grown accustomed to. 'Whose only business was to flow' is a bit of cheek, though not taking heed of its own bounty or his need does seem more generous. The final couplet is hard to take if one wants to go on admiring Wordsworth. At no time does he take his mind off his own need. Such a fond heart as his might seem to others a rather greedy one. Lazy as I was, I suppose I knew he was writing about Coleridge. My question now is whether identifying Coleridge as the turned-off fountain makes any significant difference to one's reception of the poem. Beyond this, there is the whole question of the Theophrastian voice in poetry, and how far it underwrites any particular set of circumstances. Thus, if I sit down to compose a poem ostensibly descriptive of someone's inadequacy or felony, will I cunningly put myself in the right by adopting well-tried modes of accusation? Further off lurks the worry about all those pronouns poetry bristles with. The second person pronoun has a long history of evasiveness in the accusatory mouth of the first person pronoun, well before today's slippery lyrics. Yet my initial reaction to Wordsworth's poem was not significantly different from my more measured assessment once I'd read it up. Suspicion was there from the start. Like Nipper with his head in the trumpet, I could recognize something in this voice. Let me call it egotism, and perhaps pompous outrage.

My second poem is by a man who has one of the most distinctive voices in English verse — in fact, I think only Emily Dickinson's among non-dramatic poets is as singular and powerful — that is John Donne. Reading a Donne poem is an immediate test of what we mean by sincerity. Stravinsky's aphorism helps as a start. Sincerity, he wrote, is the *sine qua non* which proves nothing. All artists are sincere and bad artists are sincerely bad. Therefore plain speaking and baroque elaboration are two kinds of sincerity. Donne's *Holy Sonnets* are especially alarming in that their strident arguing is conducted within the poet's own mind: it is not yet ready to appear dressed up as public rhetoric. The polemicist who was eager to be a bought pen for King James in his battles with the Continental Counter Reformation here turns on himself intemperately. The voice is hysterical, as is the sense of guilt. I find Donne's *idee fixe* of sin a baroque narcotic which limits my taste for these poems. I was able to understand them better once I appreciated that they are not spiritual exercises after ordination but come from the restless period of his life when he was still hoping for court preferment and was fighting a losing battle against the drift, king-propelled, directing him towards a career in the clergy. But, internal as the accusation is, we know it is tooling-up for the senate of world opinion. Those overbearing sermons are just over the horizon. You feel that in a secular age Donne would have been just as tortured — his way to God is through extremity, indeed flamboyance. He has no straight way as Herbert has. Though I don't trust this poetic voice, I can luxuriate in it. Here is No. 13 of Donne's *Holy Sonnets*.

What if this present were the world's last night?
Mark in my heart, O Soul, where thou dost dwell,
The picture of Christ crucified, and tell
Whether that countenance can thee afright,
Tears in his eyes quench the amazing light,
Blood fills his frowns, which from his pierced head fell.
And can that tongue adjudge thee unto hell,
Which prayed forgiveness of his foes' fierce spite?
No, no; but as in my idolatry
I said to all my profane mistresses,
Beauty, of pity, foulness only is
A sign of rigour: so I say to thee,
To wicked spirits are horrid shapes assigned,
This beauteous form assures a piteous mind.

Is this what Empson called 'argufying' or is it a piece of holy writhing? I am as uncomfortable with Donne's tone as I am when in the presence of Bernini's Saint Teresa. It's funny how the baroque fits music more happily than it does poetry or the architectural arts. The final couplet is a candidate for Auden's excising pencil — surely it is a sort of lie. Would you buy a map of penitence from this man? Yet could anyone with the temerity to imitate Christ so fulsomely adopt a more effective manner of doing it? It was while reading Donne that I first appreciated that meaning is the method and voice is the message. Such an insight may be poor criticism, but it is a useful nudge to composition.

There is, as I have acknowledged all through this lecture, a world of seriousness which poets must serve which is not responsive to stylistic analysis. This is the harmonious world, the mathematical universe. It is largely deaf to poets' games and contrivances. You get a chilling glimpse of it in Rochester's brief translation of some lines from Lucretius.

The gods, by right of nature, must possess
An everlasting age of perfect peace;
Far off removed from us and our affairs;
Neither approached by dangers, or by cares;
Rich in themselves, to whom we cannot add;
Not pleased by good deeds, nor provoked by bad.

In the meantime, we serve an interventionist world, raising our voices and leaving messages for anyone who'll listen to them. I think again of Auden, parting from Stravinsky one night after much talk and drink; no doubt well past his usual bedtime. 'After all,' he remarked, 'we were put on this earth to make things'; His was the voice of poetry encouraging the voice of music.

1991: London. British Academy Lecture.

CHAPTER X

The Poet's Quarrel with Poetry

As a teenager being introduced to the wonders of Geometry, the kind of induction I still regard as having as much resonance as hearing prayers in church, I was especially struck by one of Euclid's methods of proving a theorem. Where the going was hard, Euclid liked to proceed by proposing the opposite of what he intended to prove, and then, in developing his argument, demonstrate that his proposal was absurd. Ipso facto, its opposite must be true and therefore his original contention could be established.

I am sure you expect me to do just the same tonight. I shall ingeniously argue my poet's distrust of the art I love and emerge with its bona fides properly in place. Perhaps I shall, but what I want to engage in on the way is a severe questioning of the value of Poetry itself, and rather more relevantly of how far its limitations (or our limitations) disappoint us in the struggle to attain true eloquence. Eloquence is not a word you hear much of these days. Again, to visit my childhood, I hear instead of 'eloquence' the nasty word 'elocution', a form of voice-training intended to rid us of whatever accents our mentors didn't like. Generations of Australians learned to utter sounds which would never have deceived the British, but which nicely brought-up locals took to be the lingua franca of middle-class communication. I missed out on 'elocution', and I am afraid that I have sometimes been cheated also of eloquence. The reason for this, I shall suggest, is through some crucial failure of nerve and imagination. And I shall endeavour to spread the blame for this on the limits of poetry and the questionable place it occupies in our hearts and minds.

The good news about poetry, which I learned at the very start, is that writing it comes as naturally as learning to swim. That is you learn it by doing it — by plunging in, by imitation and by comparison. Your tyro's efforts are quickly judged as hopeless, but at the same time you are acquiring by reading and listening to the real stuff — phrases, sentences, syntactical structures, whole poems, which stick in your mind. You don't know it but this is the soil in which all your later verse will be embedded. The lame creations of your apprenticeship are like the fallen leaves which rot around a plant.

They will nourish the good poems you are going to write. Cannibalism is natural in the arts. W.H. Auden spoke unhappily about that forlorn category of creation he called 'the fair notion fatally injured'. But unless you are Shakespeare or George Herbert you are going to need many of these "walking wounded" before you produce an Achilles or a General Marlborough.

That good news I just spoke of is the last good news the learning poet hears for quite a long time. He or she is doing, as the song says, what comes naturally, but soon begins to doubt the value of the process. Here poetry differs radically I believe from its sister arts. The composers, painters and sculptors seldom doubt the worth of their art, though they know that in the modern world it may prove difficult for them to make a living from it. What happens to poets is that a sort of blight, like rust in wheat, comes to settle on the rightness and excitement of their chosen form. Wordsworth's 'We poets in our youth begin in gladness/But thereof come in the end despondency and madness' lies further down the track. For modern poets it is the recognition that they practice a literary form which most people care nothing about which upsets them. And in many cases shuts them up entirely. There is much which can be said to chart the glory and power of poetry and I hope that I shall be doing just this at various points in this talk, but for the moment I wish to emphasise the poet's unhappy sense of being redundant in the world of letters.

People often enjoy a rare sodality because they write verse at university. They are usually reading English literature anyway, and the utility of poetry doesn't need to be questioned. They have a ready audience among their fellow-poets, and, as Robert Graves observed, this is the best challenge to invention and finest sharpener of wits. Coming down from university changes things. Soon these fledgling poets appreciate that in the world outside not many people read poetry and even fewer value it. It has become for most of their colleagues an old resource of truth and idealism which they no longer need. I have observed in mercantile situations and in journalism that while names are worth being familiar with — of painters, novelists, and even poets — the only art form which commands loyalty and interest is the cinema. The wastage rate of varsity poets must be over 90%. I remember watching a television programme when W.H. Auden, almost at the end of his career, was talking with his old friend Dick Crossman, a member of the British government at the time. Of course, Wystan, said Crossman, I used to write poetry when you and I were at

Oxford, but I gave it up for philosophy and politics. If I'd persisted I'd have been as successful a poet as you. Well, I suppose he might have.

But perhaps the hardest option awaits those who do keep on writing. There are many collateral advantages to being known as a poet — you will be invited to review books, to perform on TV and radio, to teach at Summer Schools and the like, and, sometimes, to represent in your person the poet's very calling. Rilke's rapturous seriousness permitted him to indulge in the higher cadging — a castle from a Princess here, and an exemption from civic responsibility there. American poets this century have evoked Edmund Wilson's 'Wound and the Bow' and made their lives into tableaux of sacrifice: you don't so much read their poems as hail their martyrdoms. None of this is what poets really want. They want to be read. It may be their own fault they're not, and I shall at least try to establish whether it is their professional doubts which have shown the public the way to doubt also. Before that, however, I must protest at the attitude of many other kinds of writers to poetry. Chiefly these indulge in lip-service to our higher calling but don't bother to read it. Poets have some special narrow uses, of course, they make excellent subjects for biographers and playwrights. I see that Tom Stoppard is the latest to take a poet into the dissecting room; he has specially created a dual personality for A. E. Housman. We are loved for our eccentricities if not for our verses — we're not even treated with the sort of respectful contempt Shakespeare has his Roman crowd give to Cinna the Poet — 'tear him for his bad verses.' I suggest that all who have written about the lives of poets should pay money into a central fund to finance struggling poets of our own time — think what the life of Byron would yield. The most commonly encountered question put at poetry readings is 'What is the purpose of poetry' to which the obvious answer is 'to provide novelists and playwrights with titles.' And that at least is a tribute to the one ability which nobody has ever doubted poets possess, a knack with the memorable phrase.

I now hasten to assure you that these observations are only a divergence from my more serious intention. If poets aren't devoted to their calling, there's no reason for anyone else to be. And they are, though being human they'd like a bit of the attention other literary practitioners enjoy. But a lifetime's loyalty may still leave the poet wondering at that very purpose which members of the public choose to air at question time. I have come up with a proposal as to why poetry seems difficult for readers of literature in general. In prose you can say that your main purpose is *telling*. In poetry it is *making*. A poem is analogous to a painting, a piece of sculpture or a musical composition. Its material is language, and often that language will be almost mosaically fitted together, with words as the pieces of the mosaic. A novel, an essay and a TV sit-com also use words but without the oppressive need to honour them outside their utility in conveying meaning and feeling. These are turbulent waters: poetry is charged with feeling and meaning also. But first it has to satisfy the shapeliness of its hope. This peculiar phrase is my version of the Platonic template. A poet is snagged with an idea, or *pace* William Carlos Williams, a mental disturbance which requires shaping into a poem. Neither I nor Plato believes that such a poem actually exists in a sort of refrigerated Pantheon somewhere beyond us, but we do believe that as we write the poem we pitch it both forward into existence and backwards to its need to exist. This need may be as strongly felt, even as polemical, as anyone's exhortation or harangue, but it isn't ultimately there to change somebody's mind or win a debate. A poem is a made object which is a reaction to a mental node. That must be one of the least attractive definitions in existence. But I mean it — all the poetry I love is potential energy come to rest. I read somewhere recently that Einstein said the universe consisted of energy slowing down to become matter. Most writing when it slows down ceases to exist. Poetry goes on existing.

There are a few popular observations which support this. The excitement of reading even such a galvanic masterpiece as Dostoyevesky's *The Idiot* is not fully renewable. It is not truly 'news that stays news.' But, Shakespeare's Sonnet No.90, the one which begins 'They that have power to hurt and will do none' can be read a thousand times and its 'charge' or mystery remains intact. Of course, I must modify what I have said already: I am doing injustice to great novels and plays in suggesting that they are cases of just *telling*. Clearly they are *making* also, but what is made is still not as lapidary as in a poem. Take even a long poem, *The Prelude* or *Paradise Lost* — surely these are poetic examples of those great shapes which Auden believed made the novel a bigger undertaking altogether than a poem. Yet the power and scope of these large-scale poems can be held to break down into local effects. Perhaps poetry cannot be poetry beyond a certain length, except as a cycle or linkage of poems. Shakespeare's plays and those of his finest contemporaries, especially Jonson, Webster, Middleton and Ford, give pause to this argument. Economy, force and drama are presented in great verse: here *telling* and *making* may be said to work together. But, as in opera, so many of the great speeches, and even the ensembles and exchanges in these plays, may be excerpted and live on as poems. My fondest iconoclasm is to doubt the organic unity of large masterpieces. I like doing biopsies on them. It could be my love of the well-shaped unit which gives rise to my impatience with poetry as an art.

I really want to claim size and authority, and therefore public admiration for poetry, while knowing that it is at its most complete when it does not ape the importance of novels and the here-and-nowness of journalism.

I have been playing fast and loose with a very idealised notion of poetry. After all it is supposed to serve a cause greater than itself — so many good judges have said so. And I don't want to be seen to be upholding art for art's sake. Yet that very tortuous seriousness, that moral wrestling which such poets as Milton, Wordsworth, Matthew Arnold, and T.S. Eliot have propounded, is not more poetical than the improvised naturalness of Skelton, Shakespeare (in part), Marvell and Rochester. Eventually, as the German told the American in the gay bar in Isherwood's Berlin, we are all serious. Except that he didn't say serious but 'queer'. I think we are both. I recommend to you an exchange of poetic creeds which has just come to my attention. Last year in Loughborough you had the Australian poet John Forbes with you as a writer-in-residence for one term. John died in Melbourne earlier this year at the untimely age of 47. He was a highly gifted individualistic poet. Ostensibly avant-garde, he was very nearly the best read man I have known, almost as knowledgeable as the late Ian Fletcher. In her funeral eulogy of him, his good friend the Melbourne poet Gig Ryan remembered that they had swapped definitions of poetry. 'Truth is the only eloquence she would say to him'. He would respond 'Eloquence is the only truth'. In general, the poet's seriousness suffers continuous diversion. I've been talking for quite a while and as yet I have not said more than a line or two of poetry. So I shall now read a short poem which demonstrates in a tangential way what I mean when I suggest that poetry can reveal more in a light way than critical argument can in a serious one. Here is the American poet Howard Nemerov considering that unswervingly serious subject American poetry itself.

His poem is called 'Strange Metamorphosis of Poets'.

> From epigram to epic is the course
> For riders of the American wingéd horse.
> They change both size and sex over the years,
> The voice grows deeper and the beard appears;
> Running for greatness they sweat away their salt,
> They start out Emily and wind up Walt.

A flimsy joke, you may conclude. But for me it is a chapter heading of my discomfort with the American sublime. Emily Dickinson was possibly the

most original poet in all of English Literature, and it might be unfair to
expect anyone to keep up with her. As Angus Wilson once remarked about
a model girl's dress sense — she could wear a teatowel and make it look
like the *dernier cri*. So Dickinson can dress in the shreds of colloquial discourse
and make poems of rare profundity. The lightness tells. Too much of
Whitman's intention is signalled in advance — we are meant to give him
points for his overreaching humanity and inclusiveness. He is as colloquial
as Dickinson but he also labours, as she never does. But I don't want to
criticise Whitman particularly: rather I like to see in Nemerov's poem that
polarity which I find all through American verse. Americans themselves have
played with antithetical notions such as 'Palefaces' and 'Redskins', as the
English sometimes do with 'Gentlemen' and 'Players'. I am happier with
'Emilys and Walts'. My pleasure grows when I meet an Emily (Nemerov
himself is one) and fades when a Walt hoves in sight (a long procession
these days from Olson to Jorie Graham, though she is a woman).

Quoting Nemerov reminds me that recently I encountered in a piece of
prose of his entitled 'The Measures of Poetry' a good depiction or metaphorical
argument concerning the impulse to produce poetry. Nemerov states

> ... the measure of poetry begins far from the particular
> conformation of the poem, far out in the sea of tradition
> and the mind, even in the physiological deeps, where some
> empty, echoing abstract interval begins to beat; it is the angle
> of incidence of this measure upon the materials of the poem
> which produces in the first place what in the result will be
> called 'form'. This tidal, surging element has to do with the
> general shape of the poem, and is a prior musical imposition
> on its thought — musical in that it exists at its beginning
> independently of any identifiable content: it is the power not
> the material which is transmitted. The poem is a quantity of
> force, expended, like any human action, and is therefore not
> altogether formless even to begin with, but limited in its
> cadence by the energies present at its generation. The rise
> of the shore shapes the wave. ... The laws of this measure
> are simple and large, so that in the scope of their generality
> room may remain for moments of freedom, moments of
> chaos; the complex conjunction itself raising up iridescences
> and fantastic shapes, relations which it may be that number
> alone could enrage into being.

Here Nemerov is putting in much more eloquent words what I worried about when I proposed that poetry was *making* while fiction and discourse were *telling*. The drawback for poets is that their chosen art form, as Nemerov's wave and sea instances make clear, often fails to satisfy their more rationally aroused ambitions. Put bluntly, poets, even if they have few delusions as fictioneers, may still have the desire to function as philosophers or politicians. They will then find that poetry is a Procrustean bed for the task. I don't mean that poets don't think or that they are at their best when they appear to be divine idiots. A whole book could be devoted to the misunderstanding of unreason and madness in literature. The *non sequitur* may have charms, but disjunct madness is tedious. Kingsley Amis has a character in one of his books object to madness because the mad have no sense of humour. Their whole world is awry — a sane person finds humour in specific and occasional awryness. The world of the mad has no singularities: so those Jacobean 'mad scenes' and their operatic descendants in operas by Bellini and Donizetti, or the Bedlam poem, *Jubilato Agno*, of Christopher Smart are not products of insanity, but of reasonable minds fighting delusion.

However, many poets are attracted to the overrational discipline of philosophy. At which point I say, it would be better if they weren't. There is a war between poetry and philosophy which is as fixed as the great war in Heaven between God and his angels and the Devil and his cohorts. Let me presume that Poetry is of the Devil's party. But also let me emphasise that the poet is as much a thinker as the philosopher is. But the poet thinks along lines which are not necessarily logical. Logic is only glue after all: it sticks thought together. Poetical glue is association, language affinities sometimes beyond meaning, and metrical and sound patterning insisting on being heard. So whatever the subject matter of a poem, its development may be divergent from what it would be in another form of expression. Poetry also is tied to specifically vocal techniques, and resembles a lawyer's plea in a court more than a philosopher's linear and logical exposition. Those wonderful long poems of Alexander Pope, such as *The Moral Essays*, are often prefaced by a prose advertisement telling the reader the line which the poetry is about to follow. In practice he does nothing of the sort: he lets poetry's magical adjacence direct him: only afterwards does he try to make it respectable by paraphrasing his performance in prose. In a poem written some years ago I set out a possible reason for the headlong method of poetic creation, a sort of rush by ideas and words to get themselves born. I called the poem, keeping the title in lower case, *attacca*, which is the Italian word in musical scores for pressing on immediately, leaving no time between sounds. This is the relevant passage:

>   ... the trouble is your shock,
>   too much talent in the world, it can't absorb
>   its own creation; there are queues in Heaven
>   as the million dreams fight to be born
>   and troop before the face of vindication —

Sometimes you find an odd perversity in your own structures — secretly you become attached to practices you have severe doubts about. I stated just now that poetry is in thrall to thinking as much as philosophy is and has its own sort of philosophical discourse. Where it differs from philosophy proper is in its insistence on luminosity in the language of its conjecturing. Some of the poets whose work most excites me have a love of abstraction mixed with materialism, which gives their work a unique glow. Their language is never voluptuous in the Swinburnian or Edith Sitwell sense, but it has a lean and hard resonance. I am thinking of Fulke Greville, John Ford, Browning (on occasion), Wallace Stevens and William Empson. Consider these lines from Act Four, Scene One, of Ford's play, *The Broken Heart*. Ithocles has just been rebuked for over-ambition, for too quick and greedy an apprehension of palpable pleasure. He replies:

>   Look'ee uncle:
>   Some such there are whose liberal contents
>   Swarm without care in every sort of plenty:
>   Who, after full repasts, can lay them down
>   To sleep; and they sleep, uncle, in which silence
>   Their very dreams present 'em choice of pleasures;
>   Pleasures — observe me, uncle — of rare object:
>   Here heaps of gold, there increments of honours,
>   Now change of garments, then the votes of people,
>   Anon varieties of beauties, courting
>   In flatteries of the night, exchange of dalliance;
>   Yet these are still but dreams. Give me felicity
>   Of which my senses waking are partakers,
>   A real, visible, material happiness;
>   And then too, when I stagger in expectance
>   Of the least comfort that can cherish life.

Isn't this a very unmystical approach to worldly advantage expressed in supercharged legal language. The whole of *The Broken Heart* is the best representation I know before William Empson of language pre-empting feeling, of an incandescence of means rather than a servicing of character. My admiration for Ford's poetry, my conviction that his is among the most extraordinary feats of the empowering of language led me to write a poem honouring him. T.S. Eliot has an excellent essay on Ford in his collection *Elizabethan Dramatists*. Though I enjoy Eliot's essay, I took exception to his case against Ford and called my poem 'John Ford Answers T.S. Eliot'.

This is part of it:

> Why, three hundred years ahead of me,
> you should commend me for belief in love
> eludes me. What is there else to write of?
> ...
> You are a Psalmist doing without the smell
> of burning flesh. Good and evil mixed, you say,
> is not the way to justify a knack
> with cadencing, and further, I make occasion
> fill the cast list. And here you're wrong
> since you resort so often to that arid
> concept 'character'. Brutish husbands, vengeful lovers
> are simply steeds the words can ride — if every
> speaker were the same at each intrusion
> on a sentence, then personae might make character —
> instead, I write the only poetry
> the broken heart has known — not sympathy
> for this or that distracted humanoid
> but palaces and obelisks and tombs
> of diction, and I set before you shapes
> with names and callings, sub-contract them to
> a place of some malignity and then
> I watch. As they come into focus, syntax
> stirs and seeks its opportunity:
> for this the human race was made, to build
> its only lasting Babel, rusticate
> the puffed-up feelings and the blemishes
> of tragic pity. I have the instrument
> to deal with ruined love — to outlast thought
> by being before thought what it would say.

I can't guess whether anyone will judge this poem a good criticism of John Ford's style, but it is certainly relevant to my argument. I may move one word in my lecture's title — 'quarrel' — and perhaps replace it with another — 'disappointment'. Not that poetry disappoints in itself, but that it does so as a tool of persuasion, and vehicle of immediate feeling. Here, it seems to me, poetry is poised between the instant arousal of storytelling and the abstract immediacy of music. I have written several times about music's superiority to all the other arts — so often, in fact, I expect to be expelled from the Poets' Union, or at least be told I am 'off message' by its spin-doctors.

I once described poetry as 'a modest art'. I couldn't understand why so many poets disliked that description. Perhaps as a species we resent our low rating among our countrymen. Much of what I've said already implies that I am envious of the standing and rewards other kinds of writers enjoy. Perhaps poets are looking forward to posthumous glory, to being vindicated by the staying-power of their work. They could be taking Shelley's 'unacknowledged legislators' at face value. I would never say that poetry is a diminutive art, an unimportant art, a negligible art or, as Yeats did, a lying art. By modest I mean it breaks down grandeur into constituent parts, that for all its seriousness it keeps its nose in Blake's 'minute particulars'. Vladimir Horowitz, demon virtuoso at home with the flamboyance of Franz Liszt, none the less found these words for Domenico Scarlatti — also a virtuoso but a perfect example of the profound modesty I believe resides in poetry. Better, said Horowitz, 'grosse Kleinkunst' than 'kleine Grosskunst' — better great Little Art than little Great Art!

I have already doubted the organic unity of large masterpieces. I'll go further and suggest that it is lusting after 'greatness' — at least in its presumptuous forms — that is characteristic of much which has gone wrong in poetry this century. For Eliot and many others poetry's loss of its allegiance to Christendom has been the cause of its inflation. But there is plenty of inflated Christian art. Poetry has never found it as easy to aspire to the 'colossal' as music does. After Wagner size became a virtue in itself. So did overreaching. I would not want to portray Modernism as size-obsessed. Some of its pioneers were definitely 'Grosse Kleinkunst' specialists. But size has another concomitant — transcendence. And here I think Eliot, with his Classical and Religious orthodoxy, may be correct — especially when the original ideal possessed a transcendence established over many centuries. Nationalism, History, Pantheism, Aesthetic Beauty will all rush in when God moves out. The most peculiar example of this secular transcendence I can think of is the sequence of *Maximus Poems* by

Charles Olson. Transcendence has been an American concern since the time of Emerson, and Olson's huge agglomeration of poetic data is set in Transcendentalism's home, New England — chiefly in the fishing port of Gloucester, Massachusetts, site also of Kipling's *Captains Courageous*. I doubt that *Maximus* is much read today, but I think it has many poetic moments in it. It stands in my argument here for the unhappy effect of the colossal when its cause doesn't suit it. In Olson's case the cause is a mixture of Pantheism and American self-identification. America is a big place and the settlement of its vast land mass is paralleled in Olson's poem by his words opening up and expanding across a geographic and historic tabula rasa.

A strange paradox is built into much avant-garde poetry, namely that it intends universalism and an uncompromising seriousness while it insists on living in an Arcanum where the ordinary public is treated as a trespasser. The Cambridge School of Poets, whose usually acknowledged leader is J.H. Prynne, prides itself on an aloofness which rejects not just all poets who are not adepts but also most of the audience of readers in Britain. I have heard this encampment of poets described as the only authentic avant-garde left in the world. Elsewhere hermetic experiment has been swallowed up in the chic of 'Post-Modernism'. I can see why individual writers might experiment — indeed I admire many uncompromising souls who do just that — but I can never feel warmly towards a corps of experimenters, especially when it arrogantly refuses recognition to more traditional or successful rivals. Uttering the name 'Heaney' in Cambridge would probably clear the room. Which reminds me of another of Auden's observations, that 'the only thing which never changes is the avant-garde.' At a more serious level let me propose that much of what any avant-garde attempts is by definition that which cannot be done.

And this brings me back to my lecture theme, which I am again moderating; moving from "disappointment" to "discontent". I may settle with this abstraction from now on. Discontent is a very rich word. It implies the feeling of Adam after expulsion from Eden: he is not exactly cold, wet and hungry; he has been given choice; sex bothers him and his spouse but it also excites him, as perhaps it didn't while he was in Paradise; above all he is anxious, and no matter what good fortune beckons beyond the horizon, he knows he will have to die. The poet, for his or her part, knows that every achievement is but one stepping-stone further into an uncrossable river. Before this metaphor gets hopelessly out of hand, I shall try to bring it back from what must be a generalization about all human endeavour to specifics about poetry. Those stepping-stones are part of the trouble. They often seem too small, the wrong shape, too slippery, badly placed, and to be heading off in a questionable direction. Sigmund Freud believed that our various neurotic ills are precisely the miseries attendant on our most noble attainment — civilization. His 1930 book *Das Unbehagen in der Kultur* was given an inspired English translation, *Civilisation and its Discontents*. Freud chose 'Unbehagen', literally 'disagreeable' or 'uncomfortable' instead of the more usual 'unbefrieden' but Joan Rivière, his translator, got it right.

We are more than uncomfortable in our mental dress; we are, however timorously, Promethean. Discontent was held to be Divine in an old definition of Christian virtue. It is this discontent which both measures the frustration of the poet and also drives him or her towards creation. I shall quote from Howard Nemerov again. His poem 'Casting' is like one of those tense and quizzical Renaissance emblems.

> The waters deep, the waters dark,
> Reflect the seekers, hide the sought,
> Whether in water or in air to drown.
> Between them curls the silver spark,
> Barbed, baited, waiting, of a thought —
> Which in the world is upside down,
> The fish hook or the question mark?

Those stepping stones I just mentioned are our cause of disquiet. They are the forms which imagination must troop to if it is to cross over into poetry. It is late in the day to attempt to offer a rationale of form in poetry. Nor will any brow-furrowing about why we should, in Pound's words, 'make it new' lead to enlightenment. In each generation much of what the poet has in his mind is 'given'. Style itself may be argued about but is easily felt in practice. The Age doesn't demand any sort of allegiance, it merely subsumes and provides. I can't tell anyone — and believe me, in talking to students and aspirant poets I have had to attempt it — why you can't compose a poem today in the language and manner of John Keats. "O soft embalmer of the still midnight" is as fresh today as it was in 1820, but my or your sonnet written as lushly as Keats's would be fustian. Genius is Keats's preservative — maybe not for ever, but rather better than any gruesome mummification. Styles can be updated, the charming word 'pastiche' speaks of this. But such retreading of the past can too easily smack of knowingness. Eliot's observation that we know more than they did in the past precisely because they, the past, are what we know is also a warning. Imagination's flow can disperse itself uselessly through a delta of familiarity, of example and of erudition. Standing against that is poetry's duty to be proverbial, to sum up and to sing in our ears as the noises of his isle did in Caliban's — always, whatever their birth in pain and despondency, to return as sounds 'which give delight and hurt not'. I take a lecture to be a licensed time for a poet to try out some verses which have found no favour elsewhere. I have a poem of this name — i.e. 'That Give Delight and Hurt Not'. It goes like this.

> When Christina Rossetti, that gentle Italian lady
> Who loved the Anglican God,
> Was dying of cancer, her faith couldn't tame her body
> And her screams went abroad
> Wider than her fame to upset her neighbours —
> Thus many said her agony was imitative of her Saviour's.
>
> Apparently none of the mercantile pious understood
> That the heavenly listening post
> Which picks up signals through space and cloud
> Recycles them for the Lord of Hosts
> To hear as acceptable homage, a depiction
> As comfortably harmonized as Stainer's *Crucifixion*.

Now that is probably too knowing, and I am being unfair to Stainer who was an honest craftsman, and I certainly mean no disrespect to Christina Rossetti, a poet whose command of formality is an example to us all. But it may direct us to two doctrines which Auden liked to propound. Firstly, Dr. Johnson's dictum that the only end of writing is to enable readers better to enjoy life or better to endure it. Then his own statement that poetry makes nothing happen and his works had not saved a single Jew. But who would have expected them to? Literature can make things happen — but not usually the things we'd like it to, and not powerfully enough. The joy of poetry is in its writing and then in its being recognized. By recognized I don't mean praised and rewarded, but felt and seen by the person who reads it as both pleasurable and true. In *Siegfried*, the third of the operas in Wagner's *Der Ring des Nibelungen*, the pure-minded innocent Siegfried, after having killed the dragon Fafner, tastes its blood and immediately can understand the song of the Woodbird which he has been listening to but previously could not understand. The bird's song tells him of his own history and of the maid Brunnhilde who awaits him on the fire-ringed mountaintop. This is a good metaphor for the operation of

poetry, or indeed of any art. It is beauty, artistry, the love of the comely
which teaches us our role on earth. And the poet is rewarded for his skill
by the enjoyment he gets in its operation.

I am becoming almost Pelagian, so I must retreat a little. Since I am
known as an admirer of Auden — I was described in an Italian anthology
once as 'uno seguace di W.H. Auden' — I should like to take up another
of his assertions and alter it a little in the process. In that great poem
'The Shield of Achilles' he states of the poor and helpless of this world,
'They could not hope for help and no help came.' I used the sentence
'And No Help Came' as a title of the following brief poem.

> Where would you look for blessing who are caught
> In published acres of millennia
> By ravishments of salt and raucous saints
> Or janissaries drilling a Big Bang?
> The parish of the poor you'd seek, far from
> The high grandstands of words and notes and paints.
>
> And when you drove your flagged and honking jeep
> Among the huts of starving brutalized
> Dependants, you might chance to hear them playing
> Sentimental songs of flowers and moons
> Chiefly to keep them safe from art, whose gods
> Build palaces adorned with scenes of flaying.

Thus every art, including poetry, is wanton in its choice of subject. Who
would clean up after *Hamlet* or *King Lear* if the events in the plays were
happening in real life? Poets must, if they are honest, accept their own
selfishness and the advantages the world's disquiet offers them. They too
are among the world's victims. Their dilemma is not so much that they
cannot change things but that they are profiting from the universal instinct
to turn unhappiness into memorable art. If I were devoted to bringing
about radical improvement in the world I probably wouldn't have any time
to give to poetry — so Lenin and Marx believed despite being fond of
poetry and music. Things are not as bad as this in practice: poets may
still be radical politicians and even warriors. But their poetry will be
tangential to their politics, not necessarily an arm of it.

Have I categorized by now the restlessness of poets — see I've changed
my term yet again — or have I done no more than reflect on time's
inexorable flow and the short lifespan of humans? I can imagine a large
theme which surfaces under the rubric 'The Survival of Poetry'. Why do

so many of us, from such different backgrounds and with so various an assortment of temperaments, remain devoted to the writing of poetry? We are seldom kind to each other, though we may practise a species of camaraderie — rather like those who served in the trenches. Perhaps we have something to follow, some duty to observe greater than our own fame. Perhaps this folly we have persisted in is as inspiring as God, Philosophy and Science. Is Wallace Stevens's 'Supreme Fiction' the latter-day equivalent of Plato's pre-emptive felicity? There are warnings in the offing. Stravinsky declared that turning aesthetics into a religion leads to terrible vulgarity, and pointed to Wagner's *Parsifal* to make his point. But he also said that we should praise God with a little art if we have any, and who knows which comes first, Art or God?

To end this discursive performance, I've chosen three poems or passages of verse which highlight the turbulence poetry can produce. They are moving towards a credo for poetry. They belong to the less pompous end of the quarrel I started out with. First, here is Emily Dickinson considering the introspective force which lies behind the urge to speculate. Such an utterly original craftsman as Dickinson would be bound to choose poetry rather than philosophy. This is No 501 in her *Collected Poems*.

> This World is not Conclusion.
> A Species stands beyond —
> Invisible, as Music —
> But Positive, as Sound —
> It beckons, and it baffles —
> Philosophy — don't know —
> And through a Riddle, at the last —
> Sagacity, must go —
> To guess it, puzzles scholars —
> To gain it, Men have borne
> Contempt of Generations
> And Crucifixion, shown —
> Faith slips — and laughs, and rallies —
> Blushes, if any see —
> Plucks at a twig of Evidence —
> And asks a Vane, the way —
> Much Gesture, from the Pulpit —
> Strong Hallelujahs roll —
> Narcotics cannot still the Tooth
> That nibbles at the Soul —

I don't perceive much support for religion in this poem. It hymns the
restlessness of human inquiry, and seems to locate it in poetry itself. Now
another American, John Ashbery. I won't deny that he can be obscure.
He is usually pleasurable as well, and highly playful. This poem purports
to be a recipe for making a poem. Rather strange ingredients are called
for. Its title is 'And *Ut Pictura Poesis* Is Her Name'. The Latin is from
Horace, from his *Art of Poetry* where he discusses what pictorial subjects
go well in verse. These are extracts, not the whole poem.

> You can't say it that way any more.
> Bothered about beauty you have to
> Come out into the open, into a clearing
> And rest.
>   ... Now
> About what to put in your poem-painting:
> Flowers are always nice, particularly delphinium.
> Names of boys you once knew and their sleds,
> Skyrockets are good — do they still exist?
> There are a lot of other things of the same quality
> As those I've mentioned. Now one must
> Find a few important words, and a lot of low-keyed,
> Dull-sounding ones. She approached me
> About buying her desk. Suddenly the street was
> Bananas and the clangour of Japanese instruments.
> Humdrum testaments were scattered around. His head
> Locked into mine. We were a seesaw. Something
> Ought to be written about how this affects
> You when you write poetry:
> The extreme austerity of an almost empty mind
> Colliding with the lush, Rousseau-like foliage of its desire to
> communicate
> Something between breaths, if only for the sake
> Of others and their desire to understand you and desert you
> For other centers of communication, so that understanding
> May begin, and in doing so be undone.

If you read this poem several times, it slowly darkens and becomes a
description of the depression and pessimism involved in writing poetry.
To write a poem is a privilege, and may be a pleasure, but is never easy.
The longer the process goes on, and the more poems accrue, the greater

the doubt and anxiety of poets about their craft. Now, here is Shakespeare
to end. The most accomplished poet who ever lived. Also the most various.
I've selected a little-known passage from early in his career. It demonstrates
that while poetry claims to serve other masters it really attends to itself.
In *Two Gentlemen of Verona* one of the characters, Proteus, describes the
power of poetry in the voice of a lover. Bear in mind what Shakespeare
must have intended by calling his man Proteus. There is shape-changing
going on here; poetry is wooing itself.

> Say that upon the alter of her beauty
> You sacrifice your tears, your sighs, your heart.
> Write till your ink be dry, and with your tears
> Moist it again, and frame some feeling line
> That may discover such integrity.
> For Orpheus' lute was strung with poets' sinews,
> Whose golden touch could soften steel and stones,
> Make tigers tame, and huge leviathans
> Forsake unsounded deeps to dance on sands.
> After your dire-lamenting elegies,
> Visit by night your lady's chamber window
> With some sweet consort. To their instruments
> Tune a deploring dump; the night's dead silence
> Will well become such sweet-complaining grievance,
> This, or else nothing, will inherit her.

So Orpheus, Arion, Ariel and the rest are working for us poets. Much I
have said may strike you as cynical. But I mean it to be reassuring. As
Thomas Hardy wrote, 'if way to the Better there be, it exacts a full look
at the Worst'. Poets may even be helped in creativity by dissatisfaction
(this is my last change of term) with their means and method. I shall feel
I've done some good if I persuade anyone who does not know the poetry
of Howard Nemerov to read it. And I ask you to persist in general with
this superannuated art which at least is not the servant of coercion and
untruth.

1998: Loughborough University. Second Annual John Lucas Lecture.

CHAPTER XI

A Place Dependent on Ourselves
Poetry and Materialism

Most of us come back to one poet through our lives, not only in appreciation and for pleasure, but almost as irresistibly, in bafflement. For me this poet is Wallace Stevens. He is, in straightforward terms, a difficult writer and difficult in a modern way. I find all philosophy difficult, from the Greeks through to today's practitioners. I still find some poets difficult, but not in the same manner that philosophers are. Sheltering under a comforting umbrella of arrogance, I don't feel guilty at not understanding philosophers, since I don't enjoy them either, except for the more gamey aphorists. You might even say that Pascal, Lichtenberg and Nietzsche are poets whose assemblies of *non sequiturs* are like the end-stopped mood-pictures of the Chinese Poets of the T'ang Dynasty. They are players of anti-dominoes, and their motto is 'never connect'. These are the only philosophers for me. Except for Stevens, there are no great poets who are too difficult to understand. Many contemporary poets are obscure beyond elucidation — a good example would be Jeremy Prynne — though it is more worrying that they are all too often not enjoyable. If like me you are inclined to plead the attractions of the arbitrary at the expense of the consequent, then you may still recognize that pleasure in any art finally depends on its making sense.

Fortunately language was invented to convey meaning, with the result that it's hard to write a meaningless sentence or even concoct an unsyntactical arrangement of words which will maintain its randomness no matter how you look at it. For this reason, some contemporary poetry — especially Language Poetry — has to be carefully composed so that it may remain meaningless. And, of course, meaninglessness is not the same as obscurity. A speech in Shakespeare's *Troilus and Cressida* or a passage in Rabelais may seem obscure but can be elucidated if you put your mind to it. I'd like to find a comparison among great poets. John Milton remains difficult but not quite in the way that Wallace Stevens is. Before broaching the main topic of this lecture, which is advertised in my sub-title, *Poetry and Materialism*, I will just compare a passage from Milton with one from Stevens.

Firstly, this from *Lycidas*.

> O fountain Arethuse, and thou honoured flood,
> Smooth-sliding Mincius, crowned with vocal reeds,
> That strain I heard was of a higher mood:
> But now my Oat proceeds,
> And listens to the herald of the sea
> That came in Neptune's plea,
> He asked the waves, and asked the felon winds,
> What hard mishap hath doomed this gentle swain?
> And questioned every gust of rugged wings
> That blows from off each beaked promontory;
> They knew not of his story,
> And sage Hippotades their answer brings,
> That not a blast was from his dungeon strayed,
> The air was calm, and on the level brine,
> Sleek Panope with all her sisters played.
> It was that fatal and perfidious bark
> Built in th' eclipse, and rigged with curses dark,
> That sunk so low that sacred head of thine.

I'm not going to attempt to gloss this: you can find eloquent annotations in a dozen editions. All I need to say for my present purpose is that in lamenting his friend's early death by drowning in the Irish Sea, Milton evokes many figures from the Classics, often in their least familiar guise, and exclaims the pity of their not being there to raise a proper lamentation. The passage about 'eclipse' is more difficult, but probably refers to the Fall of Man. Now consider this excerpt from Wallace Stevens's *Notes Towards a Supreme Fiction*.

> A dead shepherd brought tremendous chords from hell
> And bade the sheep carouse. Or so they said.
> Children in love with them brought early flowers
> And scattered them about, no two alike.

(IV)

> We reason of these things with later reason
> And we make of what we see, what we see clearly
> And have seen, a place dependent on ourselves.

This is a very short extract from rather a long poem — one where Stevens shifts his examples almost from stanza to stanza, offering only what I would call free association of ideas — certainly no progressive logic in the development of his argument — if indeed there is an argument. There is a resemblance to Milton however, but it is not in richness of language, rather it is in the glory of irrelevance. Stevens, who wrote of poetry needing 'essential gaudiness', is pretty chaste in his diction at this point. What is shared is the poet's equally essential need to follow the tread of language rather than the thread of meaning. I understand this part of the poem to refer to Jesus Christ and his ambiguous message to Christians — hope of eternity and transcendence, and yet love of the quotidian and straightforward, with an extension to the usually Protestant notion that every human being is a separate soul with a separate claim to God's love and the Recording Angel's bookkeeping. Christianity is this 'later reason' which we follow, interpreting the original events the Master survived when he brought his 'tremendous chords from hell; and then comes the truly unexpected addition: everything, including the magnificence of heaven and hell, is to happen here, in 'a place dependent on ourselves'. Stevens does not say that Man made God, but he wants us to recognise that God may have no existence outside our knowledge of him. He is stuck with us, inside our materialist imagination.

At this point I try to play, if not quite the philosopher, then the unswerving monitor of ethics. Stevens's 'Supreme Fiction' poem is about all sorts of things, but to keep to just the passage I have quoted, then we may ask, 'if you want to write about the inheritance of Christianity, why do it in this roundabout and obscure way?' Forgetting for the moment that my idea of what Stevens is up to might be well off course — for instance the protagonist might be Orpheus, not Jesus — then the answer to that question may still be that all roads lead to Rome, and Poetry, eldest daughter of literature, keeps to the scenic route. For an overwhelming conviction, such as God's presence, then all of Nature must be evidence. Wallace Stevens's poetry, though formally as well as voluptuously ordered, is a constant materialist testimony to existence. Elsewhere he has written, in one of his most famous passages, from 'Esthetique du Mal'.

> The greatest poverty is not to live
> In a physical world, to feel that one's desire
> Is too difficult to tell from despair. Perhaps,
> After death, the non-physical people, in paradise,
> Itself non-physical, may by chance, observe
> The green corn gleaming and experience
> The minor of what we feel.

which continues at the poem's end:

> One might have thought of sight, but who could think
> Of what it sees, for all the ill it sees?
> Speech found the ear, for all the evil sound,
> But the dark italics it could not propound.
> And out of what one sees and hears and out
> Of what one feels, who could have thought to make
> So many selves, so many sensuous worlds,
> As if the air, the mid-day air, was swarming
> With the metaphysical changes that occur
> Merely in living as and when we live.

Stevens is not the first and will not be the last to resort to physicality, and rather used-up traditional physicality at that, when thinking about Heaven. Once I was pulled up in my tracks while reading a remarkable book about Heaven and our notions of it, all the way from those who don't have it — the Jews — to those who have too much of it — the songwriters and the Christian Apocalyptics. I'd reached the Swedenborgians whose Heaven is as 'down-to-earth' as the rules of an old-fashioned seaside boarding house. Ridiculous I thought, this Heaven where you will know even where to put your boots at night. But I thought again immediately — this is snobbish. Nobody can envisage Heaven and certainly not attempt to describe it without employing images from earthly life, and ordinary ones at that. By analogy mystic poetry must employ erotic imagery to stand in for the love of God. Agape is the big one, but Eros has the language. The poetry of Crashaw and Traherne relies on the tropes of love poetry and why not? The one insistence of the Church which must be right is its resistance to Manicheism. Palpable feelings must be the basis of transcendent ones and in a God-created universe sexual love is God-created too. Later on, in the history of Mankind, a few subsidiary rules have had to be introduced, but doctrine can never agree that the created world is essentially evil. To feel that it is, is a passing sort of depression, familiar to most of us, but no basis for a philosophy of life, unless you are a Nihilist like those followers of General Franco who marched under the banner 'Long live Death!'

Yet we know nothing of what is to come and all the furnishings of Heaven (supposedly where we are going) or of paradise (allegedly where we once were) are what Stevens calls 'minor(s) of what we feel.' In 'Esthetique du mal' he modulates from the demands of philosophy — for him what Christianity is for a believer — to the presences of reality, the wonders and predicaments of the physical. The final lines which I quoted a moment ago are Pentecostal, and their tongues of fire turn out to be bits of the here and now. This is what Poetry is about and what practically the whole of Wallace Stevens's output seeks to personify. Of course, there are many poets who seem more physical than Stevens, especially Nature Poets and Descriptive ones and the School of Wordsworth perhaps. But Stevens is not primarily Pantheistic; he is materialistic. His long haul through the observable world is taken up with the symbolism whereby we write reality. In his verse words themselves are materialist precisely because he knows that they are not things and cannot imitate what they stand for. Language is not tangible in itself: it has to be made materialist by the alchemy of the poet. I do not mean by any of the technical tropes which some critics like to point to — rhymes, sounds, assonances, onomatopoeia and so on. And definitely not anything to do with Sitwellian patternings, as dubious as Scriabin's colour-coding of sounds. Also Mimesis is a very doubtful concept. Or even perhaps the complications of verse forms — stanzas, metrics etc. And lastly certainly not styles, style-wars, 'make it new', 'the age demands' and the rest. Most of these devices may be used, and the poet who knows the craft will take them up or put them down with the same insouciance as a painter mixes colours on a palette. The alchemy needed to turn the materialist world into its transcendent self while honouring its essential lineaments is no more or less than that which we call 'poetry' itself! Like Housman we recognize it and like Francis Bacon's Pontius Pilate we don't stop to define its truthfulness. Because we can't. But we know that we have an inbuilt hunger for its existence, and an equally inbuilt certainty that it belongs in our materialist universe as certainly as we do ourselves. This is the serious and often passed-over significance of Auden's announcement in his poem on Yeats: 'Poetry makes nothing happen.' That is not poetry's purpose. Rather it is to oppose responsible happenings, to put God back in his lexicon, to assure us that churches are made of stone and poems of words.

These last couple of minutes have been a helping of rather heavy porridge. You may wonder why if I don't understand philosophy I get into such logical tangles about poetry and materialism. Here, in an interlude of light relief, comes a short poem of my own which turns the same problems into calendar-type verse. It's called *Last Words* and was written for the Festival of that name mounted in Salisbury in 1999.

> In the beginning was the Word,
> Not just the word of God but sounds
> Where truth is clarified or blurred.
> Then rhyme and rhythm did the rounds
> And justified their jumps and joins
> By glueing up our lips and loins.
>
> Once words had freshness on their breath.
> The poet who saw first that death
> Has only one true rhyme was made
> The leader of the Boys Brigade.
> Dead languages can scan and rhyme
> Like birthday cards and *Lilac Time*.
>
> And you can carve words on a slab
> Or tow them through the air by plane,
> Tattoo them with a painful jab
> Or hang them in a window pane.
> Unlike our bodies which decay,
> Words, first and last, have come to stay.

My doggerel and Stevens's high seriousness recognize equally that the real world and the world we make of it in language are contingent. I cannot envisage a poet who would go to the stake or endure torture in defence of a truth guaranteed only by words; i.e. some slogan or some creed. What is striking about those who suffer martyrdom for a cause is their belief that something serious enough to die for could ever be adequately summed-up in language. Those of us who love aphorisms, apothegms and maxims know better than to think their truthfulness is in proportion to their eloquence of expression. You might call the Bible and the Koran, each a set of fasces of axioms, a powerful bundle of stories and convictions stronger than any one statement contained within. And I suspect that the same applies to questions of faith. Armies which devastate whole landscapes are not really killing each other for a Catholic or a Protestant cause — they are team players and the creeds they espouse are the 'strip' of their allegiance. The two centuries of persecution which ended in Rome in 303 AD when Constantine rather equivocally converted to Christianity produced so many martyrdoms that people began to be convinced of the new God on the block. If these men and women could die for what they believed then that must be something worth following. It was courage rather than dogma which convinced them. Strange that later the triumphant church did not think that way when it, in its turn, persecuted its heretics.

Notes Towards a Supreme Fiction is in every sense an extraordinary poem, a kind of Mandeville's Travels across the intense landscape of the human imagination. I have used parts of it to stress the materialist ethic of poetry. But you may well conclude, when you read it, that much of it is abstract, and indeed you may feel this is true of Stevens's poetry in general. The first section of the poem, which has nine groups of three-line stanzas, is sub-headed 'It Must be Abstract'. The paradox in Stevens's work lies exactly in his lack of any fear of abstraction, which allows him to assume that realism in all its forms — description, actuality, shock of recognition — also partakes of the essential abstraction of language. Then there is the matter of generalisation, of the emotional need in humanity for the proverbial. While today's various Uniformity Acts, described by their practitioners as Theory, also wish to thrust experience into gestalts or pigeon-holes, the procedure of those poets I think of as generalisers is utterly different. I suppose no two poets could be more unlike than Stevens and W.H. Auden, yet both have the ability to sum up human emotion in wide-ranging packets of behaviour, while remaining masters of what Blake called 'minute particulars'. Language is tribally owned and must therefore generalise. The masterful poet is able to be recognisably particular while keeping to language's inherited orthodoxies. The lineaments of the human face are common to all people, yet each countenance is individual.

There is one hushed mystery at the heart of poetry which if you dare utter it will get you into terrible trouble. Poetry has its limits: it is not truly God-like, Apocalyptic, nor Utilitarian or revolutionary: in an honourable sense it is even 'modest'. When I used this adjective years ago and dubbed poetry a 'modest art', I was kicked out of the Poets' Club immediately. Notably immodest poets, George Barker and Donald Davie, sneered that of course to such a raconteur and journalistic poet as myself, the art must seem modest. But I have always believed that the achievements of poetry are great and formidable enough not to need cataclysmic claims by overreachers. For even the most fervent Apocalyptic, death must be as much part of the mensuration of existence as of its transfiguration. The mystic needs to have buttons sewn on his trousers, as Yeats's letters insist. We all want our poetry, like our music, to be perfect in form and uplifting as experience. And we hanker after any sustainable apotheosis. The point of my whole lecture tonight is that the only ingredients we have, as poets, to make this from are those abstract counters, words. Stevens sums up the abstract first section of *Notes Towards a Supreme Fiction* in these lines.

> The major abstraction is the idea of man
> And major man is its exponent, abler
> In the abstract than in his singular,
>
> More fecund as principle than particle,
> Happy fecundity, flor-abundant force,
> In being more than an exception, part,
>
> Though an heroic part, of the commonal.
> The major abstraction is the commonal,
> The inanimate, difficult visage. Who is it?
>
> What rabbi, grown furious with human wish,
> What chieftain, walking by himself, crying
> Most miserable, most victorious,
>
> Does not see these separate figures one by one,
> And yet see only one, in his old coat,
> His slouching pantaloons, beyond the town,
>
> Looking for what was, where it used to be?
> Cloudless the morning. It is he. The man
> In that old coat, those sagging pantaloons,
>
> It is of him, ephebe, to make, to confect
> The final elegance, not to console
> Nor sanctify, but plainly to propound.

That person in the old coat and ragged pantaloons is Everyman, the despair of priests and generals alike, a piece of democratic cannon-fodder. His unattractive dress is the only materialist thing in this part of the poem.

So he also stands for the poet, the singular inside the corporate, whose art nevertheless celebrates the corporate. So much of Stevens's poetry is the protest of a dazzled mind against the authority of religion and government. But nobody would call him a revolutionary, not even in technique, since his richness of language is deployed in highly traditional metrical and stanzaic shapes. He shows that scepticism is not a dry thing: rather the vistas of doubt are long and well-dressed. There's more voluptuousness in scepticism than in belief. There are rumours that he converted to Catholicism at the end of his life. If he did, then it must have been, like the death-bed conversion of the Earl of Rochester, a product of intellectual and emotional exhaustion. Cyril Connolly once pointed out that the essential sadness of the Roman Poets of the Silver Age sprang from too much carousing and love-making. Voluptuousness leaves you nowhere to go and bodies wear out. Christianity, interpreting the world as a veil of tears, can offer jam tomorrow. Those who have known jam today may well view tomorrow as more of the same thing, and they may not feel up to it.

You may find this a frivolous way of approaching a serious subject: I think contrariwise that there will always be war between Faith and Art, between Religion and Poetry, as well as between Philosophy and Poetry. Great painters and composers have served the church but perhaps they could find no other patron. Alternatively, they were probably grateful for such rich subject matter. And their arts are not controversial, other than in questions of style. Writers are in a different position: their freedom of speculation, while acceptable to the more sophisticated clerics, could frighten enforcers of orthodoxy. In our own permissive times, many poets, Eliot and Auden certainly, have stressed that art requires a subject greater than itself, and for Westerners since the Classical era that subject has been Christian Faith. Even before his return to Anglicanism, Auden wrote — about art — 'The only thing it must be is attendant,/ The only thing it mustn't, independent'. Stevens could agree with the first statement but not the second. For him no subject and no orthodoxy is greater than the ripples it makes in human experience. The world is all subject matter, even when it is destructive and pain-filled. The writer does not make the opportunities for tragedy or catharsis, but he knows when and how to take them.

I had Stevens's intense materialism brought sharply before me once when I was talking with some cultivated academics in one of our universities' Theology Departments. I had chosen to contrast Stevens's early and perhaps most famous poem, 'Sunday Morning' with Christopher Smart's, 'Hymn on the Nativity of Our Lord & Saviour Jesus Christ.' Here for sampling are the final lines of each poem. First the Stevens:

> She hears, upon that water without sound,
> A voice that cries, "The tomb in Palestine
> Is not the porch of spirits lingering.
> It is the grave of Jesus, where he lay".
> We live in an old chaos of the sun,
> Or old dependency of day and night,
> Or island solitude, unsponsored, free,
> Of that wide water, inescapable.
> Deer walk upon our mountains, and the quail
> Whistle about us their spontaneous cries;
> Sweet berries ripen in the wilderness;
> And, in the isolation of the sky,
> At evening, casual flocks of pigeons make
> Ambiguous undulations as they sink,
> Downwards to darkness, on extended wings.

This is magnificent, though you may complain that the detail is not as germane as the poet appears to think it is. But it is quite as rich in art as any Christian or other believer's dithyramb. Now the Smart, which is in quatrains; here are the last three.

> Boreas no longer winters
>   On the desolated coast;
> Oaks no more are riven in splinters
>   By the whirlwind and his host.

> Spinks and ousels sing sublimely,
>   'We too have a Saviour born;'
> Winter blossoms burst untimely
>   On the blest Mosaic thorn.

> God all-bounteous, all-creative
>   Whom no ills from good dissuade,
> Is incarnate, and a native
>   Of the very world he made.

My theologians thought Smart's poem as beautiful as Stevens's but infinitely more to the point because it illustrated the Christian doctrine that God made the world in order that it should love and praise his efforts. But both poems seem to me to emphasise also the vicissitudes of life on God's created planet. Smart has to resort to the troubles of our world and then insist that they are put in reverse by this remarkable Incarnation. Stevens says that things go on happening following Christ just as they did before he took up his ministry. Perhaps there is no beautiful conceptual shock in Stevens as there is when Smart trumps all paradoxes by making God condescend to be a creature of his own experimental universe. But both poems seem to me to offer us the chance to reflect that whatever our beliefs we will see substantiating (and this will include paradoxical) evidence of what we believe in the world about us. Stevens's doves and Smarts's ouzels are recognizably creatures of the same Bestiary. They are being called as evidence from different sides of the courtroom. Stevens, it should be emphasised, is not opposed to religion: he sees it as an hypothesis which has had a good run for its money. The theologians who found Smart more poetic than Stevens are parti-pris. How could they be otherwise? Christianity has never insisted that it has all the good tunes — only that it is true. Sceptics have replied that it has a great number of good tunes — more inevitably over the past two millennia than any other source of feeling — but this does not make its certainties the case.

I've gone on a lot about faith, so you may conclude, especially if you are the materialist I am trying to be, that I am a closet believer or at least a God-bothered person. What I hope I am doing is recognizing that poetry and the rest of the arts are rooted in a physical world and make from it, just as religion does, the temples of their adoration. The next question is — is Poetry up to it? I have outstared Donald Davie and others and called it 'a modest art'. Why then should we make it a cornerstone of our literature?

I think the reason for this is Poetry's extremist view of language. The desire to believe in some transcendent force emerges as a relish for the beauty of expression — Stevens's visible world, what he calls 'an excellence collecting excellence'. The death-bed cry of Aubrey Beardsley, 'For God's sake burn all obscene pictures' is understandable, but it is the cry of a frightened man, not of an artist. We would rather he'd recognized that his drawings of erotics were closer to the Almighty than his confessions. Similarly, I find it moving that scarcely a year before his early death Rochester wrote one of the great agnostic poems in the language. He prepared a translation of a passage from Seneca's closet drama *Troades* which is a gloss on pagan Epicureanism. This is how it goes.

After death nothing is, and death,
The utmost limit of a gasp of breath.
Let the ambitious zealot lay aside,
His hopes of Heaven, whose faith is but his pride;
    Let lavish souls lay by their fear
    Nor be concerned which way or where
    After this life they shall be hurled.
Dead, we become the lumber of the world,
And to that mass of matter shall be swept
Where things destroyed and things unborn are kept.
    Devouring time swallows us whole.
Impartial death confounds body and soul.
    For hell and the foul fiend that rules
    God's everlasting fiery gaols
    (Devised by rogues, dreaded by fools)
With his grim, grisly dog that keeps the door,
    Are senseless stories, idle tales,
    Dreams, whimseys, and no more.

This is splendid but it is almost an exercise. Being a translation, the hell it dismisses is the pagan one, with the dog Cerberus gnashing his teeth outside Hades. When Rochester was dying it was the all too palpable Christian priest, the proselytiser Bishop Burnet, who sat by his bed and ushered him into full repentance. Either way, a true defiance or an essay in scepticism, Rochester's poem shows how the artist's mind works. Artists are celebrant sceptics, engaged doubters, defiant cowards. They wish to surmount the prose of transcendence with the poetry of reality. And incidentally the pornographer in Rochester wrote the most beautiful description of the female genitals any poet has ever recorded, Milton included. Of the vagina he wrote: "It is the warehouse of the world's great trade/ On this soft anvil all mankind was made!"

Occasionally, such luminous materialism dovetails with profound belief, as in the poetry of George Herbert. For Herbert the world is transparent and the love of God shines through it. But that internal print does not affect the physical outline of Creation. One poem of Herbert's may serve to illustrate that worldly objects are the necessary jewels of devotion. Some of Herbert's poems are very strange indeed — in their own way they are as mysterious as Stevens'. But the mystery is chiefly to do with the prevailing fondness for extended metaphor so characteristic of Caroline Poetry. None does it as well as Herbert, of course, but modern readers in their impatient moods may still find it evasive. For every straightforward march of metaphor there is a distracted pilgrimage in Herbert, so we may seek out poems such as 'Easter', 'Prayer', 'Time' and 'Love' as characteristic rather than his more extravagant ones, 'Jordan', 'Artillery', 'The Pulley' or 'Dotage'. When he writes directly, as he does in the poem I am now going to quote, 'Virtue', he is the most convincing poet in the language.

> Sweet day, so cool, so calm, so bright,
> The bridal of the earth and sky:
> The dew shall weep thy fall tonight;
>   For thou must die.
>
> Sweet rose, whose hue angry and brave
> Bids the rash gazer wipe his eye:
> Thy root is ever in its grave,
>   And thou must die.
>
> Sweet spring, full of sweet days and roses,
> A box where sweets compacted lie;
> My music shows ye have your closes,
>   And all must die.
>
> Only a sweet and virtuous soul,
> Like seasoned timber, never gives;
> But though the whole world turn to coal,
>   Then chiefly lives.

The daring of the great poets is largely in their sudden blows of ordinariness. Herbert's line, 'But though the whole world turn to coal' is like Shakespeare's famous coups: of Cleopatra at the battle of Actium, 'The wind upon her like a cow in June'; of Volumnia reproaching Virgilia in *Coriolanus*, 'All the yarn [Penelope] spun in Ulysses' absence did but fill Ithaca with moths'; or of Antony, again from *Antony and Cleopatra* "Tis the God Hercules whom Antony loved now leaves him'. Whether writing of history, of human love, or in the service of God, or indeed of any matter which can be addressed poetically, the poet will have to inhabit that very 'place dependent on ourselves' which Stevens enunciated. Each century, each generation, even each decade has to find ways of forcing its worldliness into poetical harness. The hardest task the would-be critic has today is recognizing a genuinely new way of doing so. Hence, on the one hand, the indiscriminate hailing of certain innovators as geniuses, and, on the other, the denouncing of the Emperor's new clothes.

It's also the nature of Poetry to make lightning raids on the numinous when its intention is not to do anything of the sort. Poems deliberately couched in low tones may be closer to that startling revelation we look for in poetry than ones with the highest aims. Just when you are not expecting it, lines may leap out from prosaic or cynical backgrounds. Four lines by W. E. Henley, he of "Invicta" fame, have stayed with me since I first heard them.

> Mistress Life's a piece in bloom,
> Death goes dogging everywhere.
> She's the tenant of the room,
> He's the ruffian on the stair.

No wonder Joe Orton pricked up his ears when he first encountered this poem. Perhaps it is in their disenchanted moods that poets stick most closely to the poetry of realism, of the way things happen. As in Walter Raleigh's bitter lament, 'The Lie'.

> Say to the Court it glows
> And shines like rotten wood.
> Say to the Church it shows
> What's good, but doth no good.
> If Court and Church reply,
> Then give them both the lie.

There are no unpoetic subjects — not even shopping, television or machinery. The Australian poet John Forbes writes a love poem while watching the Gulf War on the box.

> Spent tracer flecks Baghdad's
> bright video game sky
>
> as I curl up with the war
> in lieu of you, whose letter
>
> lets me know my poems show
> how unhappy I can be. Perhaps.

But what they don't show, until
now, is how at ease I can be

with military technology: e.g.
matching their *feu d'espirit* I classify

the sounds of the Iraqi AA — the
thump of the 85 mil, the throaty

chatter of the quad ZSU 23.
Our precision guided weapons

make the horizon flash & glow
but nothing I can do makes you

want me. Instead I watch the west
do what the west does best.

I know, obscurely, as I go to bed
all this is being staged for me.

It's phrases like watching 'the west/ do what the west does best' which
give poetry its proverbial power, even if you think at your gloomiest that
memorability and concision doom poetry in an age of hype and journalism
to be little more than the provider of titles for novelists and playwrights
and headlines for editors.

There is more to reality, of course, than the most precise rendering of
emotion recollected in tranquility. Language itself has a torque or bias,
formed perhaps from years of ingrained use, which seems to want to make
declarations of its own. That 'trigger of the Literary man's biggest gun' as
William Empson described death, is an anthologist by nature. We all write
poems about death which honour the subject simply because like Everest
it is there. When embarking on such work the poet may well feel that
what's being done is close to automatic writing. The poem seems to be
composing itself. I'll dare to quote another poem of my own to illustrate
this. I wrote it more than twenty years ago, but I remember the process
clearly. I started out to face the strangeness of form: to wonder why I
had already written so many poems in so many different shapes and yet

wanted to go beyond this, and then to question the whole point of the corseting of feeling in arbitrary outlines. But the poem went its own way and by the time it was finished, at the end of the third stanza, I saw it was really a poem about death and how death defies the transcendence poetry might impose on it. The title speaks of my original intention — I called it 'To Make It Real'; this is the second part.

> Somewhere beyond my window (shall we say
> in Pessary, Ohio) a widowed lady
> rocks like acacia fragrance in the night
> and lets a naked light bulb close her eyes,
> the neighbour's dog her psychopomp, the
> ruttish evening full of floating dust
> as she is candled inwards, yet not fussed.

> I made this lady up: my cat ascends
> the curtain wildly clawing till she falls;
> non sequiturs of heartburn and despair
> are felt like persons in the early dark.
> My mortal lady with the finished eyes
> will not be named and will not need a grave,
> but for her benediction London kneels —
> our well-lit world goes in the Word machine,
> chaff in the jaws of God, blood in a dream.

Fiction is as germane to Poetry as it is to prose. That poem of mine is like a slightly mysterious short story. If Chekov is a kind of poet, then Wallace Stevens is a cross between Henry James and a serial aphorist. Stevens's *Notes Towards a Supreme Fiction* gave me my start in this talk and I shall end with Stevens as well. The poem is *Credences of Summer* and its burden is not so different from that of *Supreme Fiction*, namely the desire of the poet to face reality directly, the physical world, the 'place dependent on ourselves'. Firstly some things have to be put out of the way — Stevens promises to write 'without evasion of a single metaphor'. But we know him well enough to be sure that he won't deny himself a good metaphor when he needs it. In *Credences of Summer* he uses Poetry to do without Poetry, a well-followed trope by writers from Horace onwards, through Rochester and on to Ashbery. The reality the poem faces is not a terrible but a happy one, and this makes taking it at its own value even harder. There is too much chance of redundancy. Stevens writes 'This is the barrenness/ Of the fertile thing that can attain no more'. He tries various deviations including personifying the situation, with an old man on a hill and a group singing happily of the Summer's credences. But evocation gets down to work, and at the heart of the poem there is a typical Stevens challenge.

> The trumpet of morning blows in the clouds and through
> The sky. It is the visible announced.
> It is the more than visible, the more
> Than sharp, illustrious scene. The trumpet cries
> This is the successor of the invisible.

> This is its substitute in stratagems
> Of the spirit. This, in sight and memory,
> Must take its place, as what is possible
> Replaces what is not. The resounding cry
> Is like ten thousand tumblers tumbling down

> To share the day. The trumpet supposes that
> A mind exists, aware of division, aware
> Of its cry as clarion, its diction's way
> As that of a personage in a multitude:
> Man's mind grown venerable in the unreal.

This is what I have been trying to unearth in my talk — the possible replacing what is not possible, the Poetry we make from our inadequacy — inadequacy not just of our own minds but of the place we live in, the language we have developed and the moral truthfulness we espouse. Poetry has such opportunities for failure it must always be preferable to philosophy or religion. It is simply that much more human.

1999: The Nottingham Trent University. Inaugural Lecture as Visiting Professor of Poetry